HIKING the Gulf Islands

HIKING the Gulf Islands

An Outdoor Guide to BC's Enchanted Isles

CHARLES KAHN

HARBOUR PUBLISHING

Published by

Harbour Publishing Co. Ltd.
P.O. Box 219, Madeira Park, BC V0N 2H0
www.harbourpublishing.com

Text and cover design by Martin Nichols
Cover photo by Tara Gill, back cover photo by Lynn Thompson
Maps by Nick Murphy
Photos by Charles Kahn and Judy Norget unless credited otherwise
Printed and bound in Canada

Harbour Publishing acknowledges financial support from the Government of Canada through the Book Publishing Industry Development Program and the Canada Council for the Arts, and from the Province of British Columbia through the British Columbia Arts Council and the Book Publisher's Tax Credit through the Ministry of Provincial Revenue.

National Library of Canada Cataloguing in Publication

Kahn, Charles, 1945–
Hiking the Gulf Islands : an outdoor guide to BC's enchanted isles / Charles Kahn. — 1st rev. ed.

Includes bibliographical references and index.
ISBN 1-55017-315-4

1. Hiking—British Columbia—Gulf Islands—Guidebooks. 2. Gulf Islands (B.C.)—Guidebooks. I. Title.
GV199.44.C22G84 2004   796.51'09711'28   C2004-900914-1

For Judy Norget

Acknowledgements

I AM INDEBTED TO A GREAT MANY PEOPLE. In addition to the immense contribution she made to the maps and text in the first edition of this book, Judy Norget made invaluable suggestions. I was then fortunate to have two fine editors from Harbour Publishing—Craig Carpenter and Nadine Pedersen—review the manuscript, adding immeasurably to the accuracy and clarity of the book.

The following remarkably helpful island consultants provided information and read the draft manuscript of either the first edition or this revision to cull errors: Ian Stuart, John Reid, Graeme Dinsdale, Alan Shatwell, Collene Huskisson, Ross Carter (Bowen); the late Pierre de Trey, Ruth Zwickel (Cortes); Louise Bell, Rolf Ludvigsen (Denman); John Gambrill (Gabriola); John Coates, Debra Holmes (Galiano); Doug Carrick, Carol Martin, Tony Quin, Hilary Brown (Hornby); Pat Forbes, Bronwyn Preece, Betty Darwin (Lasqueti); Michael Dunn, Peter Askin (Mayne); Newell Smith, Chuck Harris (the Penders); Judy and Richard Leicester, Noel Lax (Quadra); Ishbel Elliott, Joan Combes, Donna Digance, Priscilla and Jon Ewbank, Rick Tipple, the Campbell family, Gail Trafford (Saturna); Lynn Thompson, Linda Quiring, Mark Haughey, Philip Grange (Salt Spring); John Dove (Texada); Veronica Shelford, Barbara Moore (Thetis).

I also thank Meredith Reeve of Parks Canada for reviewing the information on the Gulf Islands National Park Reserve and Jenny Eastman of Capital Regional District (CRD) Parks, who provided maps and photos of the CRD parks. Thanks also goes to the many people I interviewed, to the photographers who allowed their work to be reproduced, and to the members of the Salt Spring Trail and Nature Club who introduced me to some of the finest Gulf Islands hikes.

Contents

Preface

In its most limited sense the term "Gulf Islands" refers only to the cluster of islands hugging the Vancouver Island shore from Nanaimo south to the US border. Some consider it a stretch even to include Denman and Hornby, in the Parksville area. This book uses the term in its broadest sense, including all of the above plus Lasqueti, Texada, Quadra, Cortes, and Bowen. The main criteria used were the quality of hiking opportunities and public access; almost all the islands included have some recognized trail development and are accessible by ferry, although several marine parks easily reached by private boat are also included.

Population figures are from Statistics Canada's 2001 census, which often differ from the figures islanders *know* to be true. For historical information, I consulted materials provided by tourist offices, local newspapers, written histories and word-of-mouth accounts but relied mainly on previously published materials, most of which are acknowledged in the resource section at the end of the book. Island information is constantly changing: new roads are built, new stores open and old ones close, new trails are developed while older ones become overgrown or vanish because of new housing. Whenever more than one island history exists, there is often disagreement on details. I apologize for any errors or omissions.

How to Use This Book

This book is designed to be simple to use. The first section introduces you to the Gulf Islands, providing information on their natural features, history, wildlife and what you can expect to find when visiting them. I've also included information on hikers' responsibilities, what to bring when hiking, some safety considerations, and information about public parks and Crown (government-owned) land.

The main part of this book—the islands and their hikes—is arranged alphabetically, beginning with Bowen and ending with Thetis. In addition to information on the different walks and hikes, you'll find information on history, how to get there, accommodation and services. There is a separate section highlighting the more gentle walks, and for those who want to combine exploring on land with exploring on the water, each chapter concludes with a section containing a few paddling suggestions. Each chapter also has a map of an overview of the island, although only main roads and those mentioned in the text are labelled. This map also identifies the location of the hikes (by number), the main shopping area(s), public shore accesses, parks, Indian Reserves and, where possible, Crown land.

To help you decide which hikes to take, at-a-glance information is provided for each hiking trail described. This includes a short description of the hike, its length, the time required to hike it, its degree of difficulty, how to access it and any cautions. Of course, the time you need will vary with your speed, the time you have available and your interest in stopping to smell the Nootka roses. My estimates are based on a top speed of 6 km per hour on flat ground and 4 km per hour in hilly terrain, with additional time allowed for stops and enjoying views and flora. A full description of each hike and its special features follows the summary. Individual trail maps have been provided for difficult-to-follow trails. To further help you choose the hikes to take, each one is rated on the following five-star system:

★	One-star hikes are the least interesting or beautiful.
★★	Two-star hikes are fairly pleasant but nothing spectacular.
★★★	Three-star hikes are definitely worth doing.
★★★★	Four-star hikes are really special but lack the variety of the five-star hikes.
★★★★★	Five stars are reserved for the most outstanding hikes: Bodega Ridge on Galiano, Mount Warburton Pike on Saturna, Ruckle Provincial Park on Salt Spring, Helliwell Provincial Park and the Cliff Trail on Mount Geoffrey on Hornby, Nugedzi Lakes on Quadra, and Kw'as Park on Cortes.

Keep in mind that everything is relative; even a one-star hike in the Gulf Islands is special when the great out-of-doors gives you pleasure.

Many of these hikes require a half or full day to complete, although there are ample shorter walks. Shore and road walks are also listed for each island. For simplicity, all measurements are given in metric units (1 km = 0.6 mile, 1 m = 39.37 inches, 1 cm = .39 inches, 1 ha = 2.5 acres).

At the end of the book, there's a resource section and an index. I hope you enjoy using the book as much as I enjoyed researching and writing it. Happy hiking!

DISCLAIMER

The writer, editors and publisher of *Hiking the Gulf Islands* have made every effort to ensure the reader's awareness of accessibility, hazards and level of expertise involved in the activities described, but your own safety is ultimately up to you. We can take no responsibility for any loss or injury incurred by anyone using this book. If you spot any inaccuracies, let us know.

Introduction to the Gulf Islands

A paradise to residents and visitors alike, the Gulf Islands are graced with the grandeur of mountains and sea, lush temperate rain forests and a climate that is rarely too cold, too hot, too wet or too dry. When I first discovered them more than a decade ago, I was captivated by their charms and I remain entranced.

Whether you are a laid-back nature lover or a hard-core trekker, the Gulf Islands have it all—from gentle walks through exquisite old-growth forest to rugged hikes with breathtaking views. As you follow the hikes in this book, you are certain to come across many of the natural features that make these islands unique: sandstone shores worn by wind and water into sculptural shapes, twisting arbutus trees and towering Douglas fir, rolling farmland where sheep graze, rocky sun-kissed ridges, forest floors covered in thick layers of bright green moss and, in the spring, meadows strewn with wildflowers.

The beautifully contorted arbutus tree keeps its leaves year-round but sheds its thin ochre bark.

SERVICES AND ACCOMMODATION

Services and accommodation vary with the seasons. If you come in the off-season (roughly from Thanksgiving in October through to the May long weekend), expect fewer accommodations, restaurants and shops to be open. If you come in the summer, be sure to reserve well ahead, as accommodations, including bed and breakfasts and campgrounds, are quickly filled. (Even in the off-season, reservations are useful, as campgrounds are often closed—especially on islands with no provincial parks—and many bed and breakfasts close for the season.)

In any season, it's possible to buy food and find accommodation on every Gulf Island with ferry service. All the islands in this book have at least one restaurant, although it may not be open during weekdays in the off-season. Most islands also have at least one real-estate office, which is often the best place to obtain a free map that notes local services and points of interest. As well, most of the islands have a service station (or gas pump), a pub, liquor outlet and at least one excellent bakery. Many also have a small RCMP detachment and stores that sell items such as hardware and clothing. All have arts and crafts shops and studios, which are open in season.

A BRIEF HISTORY OF THE GULF ISLANDS

"The Gulf Islands" is actually a misnomer. When Captain George Vancouver charted the Strait of Georgia in 1792, he made a slight mistake. He at first thought he was sailing in a gulf, so he named it the Gulf of Georgia and the islands in it became known as the Gulf Islands. Although Vancouver soon discovered the land mass forming the western shore of his supposed gulf was a large island, the naming error wasn't corrected until 1865, when Captain George Henry Richards was surveying the area and renamed the gulf correctly as a strait. However, no one bothered to change the name of the islands—after all, "the Strait Islands" doesn't sound nearly as appealing.

Almost all of the Gulf Islands share a similar history. For thousands of years they were inhabited by First Nations people, many of whom lived a semi-nomadic life, moving with the seasons and gathering, hunting and fishing the abundant flora and fauna along the coast. Our knowledge of their lives and settlements is derived mainly from the research of anthropologists who studied the people, and from archaeological work connected with the many middens (shell and ash deposits) and other remains that have been found.

The first non-aboriginal settlers arrived in the Gulf Islands in 1859. Under the Land Ordinance Act of 1870, settlers were allowed to pre-empt, or claim, up to 160 acres (65 ha) of land if they lived on it for four years and made improvements equal to $2.50 per acre. When these requirements were met and the land had been surveyed, they could purchase it for a mere $1 per acre. The ownership almost completely ignored traditional First Nations claims to the land and many aboriginal people were displaced, though not without resistance.

Settlers did not have an easy go of it. Before they could begin farming, they needed to clear away the thick, towering trees, and with rocky soil and often a lack of water, farming was particularly challenging. Transportation problems added to the difficulties, as there were no public wharves or roads for many years and settlers had to rely on their own boats to get their crops to market. However, many farmers did succeed, especially in the south. Well before orchards were developed in the Okanagan, Mayne and Salt Spring were known for their bountiful crops of fruit.

Communities grew more rapidly in the 1900s. Steamship service, and ultimately ferry service, linked some islands to Vancouver Island and others to the mainland; electricity and improved roads modernized island life; and the development of the islands began in earnest.

In recent decades, tourism and the acquisition of recreational property have been strong factors in the development of most of the Gulf Islands. With improved services and the best climate in Canada, the islands now attract more and more newcomers each year, including many recent retirees seeking to spend their golden years in a golden locale. Tourism adds tens of thousands of visitors each year, which puts great pressure on available services and resources, especially water, which is in short supply on most Gulf Islands. As a result, growth is the greatest concern facing these islands in the 21st century.

WILDLIFE

One of the treats of being in the Gulf Islands is the opportunity to view wildlife in its natural habitat. Most of the easily observable animal and bird life on the Gulf Islands is in either the sea or the air. Large animals such as cougars, bears and wolves were systematically exterminated from the Gulf Islands years ago, although wolves and cougars have been reported on Quadra and Cortes and the occasional cougar manages to swim across from Vancouver Island to other islands from time to time. The largest wild animals you are likely to see in the Gulf Islands are the blacktail deer, common enough in island gardens to act as a stimulus for the local fencing industry. Joining the deer in the forests and along the shores are such smaller animals as mice, squirrels, raccoons, mink, otters, muskrats, beavers and, of course, the giant, oozing banana slugs and their smaller, shiny black cousins.

One of Texada Island's many osprey nests. Norman MacLean

Bald eagles are common in the Gulf Islands, where they are especially visible in the spring when they are rearing their young (look up to the tops of large dead trees, particularly near the sea). Among other large birds, vultures, ravens, hawks, owls, woodpeckers, grouse, jays, quail and crows are common. Ospreys are seen here and there. Among the more frequently seen smaller birds are wrens, towhees, sparrows, nuthatches, juncos, varied thrushes, band-tailed pigeons, kingfishers, hummingbirds, chickadees, robins and swallows.

Geese and ducks of many species, loons, sandpipers, cormorants, gulls, black oystercatchers and herons can all be spotted, especially during the colder months. In the winter, the Gulf Islands become a birdwatchers' paradise with large collections of waterfowl in estuaries and bays, which provide the birds with a winter haven.

The Gulf Islands' waters are home to seals, otters, sea lions, and even dolphins and killer whales, as well as an abundance of sea life along the shore and in tidal pools. When the tide goes out, you might see oysters, mussels and little squirts of water from buried clams, on some beaches. Look in the water for crabs and around rocks for black barnacles and purple, coral and white sea stars.

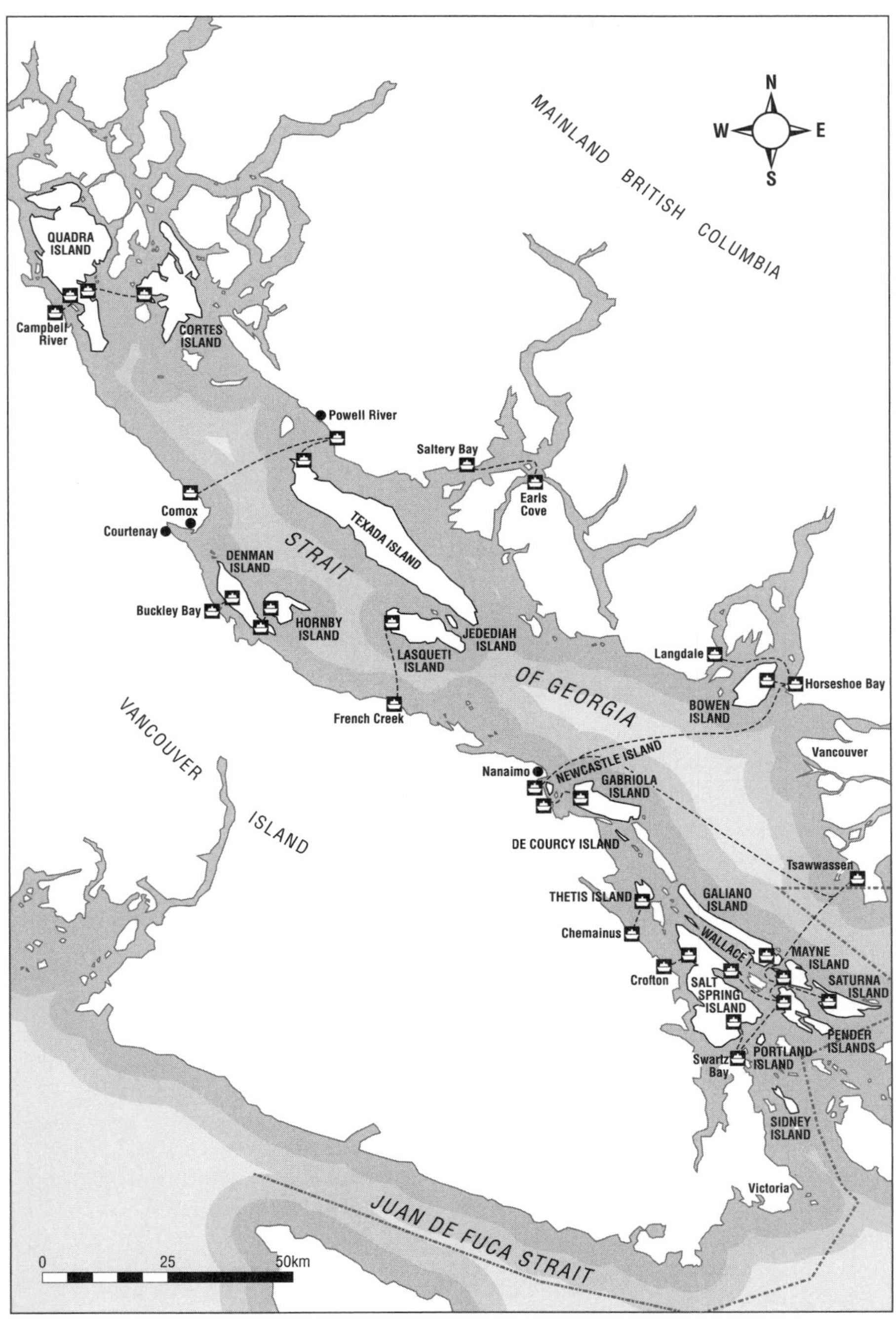

The Gulf Islands

Ferry routes   International boundary

Hiking

RESPONSIBLE HIKING

The future of hiking in the Gulf Islands is really up to us: those who walk the trails and roads. Many trails, including some of the best, cross private land and will remain available only as long as hikers respect the property rights and concerns of the owners and their neighbours. And, while it is true that you might only "pass this way but once," others will follow you, so it is imperative that, if we are to continue using many of these trails, we treat the environment with care and behave responsibly.

Responsible hiking means respecting both the land and its owners—whether it is private property, Crown land, or a national, provincial, regional or local park—and involves the following concerns:

Garbage: Waste is a problem throughout the Gulf Islands. Few of the islands have their own landfills, so garbage must be transported off-island. As well as ensuring that you leave nothing on the trails, you should take as much of your garbage as possible off the island, where it can be disposed of without cost to the locals. Many hikers carry a spare plastic bag in which they collect any garbage they see along the trail.

Fire: Fire is a constant threat on the Gulf Islands, especially in the dry period from June to October. Most islands have only volunteer firefighters, and water to fight fires is often unavailable, especially on forest trails. On many islands, fires, even on beaches, are not allowed during the summer. As well, trails in the Gulf Islands are sometimes closed if the threat of fire is severe. Be sure to check for trail closures before you visit an island during hot weather.

It takes only one careless individual to spoil a fine hike—perhaps forever—and to provide ammunition for those opposing hiking trails. If you make a campfire, when allowed, keep in mind the following procedures outlined by the BC Forest Service:

- Prepare your campfire site by removing all leaves, twigs and other flammable material from an area extending at least 30 cm around the fire and down to mineral soil.
- Never light a campfire when strong winds are blowing.
- Build your campfire at least 3 m from any flammable structure, slash or flammable debris.
- Equip yourself with a shovel and a full pail of water, before you light your campfire.
- Keep the cooking fire small and hot, for best results.
- Attend your campfire at all times and be certain it is extinguished before leaving.

- Report any suspicious fires you see to a forest ranger, property owner, the RCMP, or call 1-800-663-5555 (a free province-wide, forest-fire emergency number) or *5555 from your cellular phone.

Dogs: Dogs should be leashed, at all times. It is unfair to subject other hikers, local residents or wildlife to the noise or possibly aggressive behaviour of your dog. As well, sheep graze widely throughout the Gulf Islands and are easily spooked by dogs.

In spring, wildflowers are abundant on the Gulf Islands. Lynn Thompson

Wildflowers: Do not pick wildflowers; in public parks, this is illegal. Bring a camera and take photos instead.

Noise: Hikers are seldom loud but it's worth noting that sound carries easily in the forest. Be especially wary about noise levels on trails that border private property.

Bikes and ATVs: The increased popularity of mountain bikes, off-road motorcycles and all-terrain vehicles (ATVs), and their use on hiking trails, is a concern for many hikers. However, some trails in this book are open to both cyclists and hikers, and this combined interest group actually strengthens the lobby for the maintenance and extension of trails. If you ride a bike, use only trails that welcome you. In many places, ignoring this advice causes irreparable destruction of the land.

Camping: Camp only in designated campgrounds.

Trail markings: The trails described in this book are either well marked or self-evident, at time of writing. There should be no need to add your own markings to help you find your way back. However, if you are afraid of getting lost and decide to do this, do not blaze (slash) trees; tie surveyor's ribbon to branches and remove these ribbons on your return. Never remove trail markings already in place. In general, it is best to neither add nor remove trail markings, to avoid misleading other hikers.

Keeping to the trails: Trails in the Gulf Islands often cross land that is vulnerable to erosion and the destruction of fragile mosses, ground cover and wildflowers. Some trails are on or skirt private property and their continued existence depends on the goodwill of local property owners. For these reasons, hikers should stick to the trails at all times and avoid creating shortcuts.

Trespassing: If you are hiking on private land, be sure that you have the property owner's permission. If you are on public land, do not venture onto private land. If you are hiking along beaches, stay below the high-tide line. (In Canada, generally all of the foreshore—the land between the high and low tide lines—is public.)

Indian Reserves: All Indian Reserves, and there are many in the Gulf Islands, are private. Permission to hike is almost invariably granted to those who take the trouble to phone first. (Names and phone numbers are included with the relevant hikes.) Following this procedure will ensure that these beautiful areas remain open to hikers.

It is especially important not to remove or disturb anything from an Indian Reserve except your own or others' garbage. Aboriginal people are particularly concerned about the removal of artifacts from reserves and cultural sites. Middens, indicated by soil comprised of broken shells, often mixed with ash-black dirt, can be found fronting the shore throughout the Gulf Islands and indicate places where aboriginal people once lived.

As with petroglyphs (rock carvings) and pictographs (rock paintings), middens are of great interest to archaeologists and are protected by the Heritage Conservation Act. There are penalties for disturbing them.

Liability: When you hike, wherever you hike, be prepared to take responsibility for your own safety. Be sure you know what you are getting into before you start up a trail. If a climb is beyond your level of skill or fitness, don't attempt it.

In general, this often-given advice is still the best: take nothing but photographs; leave nothing but footprints.

WHAT TO BRING ON HIKES

I can say, with some assurance, that you'll never have everything you want with you when you go hiking. Still, if you're like me and lug along everything but the kitchen sink, you'll come pretty close to having everything you need.

Footwear: Good footwear is essential. Although I have come to prefer the security of waterproof hiking boots, for most of the hikes described in this book, running shoes with good treads would be fine, except in wet conditions.

I like wearing a pair of thick woollen or synthetic hiking socks over a pair of thin liner socks. Most hikers avoid cotton socks because they don't wick away perspiration, take longer to dry and remain cold when wet.

Clothes: I always wear a hat for protection against cold and the sun. In any season, I like the layered approach because it lets you peel off clothes as you warm up and put them back on when you cool off or it begins to rain. In cooler weather, I wear a lightweight fleece vest or jacket and a well-worn, waterproof, breathable jacket. In its pockets, I keep a pair of gloves, a small toque, paper and pencil, a collapsible umbrella (on really threatening days) and plastic bags (for garbage or new-found treasures).

Aside from cotton shorts, everything I'm wearing is synthetic, lightweight and very comfortable. My backpack contains a first-aid kit and most of what's listed in the "What to Bring" section of this book.
Craig Carpenter

Daypacks: You'll probably want to carry a daypack for extra clothes, including a bathing suit (in case there's a good place to swim). My lunch also goes into my daypack, usually in a plastic container to keep my food from getting horribly squashed. Don't forget to include water or another thirst-quenching drink. (Lots on a hot day!)

Walking sticks: Many hikers like to carry a walking stick or pair of poles. I fell in love with walking sticks when I was a teenager but never really got into the habit of hiking with one until I ruptured my Achilles tendon. I now use two poles, which help me maintain my balance, especially when going downhill. They are also useful for deflecting stinging nettles, thistles and spider webs.

Miscellaneous items: I carry my essentials—and more—in a fanny pack that opens into a backpack when my gear requires the extra space. You'll want to bring along this guidebook, of course, and any maps for the area you're hiking. My pack also contains the following:

- moleskin (to put on at the first hint of a developing blister)
- sewing kit (like the ones provided by travel agents or hotels)
- first-aid kit
- Swiss army knife (the kind with scissors, screwdrivers, a can opener, a corkscrew and other useful tools)
- pens, pencils, paper, elastics, paperclips, Post-its (for leaving messages)
- fluorescent surveyor's tape (to tie to trees to mark the path, so you don't get hopelessly lost on your return trip)
- small flashlight (in case you're still on the trail at dusk or wish to explore a cave)
- small pair of binoculars
- compass
- sunscreen
- strapping with Velcro to attach things like a jacket to your pack

- string (for use as emergency shoelaces, belt, etc.)
- tissues
- sunglasses, reading glasses or just extra glasses and a strap to hold them on
- sweatband
- waterproof matches/fire-starting kit
- packages of salt and pepper, teabags, etc.
- GPS (Global Positioning System) and extra batteries
- pack towel (which takes up almost no room and is incredibly effective for those spur-of-the-moment swims)
- cellphone for emergencies (they do not work in all areas)
- wallet
- camera and film
- plastic poncho for absolute downpours (especially when you aren't wearing a waterproof jacket)
- a whistle or other noisemaker
- a thermal blanket (garbage bags can also help you conserve body heat and stay dry in cold or wet weather)
- snacks (granola bars, chocolate bars, trail mix, etc.)
- plastic or foam for sitting on wet ground
- large garbage bag for an emergency shelter
- tide table
- flares

This is my list. At some time or other I've used every item on it. Undoubtedly, there are different lists to suit individual needs, but this should give you some ideas.

One final word about first-aid kits. Some people feel they are essential. I have started carrying most of the following items:

- oral thermometer
- antacid tablets
- tweezers
- mild antiseptic
- antibiotic ointment
- alcohol swabs
- ASA tablets/Tylenol/ibuprofen
- antihistamine tablets
- cotton swabs
- tensor bandage
- sterile gauze dressings
- roll of 2.5 cm adhesive tape
- anti-itch ointment (e.g., calamine lotion)
- absorbent cotton
- tongue depressors (for use as finger splints)
- matches
- scissors, safety pins, elastic bands
- variety of bandages/dressings

SAFETY CONSIDERATIONS

Hikers frequently get lost. I certainly have—and you might, too. If you do "misplace" yourself, you'll probably manage to find your own way out. However, it's wise to take precautions to prevent getting lost and to avoid discomfort, injury or even death. Here are a few suggestions:

- Know your limits. Don't attempt a hike that is beyond your ability, strength or the time you have available.
- Before you leave, ensure that you know where you're going. Read the maps and trail descriptions carefully and take maps and a compass along, since directions are often difficult to determine, particularly on cloudy days in a BC forest or when trail markings are limited.
- Let someone know where you're going, how long you'll be, the number of people in your party and when you plan to return, so there's someone who knows enough to look for you if you're not back at a reasonable time.
- Don't hike alone. You're much safer with someone else.
- Don't leave too late in the day; be sure there's ample time to return before dark. This is especially important in the fall and winter, when there's less daylight.
- Keep to designated trails. Some are marked only by the pathway created by the passing of many hikers, while others may be marked by surveyor's ribbon, metal markers, or slashes or spray paint on trees. In some places, cairns are used where it is difficult to mark the trail in any other way. Cairns (or sometimes double markings) are also used to indicate a change in direction. Where alternative trails exist, side trails are often symbolically blocked off by stones and branches. Take great care to follow the correct trail, as deadfalls can often obscure main trails and other trail markings are easily removed, naturally or otherwise.
- Wear appropriate clothes and footwear for the area. I favour polyester clothes because of their ability to wick away moisture and stay dry. (I avoid cotton because it absorbs moisture and takes too long to dry.) It's also important to carry extra clothes, even if it's quite warm when you leave home. Hypothermia is one of the most common causes of distress, and even death, for lost hikers.
- Carry emergency equipment as suggested under What to Bring, page 18.
- If you do get lost, keep calm and remain in a place where rescuers can see you. Do not leave the trail, even if it's obvious you're on the wrong one. It's much more difficult to find a hiker who has taken off through the bush.
- In addition to mosquitoes and wasps, hikers should beware of ticks, especially from early spring to late summer. Hikers can discourage tick bites by wearing long-sleeved shirts and full-length pants secured at the ankles. If you suspect that you are hiking in a tick-infested area, be sure to check for them when you return from your outing. If hiking with a dog, you should also check your pet. Bites by coastal ticks seldom create complications, although they may cause infection or a rare condition called Lyme disease. If you experience a rash or flu-like symptoms following a bite, see a doctor.

A NOTE ABOUT TIDES

As so many of the shore walks in this book are possible only at low tide, you should know something about tides. In general, you can expect four tides a day in the Gulf Islands: two high tides and two low tides every 24 hours. Depending on the time of year, the difference between high and low tide may range from half a metre to six metres. In general, a tide that is right out when you start your hike will be right in approximately six hours later and the beach trail you followed may have completely disappeared. Unless you are on Crown land or in a park, you may be forced to trespass on private property to make your way back. Worse, you may be completely stranded. For this reason it is essential to check the tide tables before starting out and schedule your movements accordingly if any part of your hike crosses the intertidal zone.

PUBLIC PARKS AND CROWN LAND

Many of the trails described in this book are found in public parks, which are in some of the most beautiful spots on the Gulf Islands. These parks are managed by several different jurisdictions and have been established for different reasons.

Community parks: Many Gulf Islands have parks and recreation departments that administer local parks. Increasingly, new local parks, usually for day use only, are being created under provincial laws that require developers to dedicate up to five percent of all new developments to the public. These new parks often include trail networks.

Regional parks: Each of these parks is maintained by a regional government, for a variety of recreational uses. They are open year-round and are usually larger than municipal parks and often more accessible than provincial parks.

Provincial parks: The province's parks, many of which are marine parks (often accessible only by water), provide users with outdoor recreational opportunities while conserving the natural environment. No mineral exploration or commercial development was permitted inside any of the parks described in this book at time of writing, although the provincial government was considering changes to this rule. Provincial parks are administered by the Ministry of Water, Lands and Air Protection (WLAP). You can find information on provincial parks from www.gov.bc.ca/wlap and http://wlapwww.gov.bc.ca/bcparks.

Crown land: The provincial government manages Crown (or public) land. Eighty-five percent of all of BC is Crown land that has been designated as provincial forest. A significant portion of this land is available for public recreational activities, such as camping and hiking. Some of the trails described in this book have been developed co-operatively by the Ministry of Forests and members of the community. (For further information on the recreational use of provincial forests, contact the BC Forest Service office in the area you plan to visit.) Some Crown land has been designated to be used for provincial parks or ecological reserves. Other Crown land is "vacant," which means no decision has been made as to how it may ultimately be used. Outdoor enthusiasts hope the government can be persuaded to convert this land into parks, to protect it for future public use.

Anyone has the right to enter vacant Crown land. A Ministry of Forests resource officer explained that the general rule for Crown land is "use it but don't abuse it, and don't steal from it." For our purposes, this means that you can camp and hike on this land. However, you are not allowed to remove anything (mushrooms, firewood, cedar boughs, etc.), especially for commercial purposes. For further information on the Ministry of Forests, visit www.gov.bc.ca/for.

From Mount Warburton Pike, you look over South Pender Island to Stuart Island in Boundary Pass and to the many islands that border Haro Strait.
Richard Blier

There are well-established trails, used by local residents, on Crown land throughout the Gulf Islands. Where possible, these trails are described in this book. Crown land is often surrounded by private land and can be accessed only by crossing private property. If this is the case, you must first get permission of the landowner.

Ecological reserves: Ecological reserves have been established on selected pieces of Crown land to preserve representative and special natural ecosystems; rare and endangered plants and animals; and unique, rare or outstanding features and phenomena. They are not created for outdoor recreation. Although most ecological reserves are open for non-destructive observational uses, such as wildlife viewing and photography, their recreational use is discouraged. The primary uses of ecological reserves are research and educational activities.

The Gulf Islands National Park Reserve (GINPR): This new National Park Reserve (the result of eight years of land acquisition by the provincial and federal governments) was officially established in May 2003 to protect a representative portion of the southern Gulf Islands. The park currently consists of properties on 16 islands, plus numerous small islets and reef areas. With a total area of 33 square km (including a 25-m intertidal zone), it is Canada's fifth smallest national park. The park reserve will continue to grow, as additional lands are purchased or donated. Adjacent waters, extending 200 m from the mean low-tide mark, are also protected and managed by Parks Canada.

At time of writing, the services and facilities for visitors in the park reserve were very limited. The development of any major visitor facilities will be subject to public consultation over the next several years and must be approved through a management planning process.

Bowen ISLAND

Bowen residents view their island as a rural paradise within commuting distance of Vancouver. One of the larger and more populated of the Gulf Islands, Bowen is about 52 square km and home to 2,957 full-time residents. Most of the island's amenities, including a general store, restaurants and craft shops, are centred in quaint Snug Cove, the location of the ferry terminal and a magnet for Vancouverites seeking a quick escape from the "Big Smoke." From Snug Cove, you can walk to beaches, Killarney Lake or into lush forest. Because of its steep terrain and shortage of good farmland, the centre of the island is largely undeveloped and you can easily spend a day walking its paths in quiet contemplation. Promoted by locals as the Island of Walks, Bowen has established trail networks in Crippen Park and Mount Gardner, and plans are underway to develop a more extensive trail system on the island's southwest side.

HISTORY

For centuries, the Squamish people visited the island they called Xwlil'xhwm, "fast drumming ground," to hunt and fish. In 1791, Spanish explorers named it Isla de Apodaca, in honour of a Spanish naval officer. Less than 70 years later, the British renamed the island after one of their naval heroes, Rear Admiral James Bowen. Bowen's first settlers established farms on the island in the 1870s and supplemented their income by fishing, hunting and logging. From the 1890s on, cottage communities began to develop at Snug Cove, Bluewater, Eagle Cliff, Hood Point, Cowan Point, Miller's Landing, Tunstall Bay and Deep Bay.

Early industry included two brick factories in Deep Bay and an explosives factory in Tunstall Bay. In the early 1900s, numerous unsuccessful attempts were made to mine gold and copper but, as Captain John A. Cates discovered when he began a ferry service between Bowen and Vancouver around the turn of the century, recreation was the island's real pay dirt. For more than 20 years, Cates brought vacationers to his resort in Deep Bay. In 1920, Cates sold the resort to the Union Steamship Company, which went on to build a small tourism empire that included a hotel, stables and bridle paths, tennis courts, a bowling green, a tea room, a dance pavilion, cottages, a store and picnic grounds. Until the company was sold in 1962, Bowen was like a company town centred around Snug Cove. Today, despite its large number of year-round residents, the Municipality of Bowen Island retains its rural charm.

GETTING THERE

There are hourly 20-minute ferry sailings daily, from early morning to late night, from Horseshoe Bay (near Vancouver) to Snug Cove on Bowen Island. For information, obtain a Mainland–Vancouver Island–Sunshine Coast schedule or contact BC Ferries (see Resources, page 235).

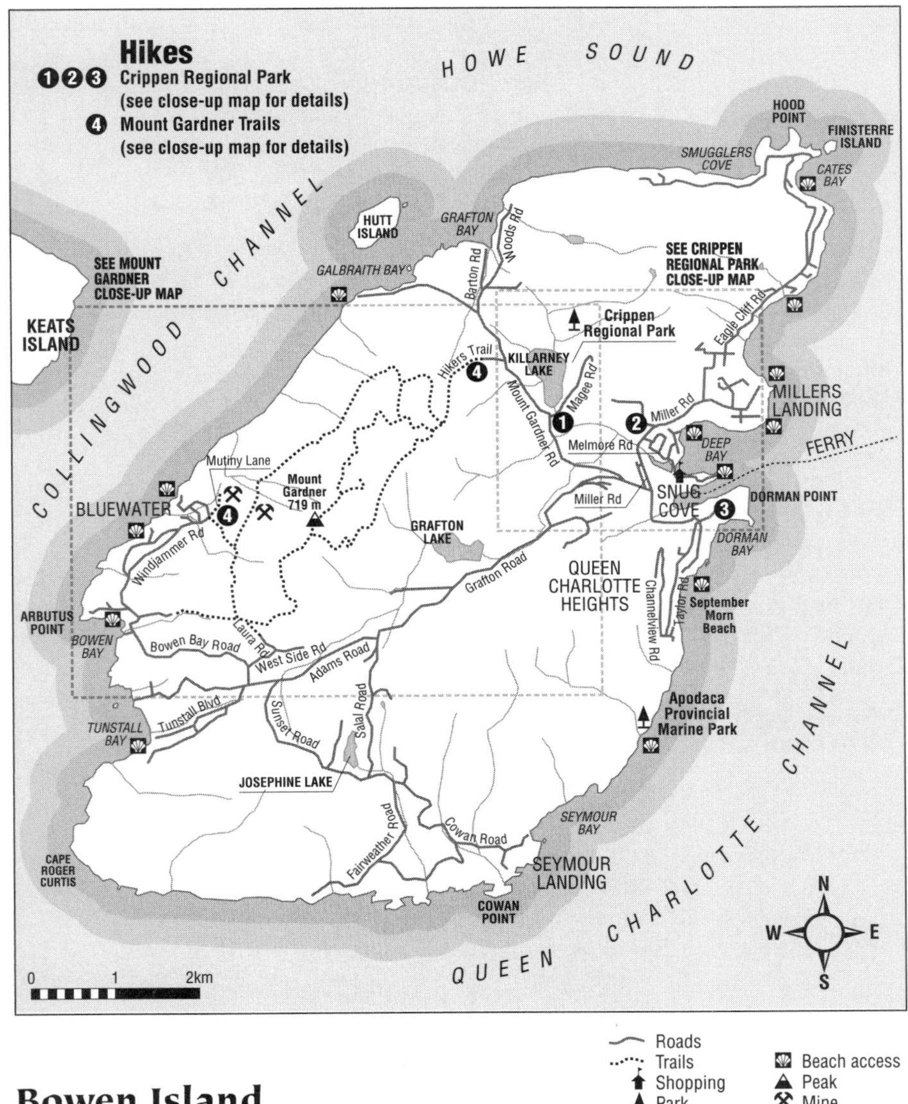

Bowen Island

SERVICES AND ACCOMMODATION

Bowen's shopping area is relatively small but includes a good range of stores, restaurants and services. Most businesses are either in Snug Cove or Artisan Square, a short walk from the ferry dock. Bowen has many bed and breakfasts and rental cottages, including some of the original Union Steamship cottages; however, the island has no camping facilities. Visitors may wish to visit the Museum and Archives (on Miller Road) run by the Bowen Island Historians (604-947-2655).

The Bowen Island Community Shuttle makes it possible to get around the island without a car (check www.translink.bc.ca, www.bowentransit.com or call 604-947-0229). As well, most of the hikes described in this chapter can easily be reached on foot from the ferry.

The Bowen Island Book, a visitors' guide that includes maps and trail information, is available from the Bowen Island Chamber of Commerce (604-947-9024; fax: 604-947-0633; e-mail: info@bowenisland.org; or www.bowenisland.org). A visitor's information centre is open in Snug Cove during the summer.

ESPECIALLY FOR WALKERS

There's lots of walking within easy reach of the Snug Cove ferry terminal and marinas. In addition to the shore and road walks described below, try Crippen Regional Park (see hikes 1 and 2). You might also explore the Bowen Island Greenway, which now connects Crown land on Mount Gardner with Crown land to the southwest. The main access is off Sunset Road, 1.3 km from Adams Road. Parking is on the right-hand side of the road. This trail network is under development and may eventually connect to trails around Cape Roger Curtis. Contact the Bowen Island Parks and Recreation Commission (604-947-2216 or biprc@bimbc.ca) for information.

HIKES

Bowen's main hikes are on trails within 240-ha Crippen Regional Park and on Crown land on Mount Gardner. A brochure on Crippen Regional Park is available from the Greater Vancouver Regional District, Parks Department, 4330 Kingsway, Burnaby, BC V5H 4G8; 604-224-5739. Limited copies are also available on the Crippen Park information board outside the library.

1. Killarney Lake Loop Trail (Crippen Regional Park) ★★★

Trail length	4 km round trip
Time required	1.5 hours, including time to enjoy the vegetation
Description	This pretty walk around a shallow lake passes through boggy areas and over boardwalks through marsh.
Level	Easy
Accesses	Either from the picnic area at the intersection of Magee Road and Mount Gardner Road or from 800 m farther north on Mount Gardner Road on the west side of the lake

Caution	Wear waterproof shoes or boots, as parts of the trail can be swampy.

Note: This hike can be combined with either the Killarney Creek Trail or the Cedar Trail, both of which run southeast from Magee Road.

Walking east from the picnic area, you pass a dam that controls the lake's water level and the flow of water to the fish ladders in Killarney Creek. Follow Magee Road for a short distance, until you regain the trail (on the left), which follows the east side of the lake. There are several creeks and some small falls within the lake area.

The trail climbs steadily to the northeast, passing a flooded area, before reaching a boardwalk that crosses a marsh at the northern tip of the lake. At the western end of the lake is a drowned forest, where you'll find Sitka spruce. Labrador tea, sundew, western bog-laurel and sweet gale grow in low-lying areas along this part of the trail. Keep your eyes open for waterfowl, especially in the spring.

2. KILLARNEY CREEK, MEADOW, HATCHERY, ALDER GROVE, SCHOOL AND MAPLE TRAILS (CRIPPEN REGIONAL PARK) ★★★

Trail length	About 3.5 km of trail in total, depending on route taken
Time required	1–2 hours, depending on route taken
Description	These interconnecting trails pass through lovely red cedar forest, as well as by a waterfall, a fish hatchery and a fish ladder.
Level	Easy
Accesses	You can access these trails from Magee Road near Killarney Lake, Miller Road, near the municipal works yard on Mount Gardner Road, and near the Union Steamship General Store (see map, page 28).

The Killarney Creek Trail runs between Miller Road (from an access opposite Lenora Road) to Magee Road. It passes through a forest of alder, maple, cedar and hemlock. The Meadow Trail, branching off the Killarney Creek Trail to the southwest, crosses a swampy meadow, passes through alder, nears an equestrian ring and ends a short distance past a fish hatchery. From between the equestrian ring and the hatchery, the Hatchery Trail leads back to Miller Road through dense red cedar forest, which also contains western hemlock and Sitka spruce.

Across Miller Road, the trail leads to a fish ladder and Bridal Veil Falls. Slightly south of here, the trail branches. If you go left (southeast) along Alder Grove Trail toward the Memorial Garden, you can descend to a trail that leads to the causeway dividing a pretty lagoon from Deep Bay. Along the way, there is a lovely view of the entrance to Deep Bay. The lagoon is a great place to observe waterfowl and, nearby, you'll find an access to the beach on Deep Bay.

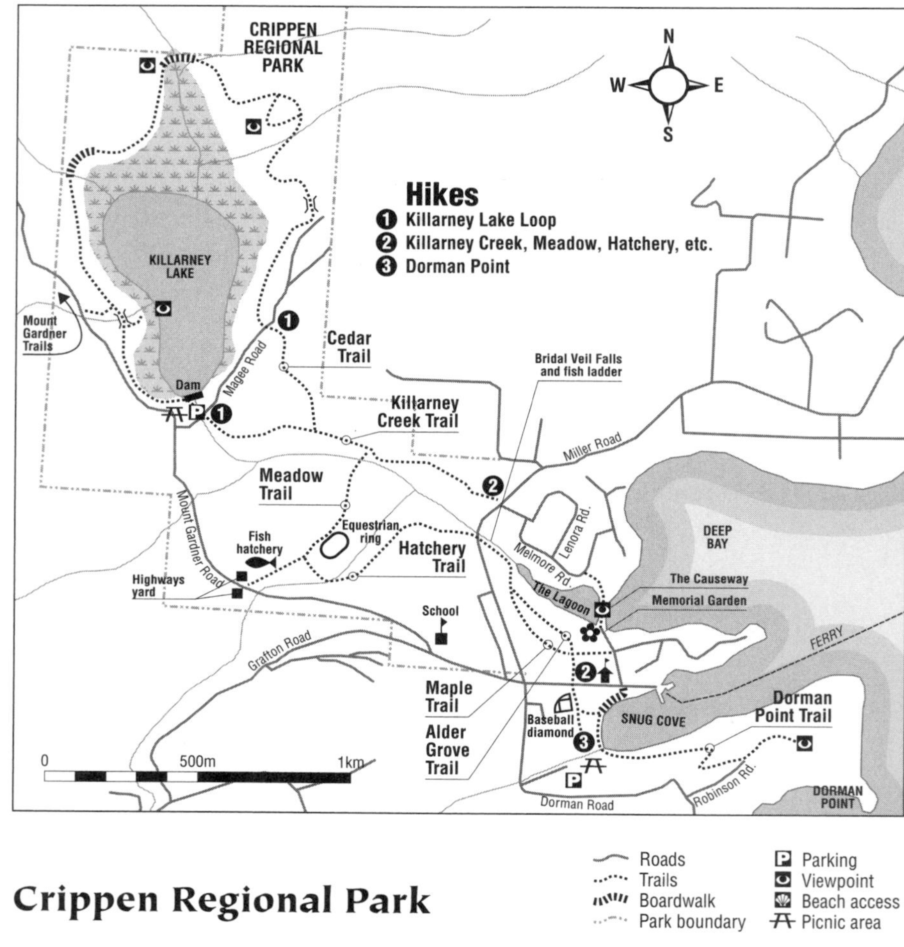

Crippen Regional Park

From the lagoon, the trail climbs to Melmore Road. Turn left on Melmore Road, then right on Lenora Road to rejoin Miller Road. Alternatively, you can follow the trail back down to the Union Steamship Store, cross the road and follow the boardwalk to the Dorman Point Trail.

3. Dorman Point Trail (Crippen Regional Park) ★★★

Trail length	2 km return
Time required	1 hour
Description	The trail climbs steadily to a point above Snug Cove that overlooks West Vancouver.
Level	Moderate, with one fairly steep ascent

Access	The complete trail starts from the picnic grounds near the marina in Snug Cove. It is also possible to take an abbreviated route to the top, from the end of Robinson Road.
Cautions	The climb is very steep, especially from the end of Robinson Road. The cliffs at the top fall off steeply, so don't get too close to the edge.

This trail ascends the hill partly on stairs and partly along an old logging road that begins at the end of Robinson Road. The picnic area at the trailhead is very pretty, as are the views of the arbutus-clad summit of Whytecliff Park in West Vancouver and the Point Grey neighbourhood of Vancouver in the distance. Ferries pass back and forth below.

4. Mount Gardner Trails ★★★★

Trail length	8 km for the loop described here
Time required	5 hours round trip, allowing time for lunch and long looks at the spectacular views
Description	The trails—partly old logging roads—climb fairly steeply. Depending on the route taken, there are excellent views of the Sunshine Coast to the west and Vancouver to the east.
Level	Moderate to strenuous
Elevation	719 m
Accesses	A. The main access is 500 m up Hikers Trail Road, a gravel road that runs west off Mount Gardner Road (between electrical poles 490 and 491) about 500 m past the entrance to Crippen Regional Park at Magee Road. The trailhead is about 3 km from the ferry dock. B. There are two alternate trails toward the end of Mutiny Lane, which runs north off Windjammer Road: Mine Trail, on the right side of Mutiny Lane, rises steeply and soon passes an old mine shaft; Bluewater Trail begins about 300 m farther, on the right side of the water-storage tank. C. Bowen Bay Trail, at the end of Laura Road (off West Side Road), is the steepest access to the summit. Follow the orange metal signs on trees, to avoid trespassing on private property.

Cautions	Follow the Mount Gardner trail map carefully, as the mountain is honeycombed with old and new trails and many old logging roads.

This description assumes that you start from access A. From Mount Gardner Road, it's about 500 m (about 15 minutes) up Hikers Trail to a steel gate. Almost immediately, on the left, look for a sign saying Skid Trail. The trail is marked with red metal markers on trees. It crosses a stream and begins to climb almost immediately. After another kilometre (about 15 minutes), the trail reaches a junction. Continue straight up Mount Gardner South Route.

Continue for about 2 km (about 1 hour), until you reach another junction. The trail to the right is a shortcut to the summit but it's very steep. I recommend that you continue straight. Within a few minutes, you reach a great viewpoint and then a wetland. About 500 m farther, you reach another junction. Continue straight ahead (north) to reach the summit. The trail to the left descends to Bowen Bay.

The trail to the summit actually descends before rising again. Just before the summit, you reach another junction, where the north and south routes meet. Go right to reach the summit. Here you have views from two helipads used to service the communications towers that dot the mountaintop. The first helipad you'll reach looks south and

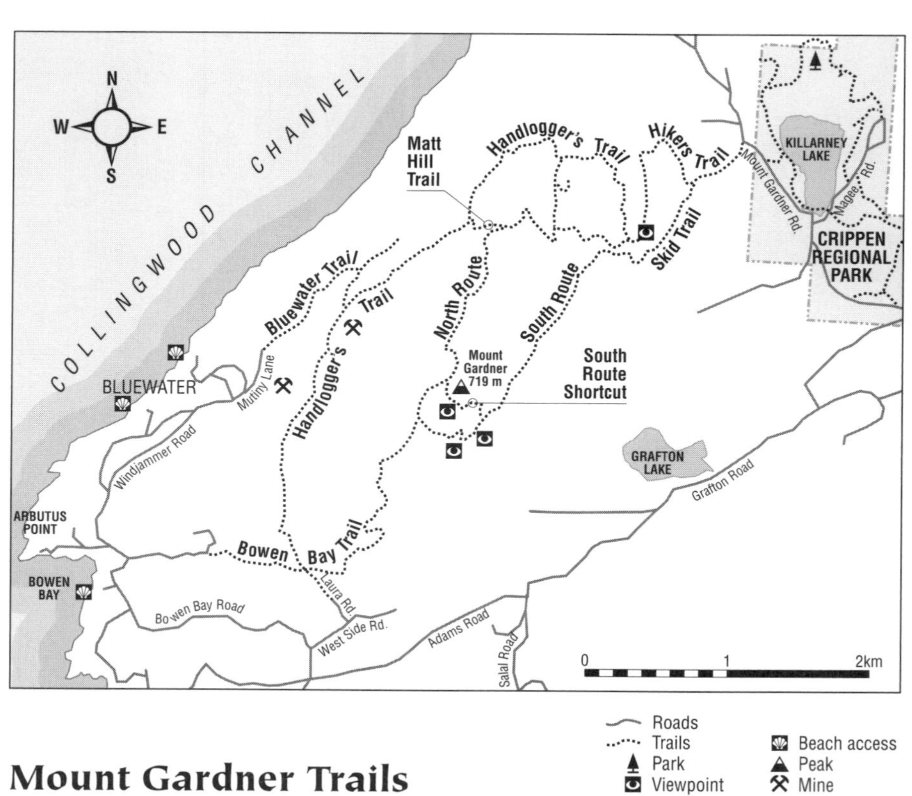

Mount Gardner Trails

west toward Vancouver Island and the Gulf Islands. The second helipad looks north toward Gambier Island and up the Squamish Valley. The Sunshine Coast is to the west.

From the summit, retrace your steps to the junction of the north and south routes. Continue right on the north route until you regain Hikers Trail Road (the old logging road). Stay on the right at the fork on this road and return down to the trailhead.

SHORE AND ROAD WALKS

Trans-Island Pathway System (TIPS): The Bowen Island Parks and Recreation Commission has been developing a trans-island pathway. The gravel trail starts at the top of Tunstall Boulevard and runs toward Snug Cove, along the road edge. Where sections of the trail are not complete, hikers walk along the road's narrow shoulder. Coming from Snug Cove, you will find the beginning of the trail across the street from the community school.

Tunstall Boulevard and Bay: Walk along Tunstall Boulevard down to Tunstall Bay, on the southwest side of the island. When you reach the sea, you can walk along the beach for a short distance, at low tide. You will pass the remains of a brick chimney from the explosives factory that once operated on this site. Behind it is the Tunstall Bay Community Association's recreation centre. An outhouse is at this beach access.

Bowen Bay: Another pretty beach at the junction of Bowen Bay Road and Windjammer Road boasts an outhouse, a wheelchair-accessible path and an extensive parking area. Walk along the driftwood-strewn gravel beach, by rocky outcrops and past the many summer cottages that line this shore.

Windjammer Road: Windjammer Road, in the same neighbourhood as Bowen Bay, makes a pleasant road walk. At the northern end by power pole number 873 (near the driveway of 974 Windjammer Road), a path leads to steps that descend to the beach. A stream enters the sea at this beach. Farther along, if there has been sufficient rainfall, another stream cascades to the ocean as a small waterfall.

Queen Charlotte Heights: The Queen Charlotte Heights area provides views of Vancouver. The Bowen Island Parks and Recreation Commission has upgraded the trail to September Morn Beach. To access this trail, follow Hummingbird Lane to the cul-de-sac at the end of the road. Stairs lead down a short trail to a pebble beach with views of Vancouver and West Vancouver.

Snug Cove: The walking around Snug Cove is delightful. Follow a trail to the viewpoint at Dorman Point (see hike 3) or a trail that climbs to Melmore Road, passing a lagoon on the left and the Deep Bay beach on your right. In the fall, you might see salmon trying to climb the fish ladder into the lagoon. The roads in this area offer water views and are interesting to explore. Melmore connects to Lenora Road, which joins with Miller Road.

Miller Road: Miller Road passes a wide variety of houses and provides many views of the sea. It is possible to descend to Miller's Landing but you can't walk along the shore.

Hood Point: Be sure to take Eagle Cliff Road north to Hood Point and visit the beach at Cates Bay. Park near the private tennis courts (on the left) and continue east along a flat, straight trail that accesses a staircase to the beach. Hood Point was originally a completely private cottage development. Although many of the cottages have been replaced by large, modern homes, the Hood Point development still looks like a cottage area. Respect private property by keeping to the road, trail and beach.

AND IF YOU PADDLE . . .

Paddling around Bowen is not for beginners. There can be a fair bit of traffic, as well as strong currents in Queen Charlotte Channel between Bowen and the mainland. This said, the Bowen shore is beautiful and fairly accessible. You will not want to miss Apodaca Provincial Marine Park. This 8-ha marine park, bordered by private property, is a beautiful spot to walk. The shore is lined by rocky cliffs, which invite exploration. The pristine gravel beaches make great picnic sites and you can climb the banks for views over Queen Charlotte Channel.

Before heading out, be sure to check your tide and current tables carefully. Here are some starting places:

Tunstall Bay or Bowen Bay: These neighbouring beaches both have good access, permanent outhouses and ample parking. You can paddle to the left (southwest) along Bowen's relatively undeveloped shore to Cape Roger Curtis. This is also the best access to the popular Pasley Island Group off Bowen's west side. Paddlers should be aware that there are few places to pull out between Bluewater and Galbraith Bay to the north.

Galbraith Bay: The government dock (Mount Gardner Dock) is a good place to launch. From here, you can explore Bowen's northern shore, as well as nearby Hutt Island. Parking is very limited in this area during all but the winter months.

Hood Point: From the access on Cates Bay at Hood Point, explore the northern tip of Bowen, including tiny Finisterre Island just offshore. To the west, there's no road access to the shore until you reach Grafton Bay.

Deep Bay: This is a good spot to launch at high tide. It gives you access to Bowen's busiest waters, so paddle carefully. Keep well away from the ferry, which docks in Snug Cove to the south, and be careful of its wash. Farther south, the shore around Dorman Point and down to Cowan Point is well worth paddling. On the way, plan to stop on one of the small beaches at Apodaca Provincial Marine Park and climb a trail to one of the viewpoints for a picnic lunch. The Deep Bay access is equipped with an outhouse.

Snug Cove: While the ferry and heavy boat traffic can make paddling here stressful, people can wheel their kayaks off the ferry and launch from the nearby government dock. Kayakers should stick close to the shore and time their arrival and departure so as not to coincide with the ferry. From here, you can paddle south toward Cowan Point or explore Deep Bay to the north.

Cortes ISLAND

Alternately grouped with the Discovery Islands and the Northern Gulf Islands, Cortes is located immediately east of Quadra. About 25 km long and 13 km wide, it covers an area of 130 square km. With a population of approximately 1,000, Cortes has a remote feel, although there is daily ferry service and public roads linking the main settlements: Mansons Landing (the largest), Whaletown, Squirrel Cove and an area known as The Gorge. Facilities include stores, a credit union, liquor outlets, accommodation, a marina, kayak rentals and a famous retreat centre, Hollyhock. With the superb hike in Kw'as Park and the fabulous kayaking provided by the island's intricate coastline, Cortes is well worth visiting.

HISTORY

Cortes is home to the Klahoose First Nation, who occupy a large reserve in Squirrel Cove. Spanish explorers named the island in 1792 after the conquistador Hernando Cortez, whose name was also given to nearby Hernando Island.

One of the first activities that caused non-Native people to stop at Cortes was whaling. Whales were once numerous in the Strait of Georgia and a whaling station flourished briefly at Whaletown from 1869 to 1871. Shetland Islander Michael Manson started the first permanent non-Native settlement in 1886, establishing a trading post at present-day Mansons Landing. A post office opened in 1893 and the first school, a two-room building near Gunflint Lake, opened in 1895 with 12 students. There were also communities at Von Donop Inlet, Gunflint Lake, Squirrel Cove, Smelt Bay, Seaford, Gorge Harbour and Carrington Bay. Ferry service began in 1969 and electricity arrived in 1970. Early settlers tried sheep ranching and fruit farming but, as elsewhere, logging was the chief occupation. An important industry today is clam and oyster aquaculture, reputedly valued at $10 million per year.

GETTING THERE

From Campbell River on Vancouver Island, take the ferry to Quathiaski Cove on Quadra Island, then make your way across the island to Heriot Bay to catch the 45-minute sailing to Whaletown Bay on Cortes. For information, obtain a Northern Gulf Islands ferry schedule or contact BC Ferries (see Resources, page 235).

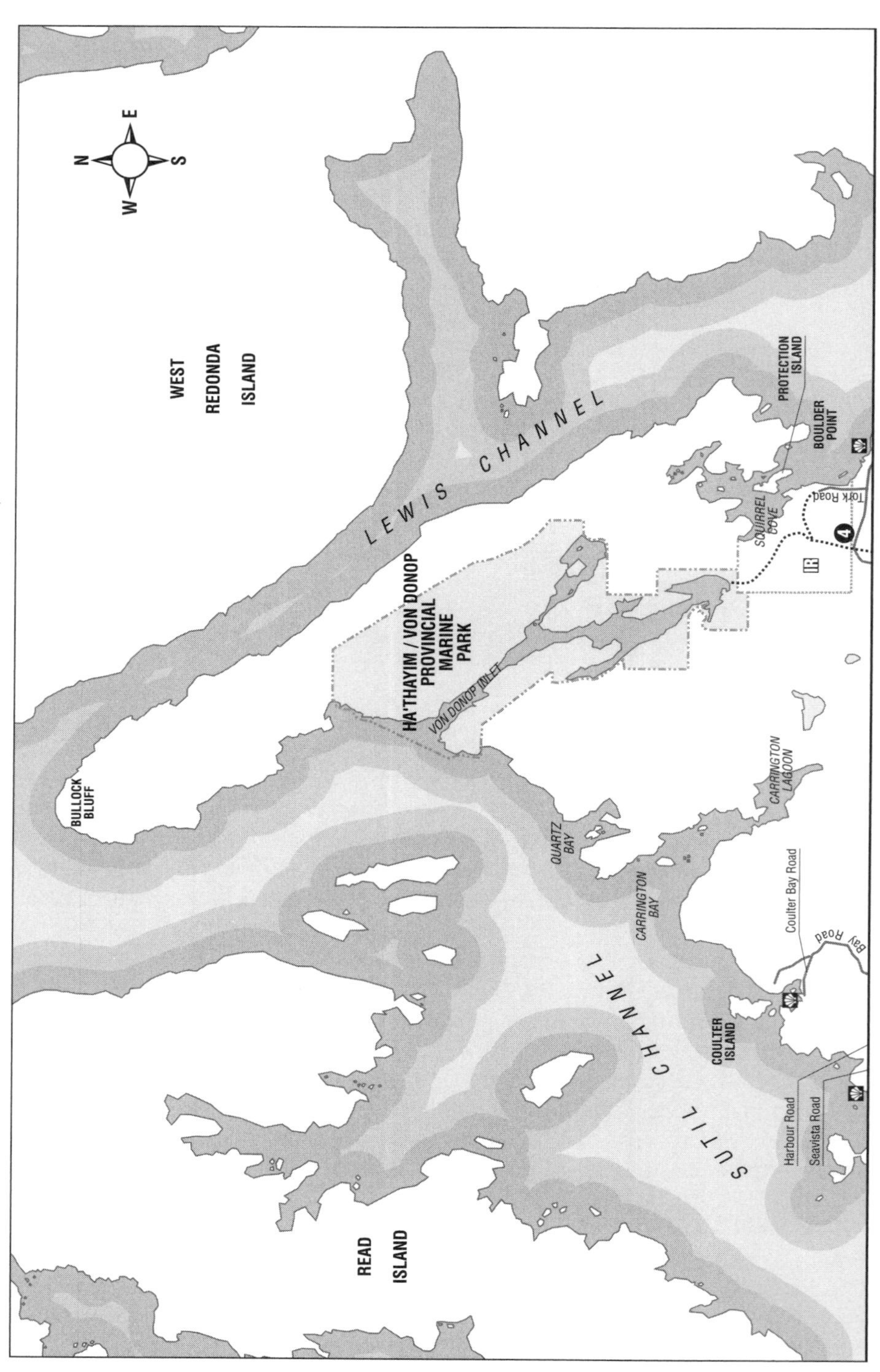
N
E
S
W
WEST REDONDA ISLAND
LEWIS CHANNEL
HA'THAYIM / VON DONOP PROVINCIAL MARINE PARK
VON DONOP INLET
BULLOCK BLUFF
QUARTZ BAY
CARRINGTON BAY
CARRINGTON LAGOON
SUTIL CHANNEL
COULTER ISLAND
READ ISLAND
PROTECTION ISLAND
BOULDER POINT
SQUIRREL COVE
Tork Road
IR
4
Coulter Bay Road
Bay Road
Harbour Road
Seavista Road

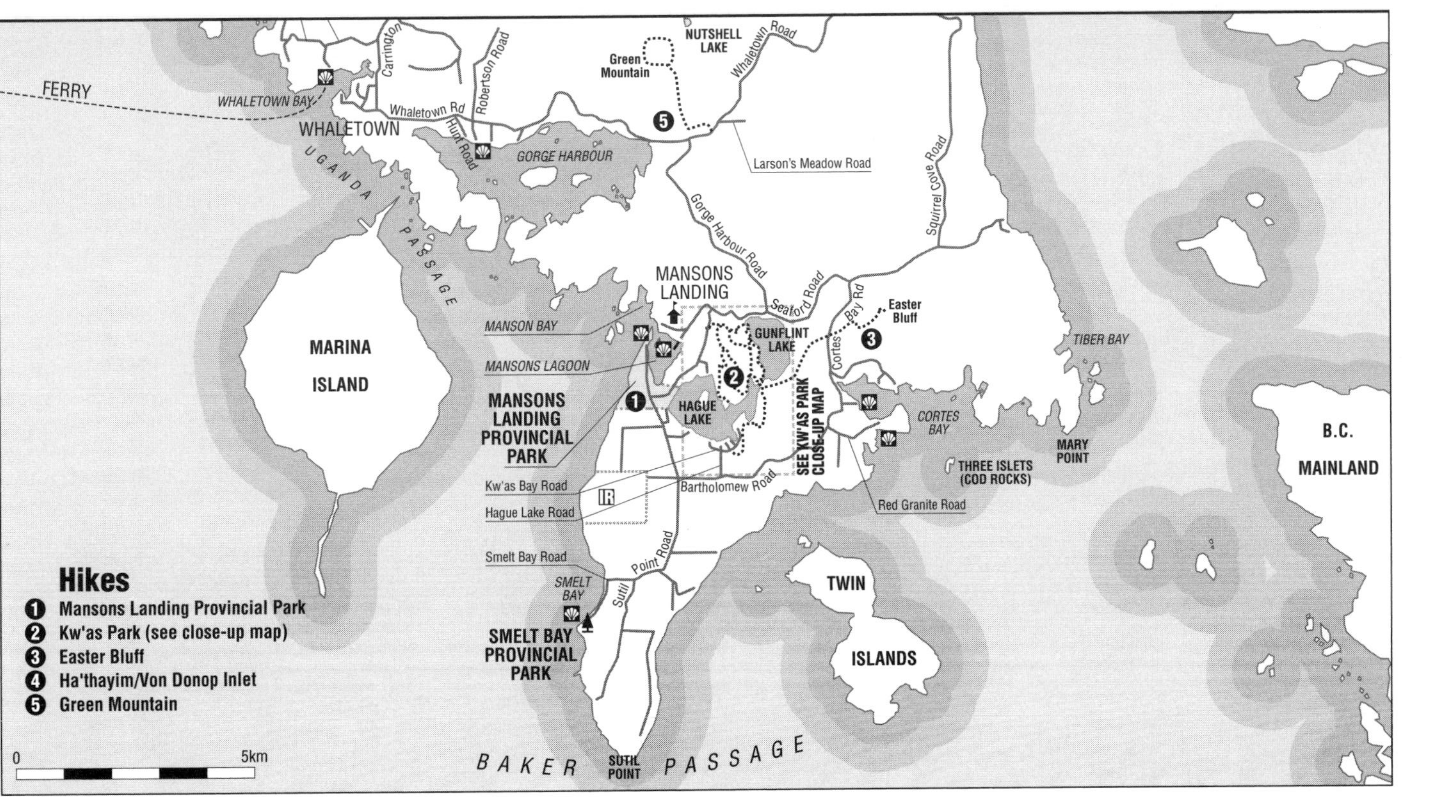

Roads
Trails
Park boundary
IR Indian Reserve
Shopping
Park
Beach access
See text

Cortes Island

SERVICES AND ACCOMMODATION

Since the island has long attracted boaters to its many naturally protected harbours, Cortes has all the basic services. There are general stores near the docks at Whaletown, Squirrel Cove, Gorge Harbour and at "downtown" Mansons Landing, which also has a motel and a credit union with a 24-hour ATM. The island also has several restaurants, several bed and breakfasts, a lodge, kayak rentals and other services, many of them seasonal. There's camping at Smelt Bay Provincial Park and an RV park and marina at the Gorge Harbour Marina Resort. For more information, check www.cortesisland.com, www.northcentralisland.com or the excellent information brochure available locally.

ESPECIALLY FOR WALKERS

Although some of the hikes described below are fairly strenuous, there are also many easy walks on Cortes, suitable for boaters wanting to stretch their legs. In addition to most of the Shore and Road Walks described on page 42, walkers might try one or more of the following:

- the trails in Mansons Landing Provincial Marine Park (see hike 1, below)
- the trails in Ha'thayim/Von Donop Marine Park (see hike 4, page 41)

You might also try the first bits of the Kw'as Park hike from either of the two accesses (page 37). You will find the going quite easy for a while, and when it gets too strenuous, you can return the way you came and try something else—or just go for coffee.

HIKES

Although one of the larger islands described in this book, Cortes is one of the least developed. The following are descriptions of a few of the more remarkable and accessible places to hike.

1. Mansons Landing Provincial Marine Park ★★★	
Trail length	About 3 km in total, depending on route taken
Time required	An hour or more, depending on pace
Description	Pleasant walk through open woods to a sand spit, along the beaches of a large and beautiful lagoon and through forest trails to a lake
Level	Easy
Access	At the end of Sutil Point Road (about 20 km from the ferry). There are signs to the right of the government dock for a trail leading to a sand spit. From the spit, you can follow a beach trail along the lagoon.

Walk along the soft sand spit, an ancient midden site, until you reach the narrow opening to the lagoon. Continue along the lagoon until your way is blocked by rocks, then duck into the forest on a trail along an old logging road. This trail takes you across Seaford Road to Hague Lake, one of Cortes residents' favourite swimming spots. There are paths both ways along the lakeshore but neither is very long. There are a number of great spots in the park for a picnic, the best being the sand spit and the beach at Hague Lake.

2. KW'AS PARK ★★★★★

Trail length	12 km in total
Time required	2–3 hours for the north loop (access A); 1–1.5 hours for the south route (access B). There are also a number of shorter trails within the north loop area.
Description	Vigorous hike through a mature forest, with views of Hague and Gunflint Lakes
Level	Moderate to challenging and definitely strenuous if you combine it with hike 3
Access	A. North entrance: east side of Seaford Road opposite the Cortes Island Motel B. South entrance: south side of Kw'as Bay Road off Hague Lake Road. There's a parking lot here.

The Regional District of Comox–Strathcona's 70-ha park contains a labyrinth of trails on the well-forested land between Hague (Kw'as) and Gunflint Lakes. The trails are well marked and maps are posted throughout the park. Most of the inspiration for this extraordinary park came from the late Pierre de Trey, who came up with the interesting names for land formations, wrote all the signs, and built the bridges, ladders and other aids you'll find on the trails.

Starting from Seaford Road (access A), you quickly enter a forest where everything seems upholstered with green moss. As you walk over a tangle of roots, you'll notice huge stumps with "gardens" sprouting out of them, remnants of the logging that took place here. Some of this area is wetland, complete with skunk cabbage and other swampy vegetation. The Spruce Grove Trail to the east follows the shoreline of Gunflint Lake, for some way. You pass the "Inca Ruins," a massive rock wall that looks as though it could have been constructed by Inca stonemasons. There are a number of access points to the lake, including one on which you'll find an old steam donkey that exploded in the fall of 1923, bringing logging in this area to an abrupt halt.

It will take you at least 35 minutes to reach the fanciful bridge over Serge Narrows (see map, page 38). From here, you can take a 2-hour side trip to Easter Bluff (see hike 3), continue on the south trail loop that leads to Kw'as Bay Road (a

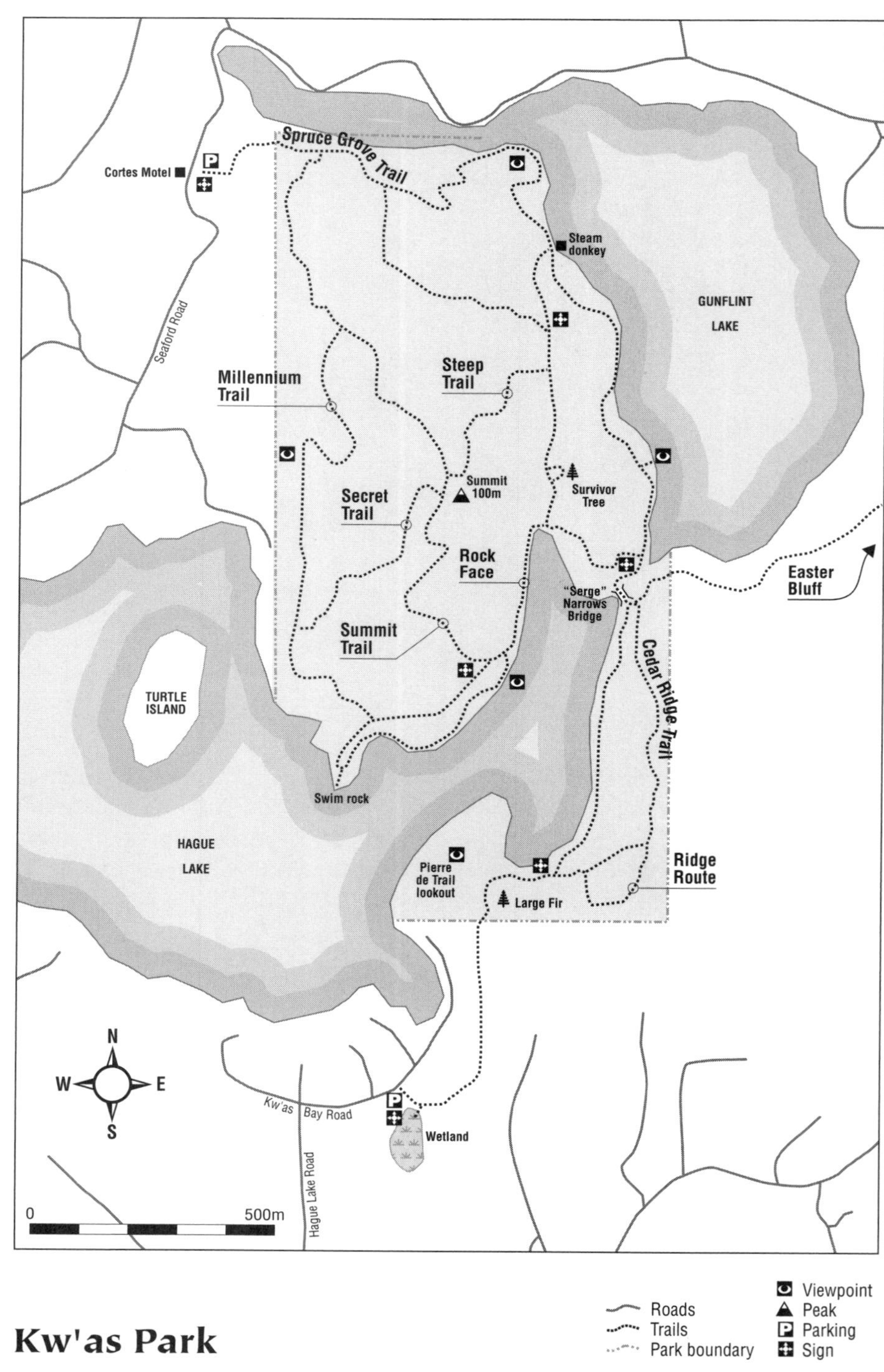
Spruce Grove Trail
Cortes Motel
Seaford Road
Steam donkey
GUNFLINT LAKE
Millennium Trail
Steep Trail
Summit 100m
Survivor Tree
Secret Trail
Rock Face
"Serge" Narrows Bridge
Easter Bluff
Summit Trail
Cedar Ridge Trail
TURTLE ISLAND
Swim rock
HAGUE LAKE
Pierre de Trail lookout
Large Fir
Ridge Route
N
W
E
S
Kw'as Bay Road
Wetland
Hague Lake Road
0
500m
Roads
Trails
Park boundary
Viewpoint
Peak
Parking
Sign

Kw'as Park

60- to 90-minute walk) or continue on the trails in the north loop. The trail to the south loop meanders for about 1.5 km through mature second-growth trees with some old-growth Douglas fir and western red cedar. The largest tree, a Douglas fir with a circumference of 8.4 m at its base, is just 500 m from the Kw'as Bay Road access (access B). There's a swamp at the access, and if you walk onto the viewing float provided, you can see a beaver lodge.

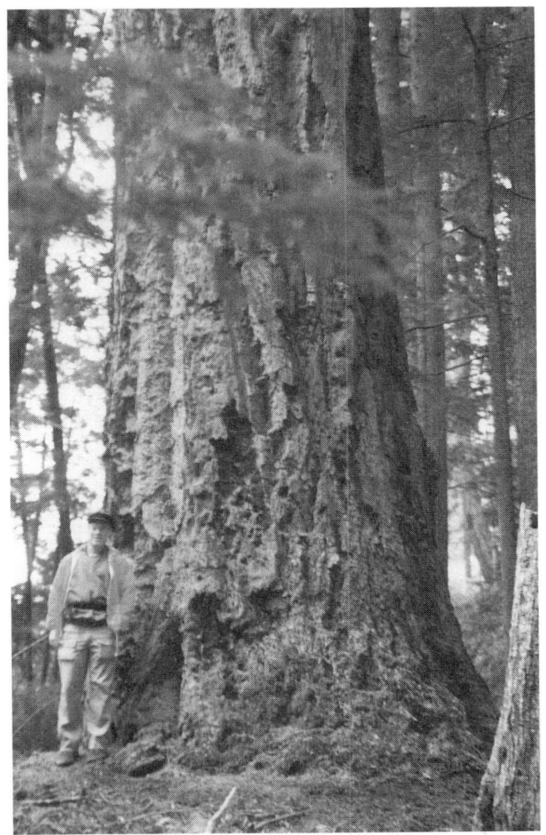

This tree in Kw'as Park is the largest I've seen in the Gulf Islands, with a circumference of 8.4 metres at its base.

Once back on the north loop, I stayed on the trails on the circumference as much as possible but did take a short detour to see the Survivor Tree, a huge fir with a large dead cedar hung up on it. I continued on the Summit trail (see map) which climbs an impressive rock face (in one place by way of a ladder) high above the lake. There is a fine view of Hague Lake and the trail passes groves of manzanita and pine trees before descending to a swimming spot (Swim Rock) on Hague Lake. The Millennium, Secret and Steep trails all meander through stands of old-growth Douglas fir. A short side trail from the Millennium Trail leads to a viewpoint overlooking Marina and Vancouver Islands. Since I was last in Kw'as Park, a memorial trail was created in honour of the trail builder who made this park unique. Named the Pierre de Trail, it starts near the park's largest fir (close to access B), climbs to a lookout over Hague Lake to Swim Rock and then descends back to the main trail.

This exceptional trail system has sufficient variety to keep you enchanted and well exercised for most of a day. There are plenty of great picnic spots, too, so don't forget your lunch.

3. Katimavik Trail to Easter Bluff ★★★

Trail length	9 km return (2 km if you begin at access B)
Time required	2 hours (45 minutes if you begin at access B)
Description	Rocky up-and-down trail leading to an excellent viewpoint
Level	Moderate
Access	A. The trail starts at Serge Narrows Bridge (see map, page 38) in Kw'as Park. The Kw'as Bay Road access (access B) to the park is the shortest access to the trailhead. B. The trail crosses Cortes Bay Road 1.5 km from its intersection with Bartholomew Road or 800 m from its intersection with Seaford Road. You can park on the edge of the road and take the trail in either direction—to Kw'as Park (35 minutes) or to Easter Bluff (10 minutes).

This trail, built by volunteers and Katimavik students led by Pierre de Trey, will give you a fair bit of exercise as it goes up and down over rocky terrain. It follows the south shore of Gunflint Lake for some distance, crosses a private driveway and Cortes Bay Road, and then climbs to the top of legendary Easter Bluff, where early settlers are said to have hidden Easter eggs for their children. The westward view encompasses Gunflint Lake below, Marina Island, and the Vancouver Island mountains in the distance.

After admiring the view from Easter Bluff you may wish to hike down to Gunflint or Hague Lake for a swim.

Easter Bluff is protected by the Linnaea Farm Society, a land trust established in 1991, which also runs an elementary school from its 127.5-ha farm. Respect private property and the protected area by keeping on the trail at all times and keeping your dogs leashed.

4. HA'THAYIM/VON DONOP MARINE PARK ★★

Trail length	3 km (more if you explore offshoot trails)
Time required	2 hours
Description	A network of grown-in logging roads through mixed young and mature forest, often leading to the shore of Von Donop Inlet
Level	Easy
Access	On Whaletown Road, 5.7 km from its intersection with Gorge Harbour Road and 1.2 km west of Tork Road. A small BC Parks sign on the north side of Whaletown Road marks the parking area and trail access to the Klahoose First Nation's Ha'thayim/Von Donop Trail.

To reach the park from the parking area, walk about 2.5 km through the Klahoose reserve on a gentle old logging road. The route is well signed by BC Parks, with helpful distance signs every 500 m. Stay on the main logging road/trail at least until you're in the park. Remember: reserve land is private land.

It takes about 40 minutes to reach the water's edge. This is a lovely spot but there is really nowhere to walk along the water. A signed path near the outhouse heads 1 km east to a little bay in Squirrel Cove. Another path heads north for 3 km (40 minutes), ending at another of Von Donop Inlet's many bays. This beautiful spot was deserted when I visited. There is no beach trail and you must return the way you came.

There are endless old logging road paths to explore in this way and you could easily meander for hours on trails similar to those described here.

5. GREEN MOUNTAIN LOOP ★★

Trail length	4 km
Time required	70 minutes return
Description	Hike up a logging road to a pleasant loop trail overlooking Gorge Harbour.
Level	Moderate
Elevation	310 m
Access	The unmarked logging road is off Whaletown Road 200 m east of Gorge Harbour Road and 500 m west of Larson's Meadow Road.

This is one of those hikes on Crown land that is familiar to locals but can be confusing to outsiders. You can start walking at the beginning of the logging road or you can drive up it 300 m, just past a private driveway on the left, to a small parking space. Do not drive farther, as it is extremely rough.

The hike will take you 35 minutes each way. You will spend 15 minutes on the logging road before branching off to the left, for 5 minutes, on a pretty little trail that leads to the attractive Green Mountain loop, which provides views of Gorge Harbour and the Vancouver Island peaks in the distance.

There are a number of side trails off the loop, including a trail to the east that leads down to Nutshell Lake—still on Crown land. The main trail is marked by cairns but the side trails are not well marked, so take a compass and be careful not to trespass on the nearby private land.

HIKING ON NORTHERN CORTES

Some of the best hiking on Cortes is found among the old logging roads and informal bush trails on the undeveloped north part of the island. Much of this wild land is Crown-owned and some private. At time of writing, much of the privately owned land belonged to the Weyerhaeuser corporation, which allowed the public to hike and picnic (no camping or fires) on its property. For more information, contact the company at 201–7373 Duncan Street, Powell River, BC V8A 1W6 (604-485-3100).

SHORE AND ROAD WALKS

There are pleasant walks along the roads bordering Gunflint and Hague Lakes and along the ocean in Smelt Bay Provincial Park. One especially pleasant walk is beside an enchanting forest on Hunt Road, which leads to Gorge Harbour Marina. Closer to the ferry, you should not miss Whaletown. Although you can't walk for very long here, Whaletown is arguably the prettiest settlement on the island, with its tiny local library and quaint little church. Whaletown's wood-heated post office still uses the brass cancelling mallet made for its 1894 grand opening.

There are several beach walks on Cortes.

Seavista Road: (first left from the ferry dock): The beach at the end of the road is quite rocky but you can scramble over it at low tide.

Red Granite Road: (near the Seattle Yacht Club's Cortes Bay Outstation): At the end of the road, there's a beach of rocky pink granite. You can walk both ways along the water at low tide, clambering over the large rocks that litter the shore.

Smelt Bay Provincial Park: This is a fantastic place to watch the sunset and it has great views, as does Sutil Point. It is also possible to collect oysters and dig for clams along parts of this long beach. The pebble beach can be walked north as far as Mansons Landing and south around Sutil Point (a.k.a. Reef Point), and then for quite a way north along the eastern shore. Along the way to Mansons Landing, there is a petroglyph on a 2-metre-high boulder on the beach.

AND IF YOU PADDLE . . .

Cortes Island's intricate coastline offers fine paddling itself and makes a great jumping-off point for exploring Desolation Sound, one of BC's prime paddling areas. The shoreline here is generally protected but sudden changes in weather can make any exposed crossing hazardous, so the usual precautions should be observed, especially at the south end of Cortes around Sutil Point. Strong currents can be encountered entering narrows in Gorge Harbour, Squirrel Cove, Carrington Bay, Von Donop Inlet and Mansons Landing. In most cases, the government docks are the best places to launch. They are also usually accompanied by parking places and telephones. Here are a few suggestions:

Squirrel Cove: Launch either from the government dock or (by permission) from the Klahoose Band beach. Explore the cove's labyrinth-like shoreline, Protection Island at the mouth and the nearby coast. This is a popular launching spot for paddlers heading for Desolation Sound.

Cortes Bay: Explore the bay, the nearby shoreline, Three Islets (Cod Rocks) just offshore and Twin Islands to the south.

Cortes Bay is a popular launching point for paddlers headed into Desolation Sound; many also come to explore its unique buildings and shore.

Gorge Harbour: Launch from the government dock at the end of Robertson Road or the marina at the end of Hunt Road. The Gorge is a large, busy harbour and interesting to explore. If you decide to go through the narrow entrance, be aware that the current runs up to 4 knots. The pictographs halfway down the cliff wall are best seen at high tide.

Smelt Bay: Launch at Smelt Bay Provincial Park or anywhere along the extensive beach north of the small park. While this is an easy place to put in, the paddling is somewhat monotonous.

Mansons Landing Provincial Park: Put in at the government dock and then explore Manson Bay, the small islands just outside it and, at a high tide, Mansons Lagoon. The tidal rush at the entrance may force even strong paddlers to portage during tide changes. The island-studded shoreline north to Gorge Harbour is also interesting to explore.

Coulter Bay: Launch from the end of Coulter Bay Road. From here, you can explore Coulter Island then continue north to tour Carrington Bay and Quartz Bay.

Denman ISLAND

LOCATED JUST OFF THE COAST OF VANCOUVER ISLAND, halfway between Nanaimo and Campbell River, Denman Island is a low-key and relatively undeveloped island. Denman covers an area of 50 square km and is home to a close-knit, artistic community of 1,016 residents. Referred to by some as the speed-bump on the way to Hornby Island, it has fewer natural attractions than its more popular neighbour. Its shoreline is mostly unindented and its highest point is a mere 120 m above sea level. While there are no major hikes on Denman, there are pleasant walks on trails in both Fillongley and Boyle Point Provincial Parks, along beaches and on country roads. While parts of Denman are badly scarred from recent clear-cutting, much of it is quite pastoral, with many productive farms on possibly the best agricultural land in the Gulf Islands. Its services include a general store, a museum, an art gallery, bed and breakfasts, and eateries.

HISTORY

For centuries, the Comox people had summer camps on Denman, where they hunted and fished. Beginning around 1870, several Scottish families moved to Denman from the Orkney Islands. By 1878, the island had a post office and a school; a church and store quickly followed, although it wasn't until 1897 that a community hall—the sign of an established community—was built.

Agriculture, especially dairy farming, was always a significant industry on Denman, but as elsewhere, locals supported themselves through a variety of means including salmon fishing and logging. This latter activity was so popular that, by 1950, most of the island was logged. From 1908 to 1915, some islanders were employed at an ill-fated local sandstone quarry, which shut down after it was discovered that the stone, used in buildings in Victoria, streaked as it weathered. Today, oyster farming is an important local industry and much of Denman's western foreshore is leased for this purpose.

GETTING THERE

The 10-minute ferry to Denman leaves Buckley Bay on Vancouver Island (about 20 km south of Courtenay) almost hourly. For specific information, obtain a copy of the Northern Gulf Islands schedule or contact BC Ferries (see Resources, page 235).

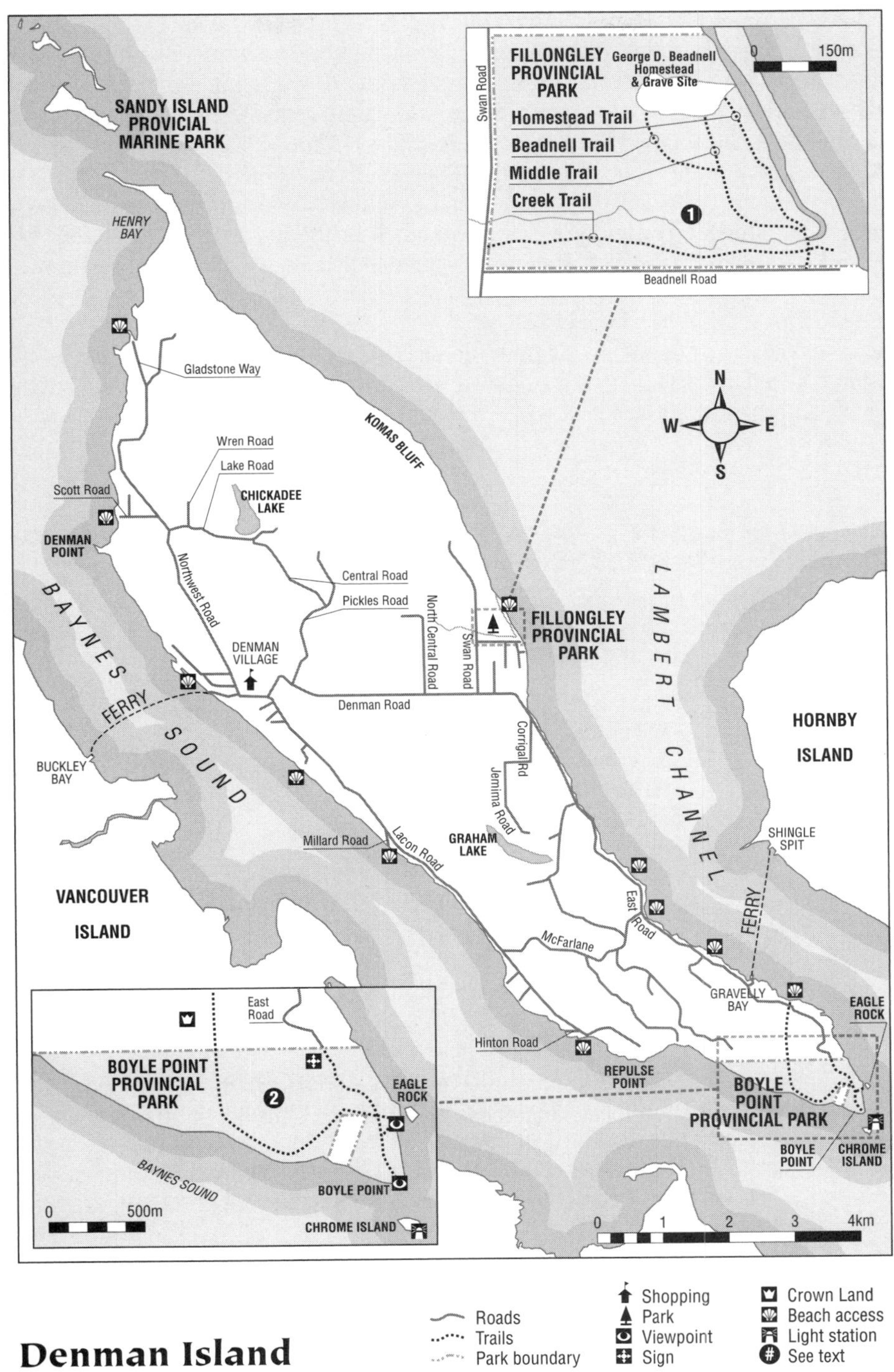
FILLONGLEY PROVINCIAL PARK
George D. Beadnell Homestead & Grave Site
Homestead Trail
Beadnell Trail
Middle Trail
Creek Trail
Swan Road
Beadnell Road
0 150m
SANDY ISLAND PROVICIAL MARINE PARK
HENRY BAY
Gladstone Way
KOMAS BLUFF
Wren Road
Lake Road
Scott Road
CHICKADEE LAKE
DENMAN POINT
Central Road
Pickles Road
Northwest Road
North Central Road
Swan Road
FILLONGLEY PROVINCIAL PARK
LAMBERT CHANNEL
BAYNES SOUND
DENMAN VILLAGE
FERRY
Denman Road
Corrigal Rd
Jemima Road
HORNBY ISLAND
BUCKLEY BAY
SHINGLE SPIT
Millard Road
Lacon Road
GRAHAM LAKE
VANCOUVER ISLAND
East Road
McFarlane
GRAVELLY BAY
EAGLE ROCK
Hinton Road
REPULSE POINT
BOYLE POINT PROVINCIAL PARK
BOYLE POINT
CHROME ISLAND
East Road
EAGLE ROCK
BAYNES SOUND
BOYLE POINT
CHROME ISLAND
0 500m
0 1 2 3 4km
Roads
Trails
Park boundary
Shopping
Park
Viewpoint
Sign
Crown Land
Beach access
Light station
See text

Denman Island

SERVICES AND ACCOMMODATION

All of Denman's stores are located in "downtown Denman," (a.k.a. Denman Village), a short stroll away from the ferry terminal. These include the general store dating from 1910 (with a gas pump and liquor outlet), a café, the community centre, and a museum and art gallery. Denman has about a dozen bed and breakfasts and there is a small public campground at Fillongley Provincial Park.

A combined visitor's guide to both Denman and Hornby, including a map of each island, is produced yearly by Hornby Denman Tourist Services, Hornby Island, BC V0R 1Z0. Contact the office or visit www.denmanis.bc.ca for more information.

ESPECIALLY FOR WALKERS

Denman has fewer public hiking trails than most Gulf Islands. However, because the island is so flat, all of them are suitable for most walkers. There are also numerous shore and road walks to enjoy.

HIKES

1. Fillongley Provincial Park ★★★	
Trail length	About 2 km in total
Time required	Plan to spend at least an hour in this beautiful, tranquil park.
Description	Lovely walks through old-growth forest and along a stream that flows into the sea, from where you can walk along the beach in both directions
Level	Easy
Access	The route to the park is well signed. From the ferry, drive east along Denman Road, turn left (north) on Swan Road and then turn right at Beadnell Road. The park runs from the corner of Beadnell and Swan down to the sea. It's about 5.5 km from the ferry.

The 23-ha Fillongley Park was once the oceanfront estate of George David Beadnell, whose parents bought the property in 1889. George and his wife, Amy, developed a park-like property that included paths, a bowling green, gates and trellises, a lily pond, rockeries, birdhouses and flower beds filled from the estate's greenhouses. The Beadnells deeded the property to the province in 1953 and it became a provincial park after George's death.

Information shelters in the park display a map of the park trails, as well as a couple of articles on the Beadnell family. You can easily walk all of the short, scenic paths in an hour or so, but you'll probably want to spend more time in this peaceful spot. Trails include:

Creek Trail: This parallels Beadnell Road from just beyond the camping area to Swan Road, passing through stately old-growth forest along the edge of Beadnell Creek.

Homestead Trail: One of three that lead to the remains of the Beadnell home and grave site, this 400 m trail starts just outside the camping area. It crosses a bridge over the creek, continues up through the forest and enters a meadow—perhaps a lawn in an earlier incarnation—in which you can see the base of a fountain from the old estate, as well as the wide variety of trees planted by the Beadnells and a profusion of flowers in the spring. George Beadnell's grave is at the entrance to the field.

Beadnell Trail: To the west of the Homestead Trail and running off of it, this trail is prettier than its counterpart and overlooks the creek, in places.

Middle Trail: A short trail that connects the Beadnell and Homestead Trails.

Shoreline Trail: Begins just beyond the turnaround for vehicles in the camping area. It parallels the shore, following a midden between the creek and the sea. The stream enters the ocean about a 10-minute walk from the campsites. From here, you can walk almost indefinitely along the beach. You can also return to the camping/parking area, by way of the beach.

2. BOYLE POINT PROVINCIAL PARK ★★

Trail length	2–3 km round trip
Time required	30–60 minutes, depending on route taken
Description	A pleasant hike through some second-growth forest to the sea, with views of picturesque Chrome Island Light Station and Eagle Rock offshore
Level	Easy
Access	The end of East Road

This 125-ha provincial park has no facilities; there is, however, a signboard containing a map of the simple trail system. The main trail starts beside a stream bed and is fairly straightforward, leading to a steep cliff overlooking Chrome Island Light Station. This is a good spot to sit on the bench provided and enjoy a picnic lunch. On your return from the viewpoint, look for a marked trail to the right (north), which leads to a view of Eagle Rock, around the point. Visitors used to explore the shore here, clambering down the steep cliff to the beach below, where it is possible at very low tides to walk right out to Eagle Rock. However, BC Parks has placed a fence here and advises against doing this because of the danger.

Once you've retraced your steps to the Chrome Island trail, you can return to East Road the same way you came or take the unmarked trail facing the trail to Eagle Rock. This 3-km trail leads through lovely open forest, following an old logging road

Disaster at Chrome Island

Chrome Island's first lighthouse was established on the east end of the island in 1891, and a second (the one used today) was built at the west end in 1898. The British originally named the island Yellow Island because of its light colour. Aside from its Alcatraz look—a flat tabletop with sheer cliff edges falling straight down to the sea—Chrome Island's main claim to fame is a spectacular shipwreck, which took place during a gale on December 16, 1900.

The British merchant steamer *Alpha* was heading for Union Bay on Vancouver Island to pick up coal before it started on its journey to Japan with a cargo of coal and canned salmon. The ship foundered on the rocks on the east end of the island and sank. Although most of the crew were able to reach safety, the captain and eight others went down with the ship. The story does not end there, however. In the days following the disaster, cases of salmon were salvaged by Denman residents. Reportedly, one case contained rum, rather than salmon, and the fellow who found it drank himself to death.

Kate Dunsmore

in a 65-ha piece of Crown land. While this trail is fairly easy to follow, there are a few offshoots—including one leading to a beach—that are not as well maintained and some people have gotten lost here. Carry a compass and make sure that you're heading in the right direction. If you have any doubts, retrace your steps and exit via the park trail. The alternate trail emerges on East Road about 2 km west of the park entrance. Turn right (east) to return to the park entrance.

SHORE AND ROAD WALKS

There are many well-signed oyster leases along Denman's shoreline. Respect the signs and do not threaten the livelihood of the oyster farmers by walking on the leased area or by picking oysters between the posted signs.

The following beach accesses can be walked comfortably only at low tide:

Scott Road (at the end)**:** West of the ferry terminal.

Millard Road (at the end)**:** Off Lacon Road about 2 km south of the ferry dock. This particularly lovely beach access is down a good but very steep road. You'll find yourself on a little promontory from which you can walk along the beach, in both directions. On a clear day, you will have excellent views of the Beaufort Mountains on Vancouver Island, across Baynes Sound.

Gladstone Way (at the end)**:** From "downtown Denman" take Northwest Road for about 6 km, until you reach Gladstone Way. A public walkway follows a fence to the beach; this involves crossing a stream, which swells after heavy rainfall. At low tide, you can walk along the beach for some distance in both directions. If you head north, you can walk along Henry Bay to the north tip of the island. From here, Sandy Island Provincial Marine Park is accessible by foot, but only at low tide.

Fillongley Provincial Park: This wonderful beach is as fine as any on Denman. You can walk along this beach in both directions, for quite some distance.

East Road: There are several beach accesses off East Road.

Denman also has a number of pleasant roads for walking:

Central Road: Near Chickadee Lake, it is a pretty, narrow, level road, which passes through ferny woods.

Lacon Road: Along the west side of the island, south from the Vancouver Island ferry terminal, this road passes by several lovely farms and provides fine views of the sea.

East Road: From near Fillongley Provincial Park toward the Hornby ferry terminal, this offers similar vistas on the other side of the island to those provided by Lacon Road.

AND IF YOU PADDLE . . .

Denman has a boringly unindented shoreline with lots of rocks in the shallow water along its coast. However, it's easy to launch a boat at the end of Beadnell Road near Fillongley Provincial Park on Denman's east side. From here, you can paddle up to Sandy Island Provincial Marine Park about 4 nautical miles (7.4 km) and explore its sand beaches. You might also launch at one of the beach accesses near the ferry dock and access Sandy Island Provincial Marine Park from Denman's west side.

Gabriola ISLAND

JUST A 20-MINUTE FERRY TRIP FROM NANAIMO, Gabriola is the second most populous southern Gulf Island, with 3,400 residents, and is one of the largest, at some 53 square km. There are settlements near Descanso Bay, Degnen Bay, Silva Bay and Taylor Bay, with most amenities, including many craft studios. The island is laced with country roads, surrounded by walkable beaches and blessed with several fine parks with developed trails. Gabriola is famous for its honeycombed sandstone grottoes, one of which, the historic Malaspina Galleries, is a provincial landmark. Known as The Queen of the Gulf Islands, Gabriola's gentle topography, park-like Garry oak and arbutus groves, snug harbours, spectacular ocean vistas and its atmosphere of pastoral balm make it an excellent choice for anyone wishing to sample the storied enchantment of BC's Gulf Islands in one easy trip.

HISTORY

Gabriola is in the traditional territory of the Snuneymuxw (Nanaimo) people, who decorated the soft sandstone shores with the intriguing petroglyphs reproduced at the Gabriola Museum, where visitors can make their own rubbings. Many of the island's first non-aboriginal settlers were Scots who farmed, mined coal in Nanaimo or worked in the sandstone quarry near Descanso Bay, producing stone for buildings in Victoria and the enormous pulp-mill grindstones that now decorate some island yards. A brickyard, whose ruins may still be seen on Brickyard Beach, operated from 1895 to 1945, employing mainly Chinese. By 1906, the island had about 200 residents, whose descendants still live there. In the 1920s, summer cottagers began to arrive from the cities, a trend that continues today.

GETTING THERE

Each day, the ferry makes 16 return crossings between downtown Nanaimo and Descanso Bay on Gabriola. For specific information, obtain a copy of the Southern Gulf Islands schedule, or contact BC Ferries. Gabriola is also serviced by Tofino Air (see Resources, page 235).

Crashing storm waves sculpt Gabriola's sandstone shores and remind islanders of their isolation. Mark Kaaremaa

SERVICES AND ACCOMMODATION

Most of the island's services are located at or close to Folklife Village on North Road, 1 km from the ferry dock. Other shops can be found in Twin Beaches Shopping Centre, on Berry Point Road, about 2.5 km from the ferry. From Victoria Day to Thanksgiving, a farmers' market takes place every Saturday from 10 a.m. to noon outside Agi Hall, at the junction of North and South Roads, just up the hill from the ferry.

There's a Visitor Info Centre at Folklife Village. Information is also available, toll free, from the Chamber of Commerce at 1-888-284-9332 or www.gabriolaisland.org. A free brochure, including a detailed map of the island, is produced annually and is available in local stores and on the ferry. The best map of the island is produced by the real estate office in Folklife Village.

Gabriola has three provincial parks, a regional park and several community parks. There's also a 32-site campground at Descanso Bay Regional Park (call 250-729-1213 for information).

ESPECIALLY FOR WALKERS

One of the highlights of Gabriola is the accessibility to easy walking and hiking along the shoreline. These walks are on sand and gravel beaches, on sandstone shelves and along the curves of bays and headlands.

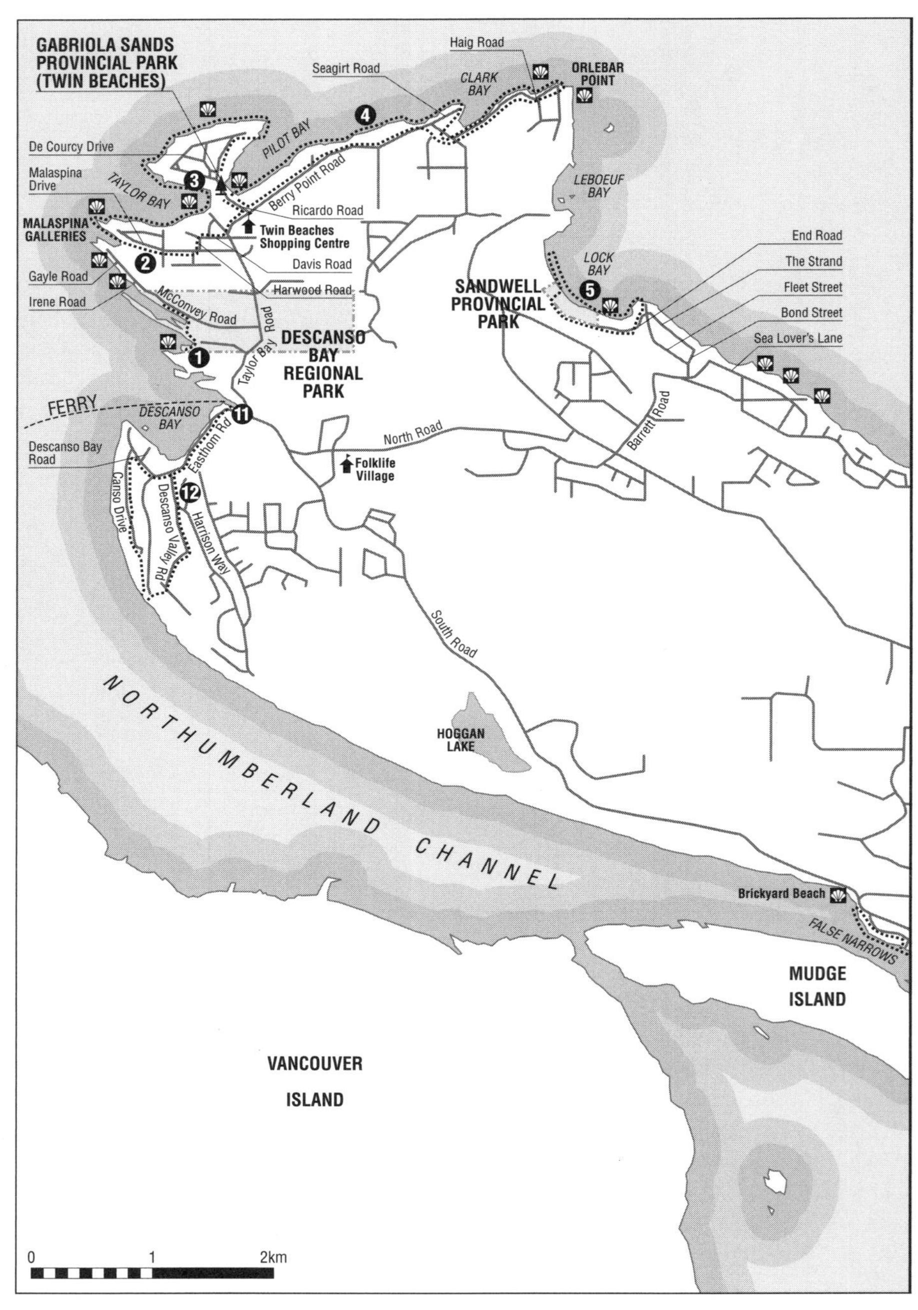
GABRIOLA SANDS
PROVINCIAL PARK
(TWIN BEACHES)
Haig Road
Seagirt Road
CLARK BAY
ORLEBAR POINT
PILOT BAY
De Courcy Drive
Malaspina Drive
TAYLOR BAY
Berry Point Road
Ricardo Road
MALASPINA GALLERIES
Twin Beaches Shopping Centre
LEBOEUF BAY
Davis Road
Gayle Road
Irene Road
Harwood Road
McConvey Road
Taylor Bay Road
LOCK BAY
SANDWELL PROVINCIAL PARK
End Road
The Strand
Fleet Street
Bond Street
Sea Lover's Lane
DESCANSO BAY REGIONAL PARK
FERRY
DESCANSO BAY
Easthom Rd
North Road
Barrett Road
Descanso Bay Road
Folklife Village
Canso Drive
Descanso Valley Rd
Harrison Way
South Road
HOGGAN LAKE
NORTHUMBERLAND CHANNEL
Brickyard Beach
FALSE NARROWS
MUDGE ISLAND
VANCOUVER ISLAND
0
1
2km

Gabriola Island

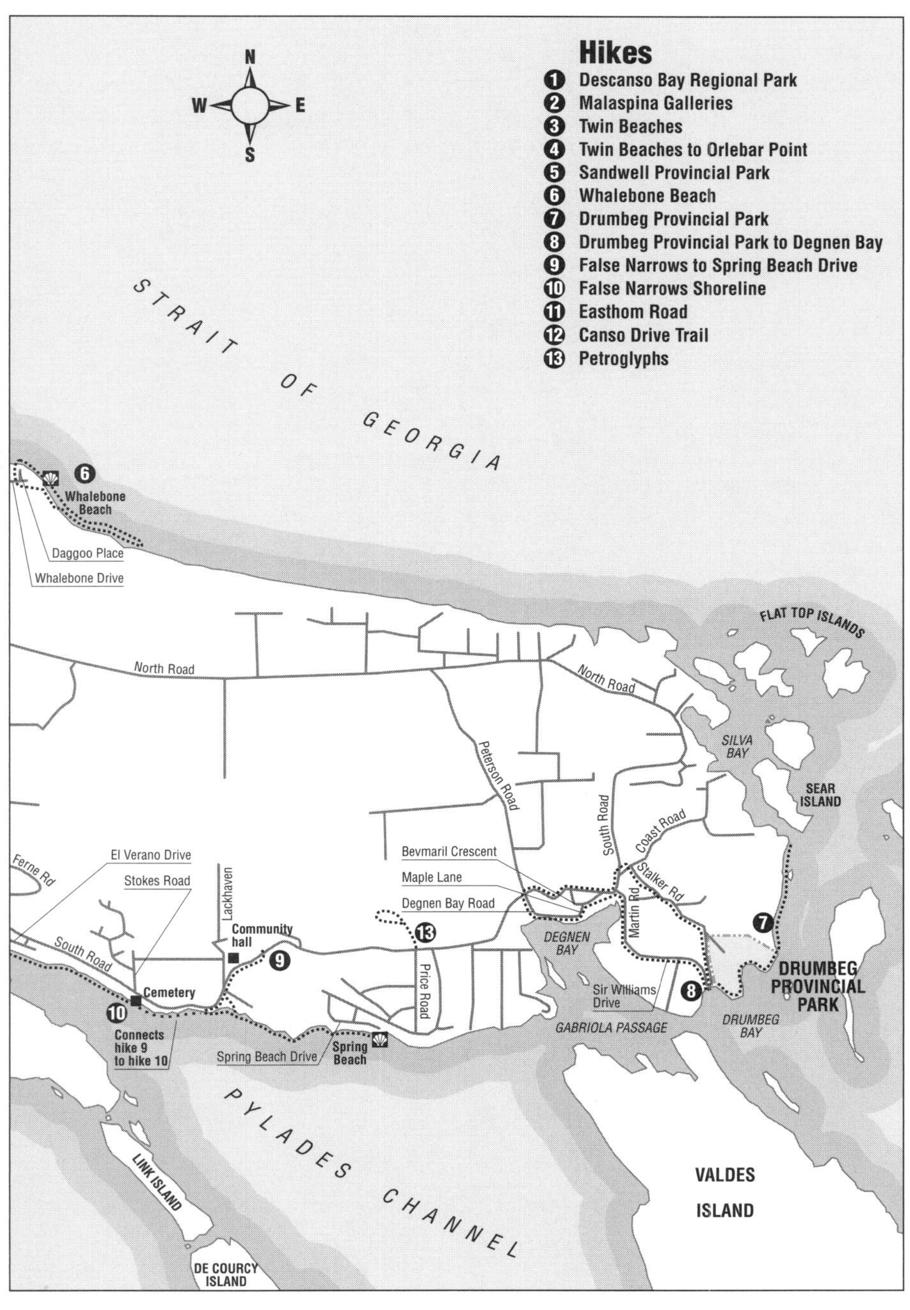
N
W
E
S
Hikes
1 Descanso Bay Regional Park
2 Malaspina Galleries
3 Twin Beaches
4 Twin Beaches to Orlebar Point
5 Sandwell Provincial Park
6 Whalebone Beach
7 Drumbeg Provincial Park
8 Drumbeg Provincial Park to Degnen Bay
9 False Narrows to Spring Beach Drive
10 False Narrows Shoreline
11 Easthom Road
12 Canso Drive Trail
13 Petroglyphs
STRAIT OF GEORGIA
Whalebone Beach
Daggoo Place
Whalebone Drive
FLAT TOP ISLANDS
North Road
North Road
SILVA BAY
SEAR ISLAND
Peterson Road
South Road
Coast Road
Stalker Rd
Martin Rd
Ferne Rd
El Verano Drive
Stokes Road
Lackhaven
Community hall
South Road
Cemetery
Connects hike 9 to hike 10
Bevmaril Crescent
Maple Lane
Degnen Bay Road
Price Road
DEGNEN BAY
Sir Williams Drive
DRUMBEG PROVINCIAL PARK
DRUMBEG BAY
GABRIOLA PASSAGE
Spring Beach Drive
Spring Beach
PYLADES CHANNEL
LINK ISLAND
DE COURCY ISLAND
VALDES ISLAND
Roads
Trails
Park boundary
Park
Shopping
Beach access
See text

There are also many woodland trails through parks, as well as country roads that are pleasant to explore at almost any time of the year. In many cases, these walks along the shore, the roads and occasionally through forest can be combined to make long, satisfying outings. Almost everything described in this chapter is accessible to most walkers. The provincial parks contain some of the most beautiful shoreline on the island.

Nature lovers and photographers will be kept busy on these walks. There is rich intertidal life and the birdwatching is good year-round. The walks around the shoreline paralleling Berry Point Road can offer stunning sunsets.

SHORELINE HIKES AND WALKS

All the walks in this chapter are best from late spring to early fall, when tides are lower. If you try them in the winter months or after rainfall, be cautious, as the sandstone shore is very slippery. To make the most of the walks, be sure to check the tide tables before starting and plan your walks around low tide.

The walks are listed clockwise around the island, starting from the ferry terminal. Some of the walks can be grouped together to make a longer day out, which is indicated in the text.

In addition to the hikes, routes and walks suggested here, you might want to join the Gabriola Walking Group, which has regular weekly outings at 10 a.m. on Wednesdays. For more information, consult *The Sounder* (www.soundernews.com), the island's weekly newspaper, which lists the group's current and upcoming activities.

1. Descanso Bay Regional Park ★★★

Trail length	About 2 km
Time required	30 minutes
Description	A marked trail allows easy access to two bays and headlands.
Level	Easy
Access	Left off Taylor Bay Road, 900 m north of the ferry. A gravel road leads to a parking area near the beach.
Cautions	Stay on the groomed trail in the winter months or after rain, as slippery rocks make this hike hazardous.

Walk down to the shoreline, where you'll find a trail that goes both left and right to the park boundaries. Turn left and follow the marked trail out to the headland, which offers views to Nanaimo, Mount Benson and Protection Island. Signs indicate the boundary of the park and neighbouring private land.

Return by the same path, to your starting point, and continue along the shoreline in the other direction. The path takes you out around another headland, past an early residence, through an orchard and to a trail that climbs up the rock bluff to McConvey Road. From here, retrace your steps to the starting point. There are plans to expand the park trails, so check the information board in the park for any additional paths.

2. Malaspina Galleries to Twin Beaches and Return ★★★

Trail length	About 3 km
Time required	60 minutes or more, as the Galleries are particularly beautiful
Description	A walk that follows a unique sandstone shelf to a sandy beach, offering panoramic views and intertidal life
Level	Easy
Access	A parking area at the end of Malaspina Drive (off Taylor Bay Road)
Cautions	Following rain or high tide, slippery rocks make this hike hazardous. Be careful of the steep drop-off near the starting point.

Note: This hike can be combined with hikes 3 and 4 to make a large loop. If you combine the hikes, take a picnic lunch and allow 4 hours to complete the loop.

This is a must-see. A community park on a beautiful little point includes an unusual natural phenomenon—a hooded sandstone ledge sculpted by the elements. For about 100 m at the edge of the sea, the rounded sandstone overhang extends several metres out from the solid rock cliff from which it was formed.

This rare geological feature was originally named Galiano Gallery after the Spanish explorer Dionisio Alcala Galiano who visited the area in 1792 and described the Galleries in his reports. The Galleries reminded the Spaniards of the cloisters commonly found in Europe but with a floor of honeycombed, pock-marked rock and a ceiling of smooth, curved sandstone.

Take the short access trail from the parking area, through trees to an open sandstone cliff top. Walk to your left and out to the edge of a sheer drop to the sea below. Be very careful, especially if you are with small children. At this point, you are standing on the roof of the open sandstone Galleries. To enter or view the Galleries, walk out toward the headland and down the sandstone slope.

After leaving the Galleries, go out to the headland for spectacular views, especially at sunset. From the headland, continue right along the sandstone ledge to Taylor Bay, about 1.2 km to the east. The sandy beach at Taylor Bay is part of Gabriola Sands Provincial Park (known locally as Twin Beaches).

From here, you can continue with hike 3 and/or 4. If you wish to return, either retrace your steps along the shoreline to the Malaspina Galleries or take an alternate route along the country roads by crossing the open grassy area behind the beach to

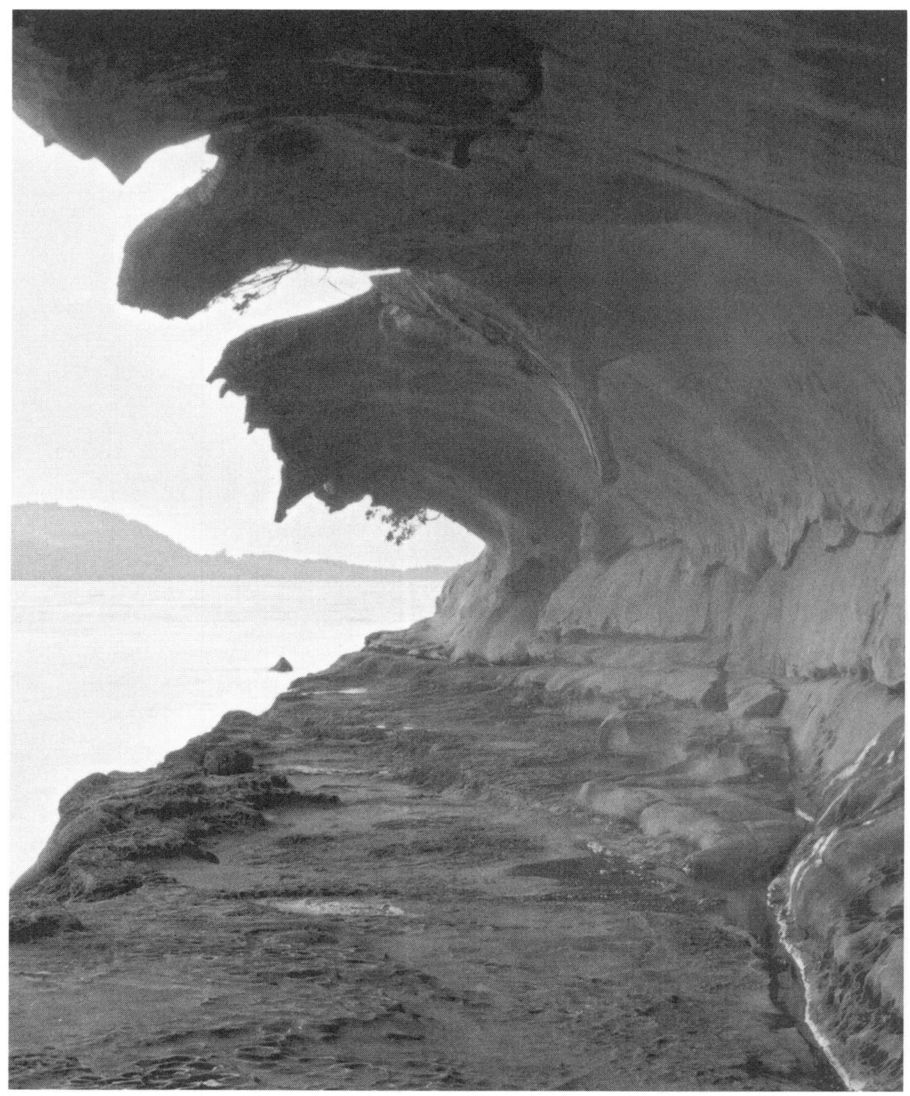

The Malaspina Galleries—also known as the Galiano Galleries—formed by wind and salt spray over past millennia, attract hundreds of visitors every year. A famous portrayal of the galleries by Jose Cardero hangs in the Museo Navel in Madrid. Carolyn Davey

Ricardo Road. Turn right on Ricardo Road and walk southeast to Berry Point Road. Turn right on Berry Point Road and, at the next intersection, turn right again on Davis Road and then left on Harwood Road. This returns you to Malaspina Drive, where you turn right and walk to the end of the road to where you began.

3. TWIN BEACHES HEADLAND LOOP ★★★

Trail length	About 3 km
Time required	45 minutes
Description	A walk along beaches and a sandstone shore offering panoramic views, rock formations and intertidal life
Level	Easy
Access	The parking area at Gabriola Sands Provincial Park toward the end of Ricardo Road
Cautions	Following rain or high tide, slippery rocks make this hike hazardous.

Note: This hike can be combined with hikes 2 and 4 to make a large loop. If you combine the hikes, take a picnic lunch and allow 4 hours to complete the loop.

Gabriola Sands Provincial Park (Twin Beaches) spans two sandy beaches on either side of a narrow neck of land. This hike starts on the beach at Taylor Bay, which is the end of hike 2. From the Gabriola Sands parking area, walk over the grass field to Taylor Bay beach. Walk to the north end of the beach and follow the rocky shelf close to the high-tide line. For the first 100 m or so, you have to pick your way among the rocks but will soon find yourself on a smooth sandstone shelf.

Follow the sandstone ledge around the headland. As you round the headland, in the distance to the east you'll see the Entrance Island lighthouse. Continue to Pilot Bay and look for a yellow marker on your right, indicating a wooden stairway. Climb the stairs and follow the short trail to Decourcy Drive. Turn left and follow the road, turning left again at Ricardo Road to return to your starting point at Gabriola Sands Provincial Park.

4. TWIN BEACHES TO ORLEBAR POINT ★★★

Trail length	About 8 km
Time required	2 hours
Description	A walk along a sandstone shore and a scenic road, with views, rock formations and interesting intertidal life
Level	Moderate
Access	From the parking area at Gabriola Sands Provincial Park (see hike 3)
Cautions	Following rain or high tide, slippery rocks make this hike hazardous.

Note: This hike can be combined with hikes 2 and 3 to make a large loop. If you combine the hikes, take a picnic lunch and allow 4 hours to complete the loop.

Start from the shore at Pilot Bay, to the east side of the parking area. Turn right along the shore and follow the sandstone ledge, heading northeast toward the lighthouse on Entrance Island. Continue along the sandstone ledge for about 2.5 km to a headland at the end of Seagirt Road.

To get to the sandstone ledge on the other side of Clark Bay, you must take a short diversion along Seagirt and Berry Point Roads. To find the trail to Seagirt Road, stand at the headland, with your back to the lighthouse. Walk along Seagirt Road and then turn left onto Berry Point Road. Follow the path along Berry Point Road.

After about 100 m, you'll see several beach-access trails down to the sandstone ledge. Follow the sandstone shelf toward the lighthouse. Alternatively, you can stay on the road, which runs parallel to the seashore. Either way, it is about 1.2 km farther to Orlebar Point, which is a good place to rest and view the lighthouse.

To return to where you started, either retrace the beach route or follow Berry Point Road all the way back to Ricardo Road, opposite the Twin Beaches Shopping Centre. Follow Ricardo Road down the slope to your starting point at Gabriola Sands Provincial Park.

If you are returning to the starting point of hike 2, instead of turning onto Ricardo Road, continue along Berry Point Road to Malaspina Drive. Then refer to the directions for hike 2, page 55.

5. Around Sandwell Provincial Park ★★★

Trail length	About 3 km
Time required	45 minutes
Description	This trail leads to a sandy beach where you can walk at low tide.
Level	Easy, although there is one short, steep section on the trail
Access	The parking area at the end of The Strand
Facilities	Pit toilets, picnic tables
Caution	Beach access is limited to periods of low tide.

From the parking area, take the trail into this 12-ha park. The trail—an old logging road—is flanked by high rocky cliffs to the west and the sea, below the trail, to the east. After 1 km, the trail descends steeply toward the shore. Take care going down. At the bottom of the slope, continue straight to an open meadow area. At the end of the meadow, look over the fence at the small, marshy area. This is a wintering area for many species of ducks, which start arriving in late September and stay until April.

Follow the fence down to the beach and walk along the beach as far as the private residence at the north end of the bay. If the tide is high, return by the trail you took into the park. If the tide is low, continue south around the bay. You'll know you're out of the park when you round a point and reach another small bay with residences off the beach.

At the south end of this bay, make your way over the sandstone ledge to a straight stretch of mixed sandstone shelf and shingle beach. About 100 m along this beach, look for a boat launch and take it up to End Road. You'll find a large parking area at the top. Walk to the next road (The Strand), turn right and continue about 400 m along the road to the starting point of the hike.

6. AROUND WHALEBONE BEACH ★★★

Trail length	About 2 km
Time required	30 minutes
Description	A short walk on a pebble beach, a sand beach and a woodland trail
Level	Easy
Access	At the end of Whalebone Drive
Caution	Beach access is limited to periods of low tide.

Walk back along Whalebone Drive to just past Daggoo Place, where you will find a signed trail on the right (east) leading to a community park. This trail opens onto a grassy area and ends at steps that descend to the beach. Turn right on the beach and walk along the high-tide line. Just offshore is a rock outcropping that is home to a colony of harbour seals. After about 500 m, you will round a headland that opens onto Whalebone Beach. Walk along the beach toward the cliffs, at its east end. At low tide, you can reach an extensive sandy beach with tide pools.

To return, walk back along Whalebone Beach, looking for a trail up the bank to the top of the beach. At time of writing, this was marked by a rope swing hanging from a tree near the high-tide line. Take this trail up the bank, where you'll join a woodland trail that follows the top of the bank. Turn right and take this trail until you reach your starting point on Whalebone Drive.

There are a number of community parks along Whalebone Drive, all with marked accesses and steps down to the beach. You can make this hike longer by exploring these parks.

It is also possible to walk all the way from Sandwell Provincial Park to Whalebone Beach, at low tide. But beware: the loose, round beach stones make for tough going. Locals consider this more of an endurance test than a pleasant stroll.

7. DRUMBEG PROVINCIAL PARK ★★★★

Trail length	2.6 km in the park; 4.8 km if you add the beach walk
Time required	At least an hour
Description	A walk along established park trails and a picturesque sandstone shoreline

Level	Easy
Access	The end of Stalker Road or from the park's parking area off Stalker Road

Note: This hike can be combined with hike 8.

The trail runs from Stalker Road to the northern boundary of this 20-ha park. It follows the shore, which is made up of sculptured sandstone shelves weathered into fascinating formations. You can walk along the Garry-oak-lined trail or along the sandstone shore. (Try going along the trail one way and returning by the shore, or vice versa.)

At low tide, you have the option of continuing north for 1.2 km along the beach beyond the park boundary to the channel between Gabriola and Sear Island (one of the Flat Top Islands) and then retracing your steps to Drumbeg Park.

If you decide not to do this, return the way you came. Be sure to walk the southern part of the trail, between Stalker Road and the parking area. This part of the trail gives you a chance to see the strong tidal current through narrow Gabriola Passage, which can reach as high as 7 knots. To the south of this point, across the passage, is Valdes Island.

From Stalker Road, continue along the path outlined in hike 8 or return to the parking area.

Located next to Gabriola Passage, Drumbeg Provincial Park has a bit of everything—a lovely trail through a grove of huge Garry oaks, sandstone formations, and views of the busy boat traffic through the Flat Top and Passage Islands. Richard Blier

8. DRUMBEG PROVINCIAL PARK TO DEGNEN BAY ★★★

Trail length	7 km
Time required	90 minutes
Description	A walk along sandstone shoreline and country roads
Level	Easy
Access	The end of Stalker Road or the parking area in Drumbeg Provincial Park

Note: This hike can be combined with hike 7.

Take the trail onto the beach from the end of Stalker Road and walk right (southwest) along the high-tide line for 100 m. Look for steps made out of old car tires. At the top of the steps, continue on the trail that leads away from the beach. Follow the trail signs.

The trail goes through low bush and enters onto what appears to be a private driveway but is an undeveloped section of Sir Williams Drive. Continue to your right (northwest) for 150 m until you reach a gravel road (Martin Road). Turn right and follow the road for about 1 km, at which point you will see Degnen Bay to your left.

Continue along Martin Road until you reach the paved road (South Road), where you turn left. On the opposite side of South Road is a large Garry oak with a sign saying Gossip Corner nailed to it. Early settlers on this end of Gabriola Island would gather here to await the mail delivery by boat into Degnen Bay. Continue past the oak tree and turn left onto Bevmaril Crescent. After 100 m, turn left again onto Maple Lane, which ends 50 m farther at the top of a bluff. Take the narrow trail that starts beside a fire hydrant supply line and descends to Degnen Bay Road, on Degnen Bay.

Turn right (west) on Degnen Bay Road and follow it until you reach South Road. Turn right and walk along South Road for about 1.2 km past Gossip Corner until you reach Coast Road. Turn right (east) on Coast Road and continue until you reach Stalker Road, then turn right once again. Follow Stalker Road until it reaches the sea, where you began.

9. FALSE NARROWS TO SPRING BEACH DRIVE ★★★

Trail length	About 5 km
Time required	About 2 hours return
Description	A beach walk with views of De Courcy and Mudge Islands
Level	Easy
Access	From the Gabriola Community Hall parking area on the north side of South Road just east of Lackhaven Road

Note: This hike can be combined with hike 10.

Turn right (west) on South Road and continue toward the shoreline. At the bottom of the hill, a lane gives access to the beach. Once on the beach, turn left and walk east. Note the collection of small boats on the logs above the high-tide line. This is a useful marker for the beach access if you choose to return via the shoreline.

The easiest walking is on the fine shale at the high-tide line. Ahead you can see Pylades Channel between Valdes Island on the left and De Courcy Island. After about 1 km, you will see a large meadow behind the beach, where farmland runs right down to the shoreline.

Continue along the beach for another 500 m. You will reach a steep, impassable cliff with interesting erosion patterns in the large sandstone rocks at its base. From here, return to your starting point by retracing your steps along the beach. You are now looking toward False Narrows, which runs between Gabriola Island and Mudge Island. Look for your landmark (the small boats on the logs) for the beach access that will return you to South Road.

If you wish to combine this hike with hike 10, stay on the beach and continue west toward False Narrows. After 500 m, look for the wide trail that comes down to the beach from the steep bank above; this is the start of the next hike.

10. False Narrows Shoreline ★★

Trail length	About 4 km
Time required	1 hour
Description	A walk along a shale shore with views of Mudge, Link, De Courcy and Valdes Islands, as well as the tidal action in False Narrows and herons feeding at low tide
Level	Easy
Access	A short unmarked road access to the shore across from Stokes Road (off South Road about 9 km east of the ferry), between a row of mail-boxes and Gabriola's cemetery

Note: This hike can be combined with hike 9.

Take the wide trail to the shore and walk right (northwest) along the shoreline. The easiest walking is on the fine shale at the high-tide line. After about 100 m, turn around and look back at the beach-access trail you just descended; you will need to be able to find it again on your return. Then continue along the shoreline, with a view of downtown Nanaimo in the distance.

False Narrows runs like a river between Gabriola and Mudge Islands. The tidal flows in the narrows are significant. On an incoming tide, it flows toward Nanaimo; on an outgoing tide, it flows in the reverse direction. At low tide, there is a large, exposed sandbar which is a favourite fishing spot for blue heron.

You will soon see a boat-launch area used by residents of Mudge Island, who leave their cars parked on the Gabriola side of the crossing. As you continue, the narrows opens into a wider bay. When you can no longer see residences, you have reached Brickyard Beach. You can still find remnants of the clay bricks once made here.

At this point, simply retrace your steps or take this short diversion: leave the shoreline and go up to South Road, above the beach. Turn right and walk along the road until you reach El Verano Drive. Turn right (east) once more onto El Verano and walk along this residential road until you reach the boat-launch access on your right. Take this access back to the shore, turn left (east) and follow the shoreline back to where you began.

OTHER WALKS

There are a few other, shorter walks that you might like to try. For example, at the beginning of Harrison Way (off Easthom Road), you'll see old logging roads heading inland. Some of these lead to the old sandstone quarry, where you can still see piles of the old grindstones once quarried here. These meandering logging roads are on private property, so check with the owner before accessing.

The following are three additional walks. Almost all beach walks should be hiked only at low tide.

11. Easthom Road: From the ferry, walk south along Easthom Road as far as Harrison Way. This quiet back road is very pretty, with views toward Nanaimo. You can retrace your steps at the end of Harrison Way. If you're feeling energetic, continue south along Easthom Road to Canso Drive and continue with walk 12.

12. Canso Drive Trail: Drive along Easthom Road (to your immediate right after leaving the ferry terminal) to Canso Drive and drive to its end. Follow the old logging road south along the high sandstone cliffs. Make your way down to a beautiful flat rock that projects over the water. This shelf-like piece of sandstone is just large enough to shelter two people and a picnic lunch. It's particularly tranquil, as you are shielded from the views of Nanaimo and the Harmac pulp mill across the channel.

13. Petroglyphs by the church: There are a number of petroglyphs in an open area of moss- and grass-covered sandstone behind the United Church on South Road, just east of Price Road. Look for the petroglyph sign by the church and follow a trail beside the barbed-wire fence for about 5 minutes. Foot traffic and rubbings are rapidly eroding the petroglyphs, which are becoming fainter and fainter each year. Treat them with care, so that others may be able to enjoy them. Alternatively, you can see the copies of these and other petroglyphs at the Gabriola Museum.

AND IF YOU PADDLE . . .

Gabriola is a paddler's delight—endless beach accesses from which to launch, kilometres of interesting shoreline and bays to explore, and aside from the strong currents in False Narrows and Gabriola Passage, generally placid waters to negotiate. As a rule of thumb, if the wind is from the southeast, the Gabriola Sands or

Descanso Bay launch sites will provide calmer waters. If the wind is from the northwest, choose the Drumbeg Park or El Verano Drive launch sites. Here are some suggestions:

Gabriola Sands Provincial Park: The sheltered sandy bays here make for easy launch access. With this as a starting point, you can paddle the shoreline from Malaspina Galleries to Orlebar Point, where you'll have a good view of the Entrance Island Lighthouse.

Descanso Bay Regional Park: The small cove at the beach parking lot is a good place to launch to see sunsets or to paddle north to view the Malaspina Galleries.

From a short side road off El Verano Drive: This easy launch site gives you access to False Narrows and the northeastern shore of Mudge Island. Check your tide and current tables and be careful to pick your times carefully: the river-like current through False Narrows flows swiftly.

Drumbeg Provincial Park: Put in at the sandy beach by the parking lot and explore the sandstone formations along the Drumbeg shoreline, the Flat Top Islands to the north and Silva Bay. Check your tide and current tables and keep away from the strong tidal flows through Gabriola Passage.

Galiano ISLAND

Long and skinny Galiano is the second largest of the southern Gulf Islands, covering 57 square km. Its 1,071 residents enjoy a distinctly Mediterranean climate, with the lowest rainfall on the southern coast. Well-protected Montague Harbour is one of the most popular anchorages in the Gulf Islands and, along with Whaler Bay–Sturdies Bay, is home to most of the island's services. Galiano's mature forests and sandy beaches, combined with its excellent hiking, give credence to the locals' claim that it is the "gem" of the Gulf Islands. The views from Bodega Ridge and Mount Galiano alone are worth the trip.

HISTORY

Long before the arrival of European explorers, the Coast Salish had summer camps on Galiano. The island was named in honour of Commander Dionisio Alcala Galiano, who explored the Strait of Georgia during the summer of 1792.

One of the earliest non-Native settlers was Henry Georgeson, who came from the Shetland Islands and built a cabin in Georgeson Bay in 1863. Farming was never very successful on Galiano, due to the lack of good farmland and the shortage of water. Most people also hunted deer, raised sheep and fished, to support themselves. Herring was salted in five different places on Galiano, four of them run by Japanese and the fifth by Chinese. Settlement centred around Whaler Bay, Sturdies Bay and Georgeson Bay—areas where the majority of Galiano residents live today.

GETTING THERE

There are several ferry sailings each day from Swartz Bay (near Victoria) to Sturdies Bay on Galiano, two sailings from Tsawwassen (near Vancouver) and two sailings most days from Salt Spring Island. For details, obtain a Southern Gulf Islands schedule or contact BC Ferries. Harbour Air and Seair Seaplanes fly to Galiano (see Resources, page 235).

SERVICES AND ACCOMMODATION

Most of Galiano's services are in the Sturdies Bay–Whaler Bay area, near the ferry terminal, and include grocery stores, restaurants and an ATM machine, but no bank or laundromat.

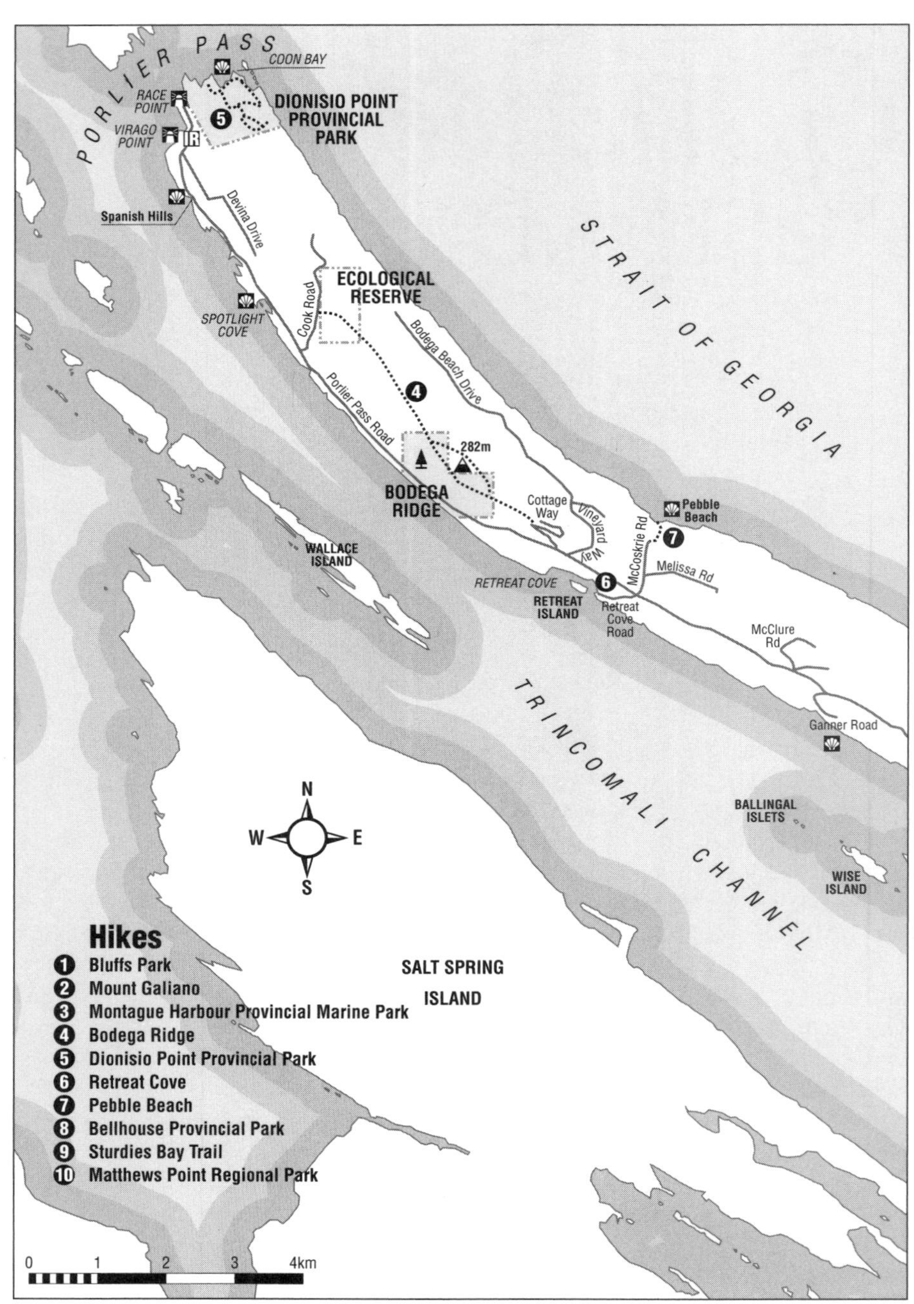

Galiano Island

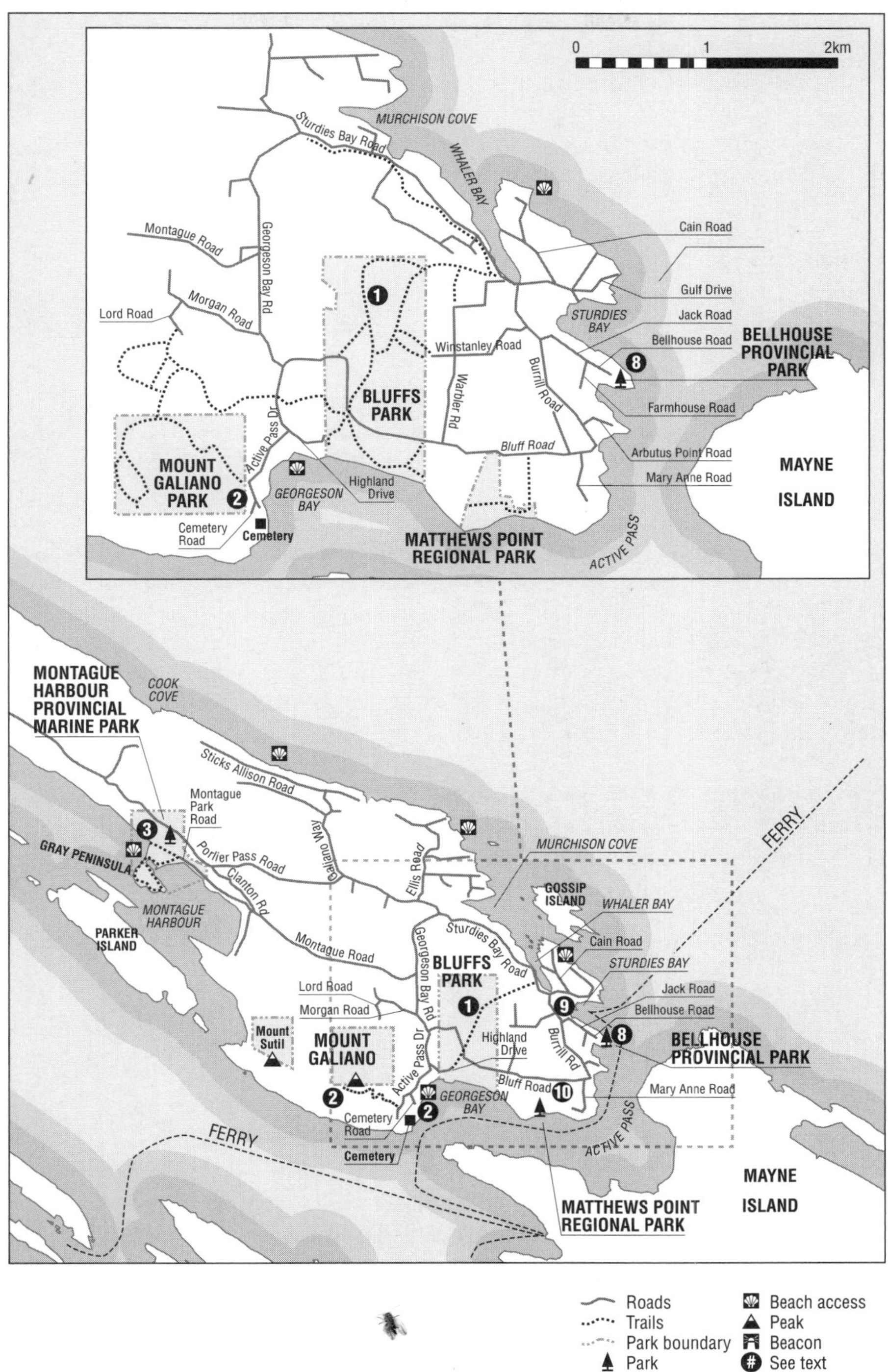
0
1
2km
MURCHISON COVE
Sturdies Bay Road
WHALER BAY
Montague Road
Georgeson Bay Rd
Lord Road
Morgan Road
Cain Road
Gulf Drive
Jack Road
Bellhouse Road
STURDIES BAY
BELLHOUSE PROVINCIAL PARK
Winstanley Road
Warbler Rd
Burrill Road
BLUFFS PARK
Farmhouse Road
Active Pass Dr
Bluff Road
Arbutus Point Road
MOUNT GALIANO PARK
Highland Drive
Mary Anne Road
MAYNE ISLAND
GEORGESON BAY
Cemetery Road
Cemetery
MATTHEWS POINT REGIONAL PARK
ACTIVE PASS
MONTAGUE HARBOUR PROVINCIAL MARINE PARK
COOK COVE
Sticks Allison Road
Montague Park Road
GRAY PENINSULA
Porlier Pass Road
Galiano Way
Ellis Road
MURCHISON COVE
FERRY
GOSSIP ISLAND
WHALER BAY
Clanton Rd
MONTAGUE HARBOUR
PARKER ISLAND
Montague Road
Sturdies Bay Road
Cain Road
STURDIES BAY
Lord Road
Morgan Road
Jack Road
Bellhouse Road
Mount Sutil
MOUNT GALIANO
Highland Drive
Burrill Rd
BELLHOUSE PROVINCIAL PARK
Bluff Road
Mary Anne Road
GEORGESON BAY
Cemetery Road
Cemetery
FERRY
ACTIVE PASS
MAYNE ISLAND
MATTHEWS POINT REGIONAL PARK
Roads
Trails
Park boundary
Park
Beach access
Peak
Beacon
See text

Accommodations are spread throughout the island and include bed and breakfasts, inns, lodges and cottages. There are two public campgrounds: at Dionisio Point Provincial Park in the north (water access only) and Montague Harbour Provincial Marine Park in the south.

For more information, pick up a visitors' guide at a store or on the ferry, contact the Galiano Island Chamber of Commerce (250-539-2233) or visit www.galianoisland.com.

ESPECIALLY FOR WALKERS

Galiano has several enchanting walks. If you are not interested in the more strenuous hikes, concentrate on the Shore and Road Walks listed at the end of this chapter and especially the following:

- Montague Harbour Provincial Marine Park (see hike 3, page 72)
- Bellhouse Provincial Park (see shore and road walk 8, page 75)
- Sturdies Bay Trail (see shore and road walk 9, page 76)

HIKES

If you want a day trip to Galiano without a vehicle, consider walking from the ferry to Bellhouse Provincial Park and then continuing on to Bluffs Park and Mount Galiano. As you can combine the hikes here in a number of different ways, I suggest you read the following hike descriptions carefully before planning your itinerary.

Some of the hikes described below are on private land. While signs encourage public access to these trails, changes in land ownership could result in changes to public access.

1. Bluffs Park ★★★

Trail length	1–4 km each way, depending on route taken
Time required	30–90 minutes, depending on route taken
Description	This pleasant hike along a short ridge combines splendid views with beautiful forest.
Level	Easy
Elevation	About 180 m
Accesses	A. From Bluff Road, 4.5 km from the ferry. Look for the small parking area in the woods on the edge of the bluffs. Try accesses B and C if you want a longer hike through forest to the bluffs. B. Just off the Sturdies Bay Trail (about 1 km from the ferry, on the west side of Sturdies Bay Road, opposite the log booming site in Whaler Bay) C. The east side of Georgeson Bay Road, 200 m south of Bluff Road

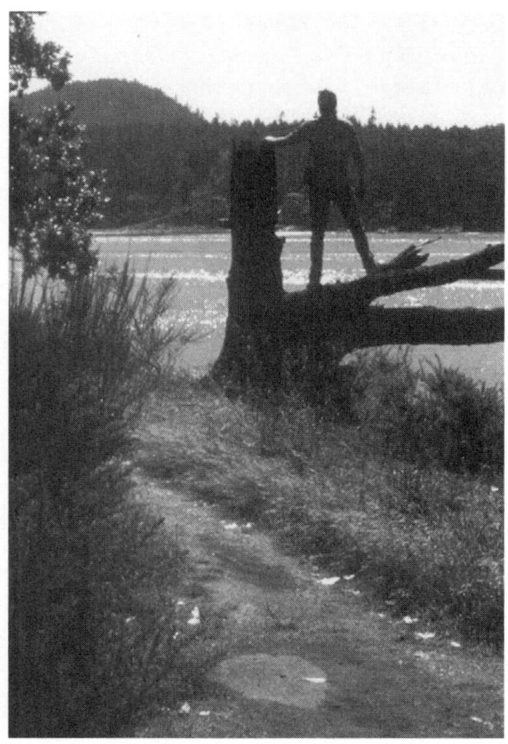

Bellhouse Provincial Park is a treasure of lovely seaside walks, spring wildflower meadows, sandstone formations, and spectacular views across Active Pass.
Richard Blier

In 1948, Marion and Max Enke sold 15.4 ha and gave another 37.2 ha of land on the bluffs to the Galiano Island Development Association. The ownership of the land was turned over to the Galiano Club, in trust, and Bluffs Park opened in 1948.

From the parking area (access A), you can walk both ways along the ridge, with wonderful views across Active Pass and down Navy Channel between Mayne on the left and North Pender Island on the right.

If you follow the trail west along the bluffs for about 10 minutes, you'll find yourself at a turnaround off Bluff Road. Here there are two trails descending the slope. The one to the left leads to a driveway at the end of Highland Drive (a 10–15 minute walk). From there, you can either return the way you came or walk down Highland Drive and turn left onto Active Pass Drive, continuing south to the main trailhead for Mount Galiano. If you take the trail to the right in the Bluffs Park turnaround, you will end up farther north on Georgeson Bay Road (a 15-minute walk), 200 m south of Bluff Road. Almost directly across Georgeson Bay Road, you'll find Grace Trail, which is one of the alternate routes to the top of Mount Galiano (see hike 2, access C).

From access B, almost as soon as you begin walking along the Sturdies Bay trail you will see a signed turn-off on the left leading to Bluffs Park, 3 km away. The path climbs gradually to the bluffs. Most of the trail choices are well marked. However, after you've walked for about 30 minutes, you'll reach a fork that isn't signed. Take the left trail, and within 10 minutes, you'll come out at an unmarked spot on Bluff Road. Turn left and continue on the road for 5 minutes, until you see a vehicle turnaround on the right. From here, you can take the trail east along the bluff or one of the trails south (described above, in access A).

From access C, the trail from Georgeson Bay Road to the bluffs is an easy 15-minute climb through Bluffs Park. There are a number of trails leading to private properties, so be sure to follow the marked trail. Toward the end, there's an unmarked choice. Take the trail to the left, which leads to the turnaround on Bluff Road. (The trail to the right connects with the route from access B.) Once you reach the top, the trail along the bluffs continues to your right (west) from the turnaround (see access A).

2. Mount Galiano ★★★★

Trail length	Up to 3 km each way, depending on route taken
Time required	About 2 hours return
Description	A pleasant hike through beautiful mixed forest in an 81-ha park with a spectacular view from the top of the southern Gulf Islands and the San Juan Islands
Level	Moderate
Elevation	311 m
Accesses	All of the following trails merge part way up to the summit. The accesses for all of them are well signed. A. Near the end of Active Pass Drive, on the west side of the road. This is the steepest ascent to the summit. B. Lord Park Trail from the northwest side of Lord Road at Morgan Road. This is the most gradual ascent to the summit. C. Grace Trail from the west side of Georgeson Bay Road, 200 m south of Bluff Road
Cautions	Fire is a constant danger on Mount Galiano. Do not smoke or create any sparks in this very dry and unprotected area. This and other areas on Galiano are closed in times of extreme fire hazard.

The Dionisio Alcala Galiano Trail (referred to here as Mount Galiano Trail) was opened in 1992, the 200th anniversary of Galiano's explorations in the Strait of Georgia.

From access A, the trail climbs mainly north-northwest for about 10 minutes and then swings left (south) for a while. It climbs fairly steeply and, in some places, runs very close to the edge of the cliff. This trail is signed with unpainted metal arrows.

After you have hiked about 40 minutes, you'll see that the trail merges with an old logging road. This is where the trail merges with the Lord Trail and the Grace Trail. Turn left (south). From here, it's a 15–20-minute climb to the top (south and then east). You'll find some offshoot trails but the main one is easy to follow and marked with metal arrows.

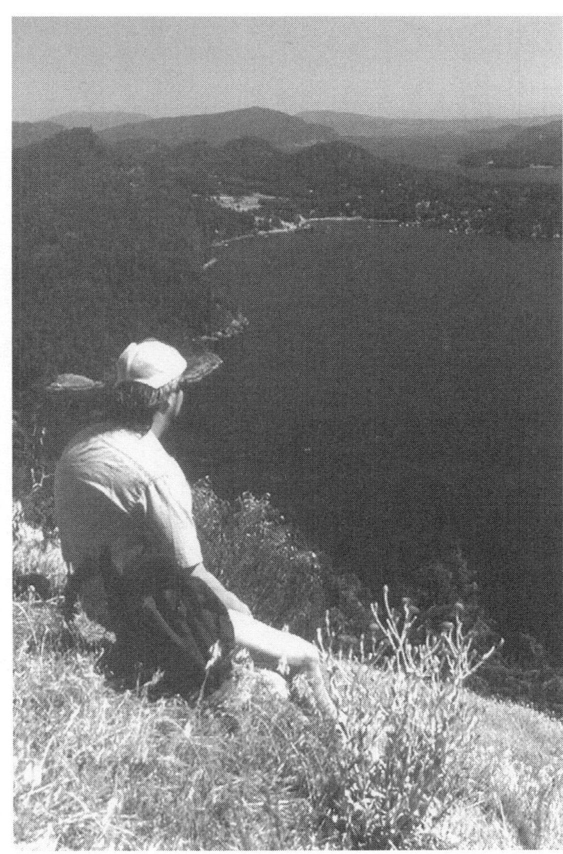

Views from the top of Galiano include a large stand of Garry oaks, other Gulf Islands in the distance, and the San Juan Islands. Richard Blier

At the top of the mountain, there is a stand of Garry oak and fantastic views of the southern Gulf Islands. Unfortunately, you can walk only a short distance in either direction along the top of the mountain before the trail starts to head down the cliff. Be careful not to get too close to the edge, as some of the rock has begun to fall away. When you have had enough of the splendid view, return the way you came. After about 1 km (15 minutes), look for the trail to the right, off the logging road. If you miss it, you'll end up on the Lord Trail (to Lord Road) or the Grace Trail (to Georgeson Bay Road).

From access B (the trailhead on Lord Road), the Lord Trail climbs fairly gradually through cedar woods. The first half of the trail is marked with wooden signs. After 10 minutes, you'll reach the junction of the Grace Trail from Georgeson Bay Road. After another 5 minutes, you'll see signs for Mike's Trail, a logging road continuing uphill to the right. Don't take Mike's Trail. Instead, turn left (east) on the logging road to continue on the Mount Galiano trail. The trail bends right (south), and after about 25 minutes from the start of the trail, you'll come to a junction. Continue straight ahead, avoiding the trail on your left. Here, the trail signs shift to unpainted metal arrows.

The rest of the trail to the summit, heading mainly south along an old logging road, is well trod and well marked with the metal arrows. See the description for access A above for more detail.

From Georgeson Bay Road (access C), the Grace Trail climbs for 10–15 minutes until it merges with the Lord Trail (access B). Follow the description above.

3. Montague Harbour Provincial Marine Park ★★★★

Trail length	About 3 km return
Time required	1 hour
Description	A very enjoyable trail following the shoreline of the park, around Gray Peninsula and along a lagoon. Other trails behind the campsites explore the woods on the park's north side.
Level	Easy
Access	From the end of Montague Park Road (a continuation of Montague Road)

Known for its spectacular beauty, this 89-ha park receives many visitors each year. In one place, the trail parallels a white shell beach, one of six shell middens found here, estimated to be more than 3,000 years old. Archaeologists have found spearheads, stone carvings and arrows on this site. As with other archaeological sites, care should be taken not to damage or disturb the area. Use the stairs provided to reach the beach, rather than climbing the bank.

You will find excellent, though chilly, swimming here. Gray Peninsula was named after a Captain Gray who planted an orchard here to supply fruit for the Victoria market.

The lagoon, a tidal salt marsh, contains reeds, sedges and glasswort. Although it is possible to walk around the lagoon past the walk-in campsites and the wharf until you reach a park road that will bring you back to your starting point, it is probably more interesting to turn around and return along the water.

4. Bodega Ridge ★★★★★

Trail length	6 km (4 km in the park) each way
Time required	70 minutes each way but you'll want to spend longer in this beautiful spot
Description	A ridge walk with constant views over Trincomali Channel, looking west to Salt Spring Island
Level	Easy
Elevation	282 m
Accesses	A. The end of Cottage Way, which runs off Porlier Pass Road B. The Bodega Resort driveway on Cook Road near its junction with Porlier Pass Road

Bodega Ridge was named for Juan Francisco de la Bodega y Quadra, the Spanish commander of the *Nootka*, who explored the Strait of Georgia in 1792. The land was slated to be clear-cut until the Galiano Island Forest Trust bought a key section of it from the logger and then made payments on the mortgage while fundraising to buy the land. In 1995, the Nature Conservancy of Canada and the BC and Canadian governments contributed the remaining funds required to purchase the property. One of the highlights of Bodega Ridge, besides the great views of Salt Spring and other islands, is the manzanita that grows all along the edge of the ridge and blooms in April.

From the end of Cottage Way (access A), the first kilometre of the hike is on private land. You then reach a sign indicating a trail for hikers to the left along the ridge, where the terrain is fragile, and an old logging road to the right for cyclists. It will take you up to 30 minutes to reach the ridge from the trailhead. Once on the ridge, you soon pass a natural rock bench with a spectacular view of nearby Wallace Island and its sister islands, and Salt Spring and Vancouver Island in the distance. The walk continues along the ridge, with ever-increasing views toward the north.

You can continue past the BC Parks sign on the north end of the park and, after descending a bit, continue along the ridge edge. Eventually, the trail leaves the ridge edge and descends to Cook Road (20 minutes away) via the Bodega Resort driveway. This part of the hike is not very scenic, so you might decide to skip it and return to the trailhead. The old trail leading down from the ridge continues west through conservancy land toward a piece of Crown land that forms part of the ecological reserve adjacent to Cook Road. At time of writing, some unoccupied private property linked these public pieces of land.

The fantastic views from Bodega Ridge include a group of small islands—Wallace, Jackscrew, South and North Secretary, Mowgli and Norway. Across Trincomali Channel is Salt Spring and to the north you can see Kuper, Thetis, and even Chemainus and Ladysmith on Vancouver Island.

If you start from Cook Road (access B), you will do the hike described above in reverse. The main drawback to this approach is that the first 20 minutes are not scenic.

5. Dionisio Point Provincial Park ★★★★

Trail length	7 km in total
Time required	2 hours, once you're there
Description	Sensational walks along the Porlier Pass shoreline and strolls through mature forest
Level	Easy
Accesses	People are expected to access the park by water and there is no public land access.
Cautions	Porlier Pass between Galiano and Valdes Islands is known for its strong currents, which run up to 9 knots at spring tides. These currents and the many exposed rocks have caused numerous shipwrecks over the years, making it one of the most respected stretches of water in the Gulf Islands. The land to the southwest is part of an Indian Reserve, which is home to members of the Penelakut Band. If you want to walk on this land, you must get permission from the band office (250-246-2321) and you are not allowed to disturb the middens or burial sites.

Perhaps the most interesting shore walks on Galiano are at Dionisio Point Provincial Park. This 142-ha park, which includes most of the northern tip of the island around Coon Bay, was a gift to the community from MacMillan Bloedel when the logging company sold off most of its Galiano holdings. There are some trails through the woods but the highlights are the shore walks.

Porlier Pass Trail connects the western edge of Maple Bay with the short trail to Dionisio Point. The Raymond V. Smith Interpretive Trail (1.3 km) connects the tidal lagoon at Dionisio Point with the camping area on the park's east side and beyond. Interior trails—the Maple Bay Trail and the Sutil Ridge Loop Trail—provide access to the mature forest in the park's interior. There are maps of the trail system on signboards in the park's camping areas.

You can walk along the sandstone formations of the shore at Dionisio in both directions, as well as along the shore of a small wooded peninsula that abuts Coon Bay. If you walk east and then south along Galiano's long, unsettled Strait of Georgia shore, you can walk almost indefinitely at low tide, with views of the Coast Mountains far away on the mainland. If you walk west along the Porlier Pass Trail, you can walk from Coon Bay to Maple Bay, then past the light at Race Point and, finally, along a boardwalk, for a total of about 1 km.

Dionisio Point Provincial Park is the perfect place to watch the sun set over the Gulf Islands and the steady boat traffic navigating the swirling waters of Porlier Pass. David Norget

SHORE AND ROAD WALKS

Despite its long coastline, Galiano has relatively little public beach access, although once on the shore you can often walk quite far. Much of the island's west side is sheer cliff and there's limited road access to the east side. On both sides, most of the waterfront property is privately owned. It's possible to walk the shore in the following places:

6. Retreat Cove: One of the few public water-access points on the west shore, at the end of Retreat Cove Road, about two-thirds of the way up the island, off Porlier Pass Road. There is a public dock here (in bad condition at time of writing), a small beach and a very short walk through a gate and along a path overlooking the cove. All the surrounding land is private. The rocks along the shore form a wonderful overhanging gallery and cave.

7. Pebble Beach: Take McCoskrie Road east (opposite Retreat Cove Road) and continue past Melissa Road until you reach a T-junction. Turn right and continue south along the dirt road for 700 m. You'll see an obvious parking area and a trail to your left (north) heading through thick forest on Crown land. A half-hour hike will take you to Pebble Beach, from where you can walk along Galiano's east shore for some distance, in both directions. This beach is well known as a place to find agates and other semi-precious stones.

8. Bellhouse Provincial Park: Although this 2-ha park on Burrill Point has only a 1-km-long trail, it is one of the most scenic little paths in the Gulf Islands. The park is 2.5 km from the ferry. Follow Sturdies Bay Road to Burrill Road. Turn left (south)

and follow the signs to the end of Jack Road, where it becomes Bellhouse Road. The trail follows the bluffs around the point. At low tide, you can descend to the sandstone that lines the shore in several places; from here, it is possible to walk northeast toward Sturdies Bay along the rocks. While in the park, keep to the trails, as the mossy vegetation is very fragile. The sandstone formations are especially intricate. The park has picnic tables, benches and outhouses but no overnight camping is allowed.

9. Sturdies Bay Trail: This commuter/neighbourhood trail starts on the south side of Sturdies Bay Road across from the head of Whaler Bay, about 1 km from the ferry landing. The trail roughly follows Sturdies Bay Road for about 2.5 km, returning to the road across from the Hummingbird Pub. At one point, the trail follows the road toward Galiano Island Community School and then continues northwest before returning to parallel Sturdies Bay Road. An offshoot close to the beginning of this trail goes west for about 3 km to emerge on Bluff Road in Bluffs Park (see hike 1, access B).

10. Matthews Point Regional Park: This 14.7-ha park was established in 1999 by the Capital Regional District. The access is on the south side of Bluff Road, 400 m west of Mary Anne Road. At time of writing, the sign to this access was partly covered by trees and easy to miss. It takes 10 minutes to get down to the beach, which is only exposed at low tide. For the first 5 minutes, the trail runs over mainly flat, cleared land alongside a neighbouring property before it descends steeply through forest to the sand beach below. The park contains stands of mature Douglas fir and pockets of arbutus and Garry oak. There are also a couple of trails running from east to west across this narrow property. Be aware that the ferry wash and the currents in Active Pass can be dangerous.

The following shore accesses are signed and easy to find:

Spanish Hills: A public dock at Spanish Hills gives boaters access to Trincomali Channel. There used to be a store here but it is now a private residence.

Spotlight Cove: The beach at the end of a trail at Spotlight Cove can be walked for quite some way, in either direction.

Ganner Road: A trail off Ganner Road leads to a pretty pebble beach on Trincomali Channel but it isn't possible to walk very far along it.

Montague Harbour Provincial Marine Park: The best beach accesses on the island are at Montague Provincial Marine Park (see hike 3).

Cain Road: At the end of Cain Road, just off Sturdies Bay Road, less than 1 km from the ferry, you can clamber along the rocks on the beach for quite a distance.

Morning Beach (local name)**:** A short trail from Ellis Road leads to this pretty beach facing the Lion Islets.

Galiano also has some lovely road walks, made more enjoyable because of the light traffic. Try the following:

Georgeson Bay Road: Walk south from Bluff Road and continue along Active Pass Drive. This is a little like walking along an old country lane—well treed, green, with glimpses of the sea. Continue to Galiano's cemetery, on Cemetery Road at the end of Active Pass Drive, where you will find headstones bearing the names of most of Galiano's early settlers. Originally a Native graveyard, this land was deeded to the Synod of the Anglican Diocese of BC for use as a cemetery, in 1928, by George Georgeson, whose family first settled on Galiano in 1863. On your way back, consider walking along Highland Drive, which runs off Georgeson Bay Road just east of Active Pass Drive. Highland Drive climbs steeply and provides glimpses of Active Pass, so turn around and look behind you, from time to time.

Sturdies Bay Road: The walk from the ferry is pleasant, with the views along narrow Whaler Bay especially satisfying. You might combine this with the Bluffs Park hike (see hike 1). At Murchison Cove (north of Whaler Bay), look for the oldest house on Galiano, a square-timbered building that dates from about 1885.

Trails: Although not a road walk, the network of trails behind Galiano Community School and Activity Centre on Sturdies Bay Road cannot be omitted. These pleasant trails wind around Centennial Park, a small community park that was a gift to the island from the Fred Robson family.

AND IF YOU PADDLE . . .

Galiano's mainly unindented shoreline is not the most interesting for paddling. Nevertheless, aside from Porlier Pass and Active Pass, where there are very strong currents, paddling around Galiano is fairly safe, though kayakers should also be careful of the heavy boat traffic in Montague Harbour:

Whaler Bay and Gossip Island: Although most of the east side of the island is unprotected shoreline open to the Strait of Georgia, you might consider paddling here.

Retreat Cove: You can put in beside the old government dock, on the west side of the island, and paddle south to Montague Harbour (see hike 3) or out to Wallace Island, where you will find numerous hiking trails (see page 233). At time of writing, the Retreat Cove dock was in very poor condition.

Dionisio Point Provincial Marine Park: You can paddle to the park from the beach access at Spotlight Cove or the dock at Spanish Hills. Dionisio is in Porlier Pass, so either enter at slack tide or try to obtain permission from the Penelakut Band (250-246-2321) to land on their reserve just past the first light on Virago Point in Porlier Pass. This historic little inlet is connected with the provincial park by a beautiful trail that follows the rocky edge of the shore.

Montague Harbour Provincial Marine Park: A good place to put in; from here you can explore the harbour and nearby Parker and Wise Islands. Be cautious of approaching the Ballingall Islets Provincial Park, a provincial ecological reserve where public access is not allowed, although the cormorants, which don't like being disturbed, now tend to nest on the Galiano cliffs to the north.

Hornby ISLAND

Although farther from Vancouver Island than Denman, Hornby was settled first and continues to be the more popular of these sibling islands, hosting about 10,000 visitors each summer. Hornby's shoreline is punctuated with many bays, coves and spits. Its topography features the bluffs of Mount Geoffrey in the southwest and cliffs along Tribune Bay and into Helliwell Provincial Park in the east. Combine this with forest, sandy beaches and the warmest water in the Gulf Islands and you have an unbeatable combination for an island of just over 30 square km. Although it has only 966 permanent residents, Hornby offers more services than some of the larger, more populated islands including a credit union, gas bar, restaurants, bed and breakfasts, food store, pub and art galleries. With some of the most scenic hikes in the Gulf Islands, Hornby is well worth visiting.

HISTORY

Comox Natives camped and fished at Whaling Station Bay on the northeast side of the island, long before Europeans gave it that name. Beginning in 1871, the bay was used as a base for the BC Whaling Company until whales became too scarce a few years later. Two of Hornby's first settlers, George Ford and Horatio Maude, were friends from Devon, England, who arrived in the late 1860s, and by 1885, owned about 40 percent of the island. Although the 1905 population was only 32, by then most of the island had been claimed. As on other Gulf Islands, the settlers supported themselves by farming, fishing and logging. Most of Hornby's original forest was logged between 1910 and 1920.

Hornby has a strong tradition of public involvement and community building. The Women's Institute and the Farmer's Institute were founded in 1921, the Credit Union in 1942 and the Hornby Island Co-operative Store in 1954. Today the Hornby Island Residents and Ratepayers Association helps administer a number of island facilities and services, and Conservancy Hornby Island recently raised $300,000 to help establish the new 182-ha provincial park on Mount Geoffrey.

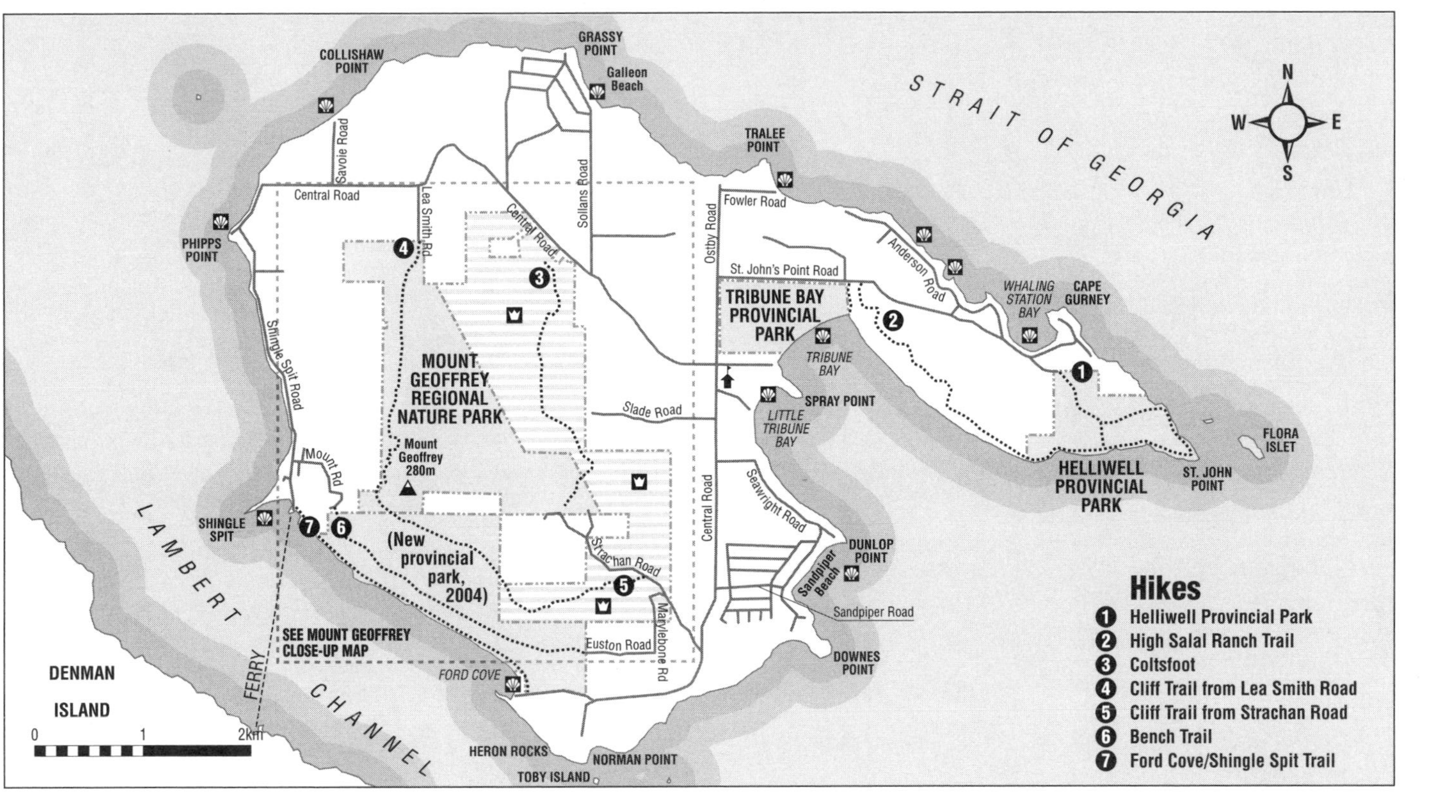

Hornby Island

The Story of Yick Shing

Yick Shing was a Chinese farmer who grew produce on his large farm for the Nanaimo market. Yick imported large amounts of rice from China, ostensibly to feed his Chinese workers. In reality, he made rice whisky in a still, camouflaged by hay, in his barn near Heron Rocks. This was around 1920, during prohibition, when whisky was a valuable product. The bottles of whisky were packed in sauerkraut to hide them, placed in waterproof boxes that were placed under the vegetables, and shipped to Nanaimo.

Eventually, Yick's "business" was discovered and he was jailed for three years. But the story doesn't end there. Yick took advantage of the fact that his jailors could not tell Chinese men apart and managed to avoid serving his entire sentence by changing places with a cousin who came to visit him from time to time. When the guards weren't looking, Yick and his cousin would exchange clothes and identities. After some time, they would switch again.

GETTING THERE

To get to Hornby, you must first take the 10-minute ferry from Buckley Bay on Vancouver Island (about 20 km south of Courtenay) to Denman Island, cross Denman Island (another 15 minutes) and then take the connecting 10-minute ferry to Hornby Island. For more information, obtain a copy of the Northern Gulf Islands schedule or contact BC Ferries (see Resources, page 235).

Hornby offers some of the most spectacular cliff walks in the Gulf Islands.
Mark Kaaremaa

SERVICES AND ACCOMMODATION

Most services are centred around the Hornby Island Co-op, near Tribune Bay. The co-op is a wonderful store that sells a wide variety of fresh and prepared foods at reasonable prices, as well as almost everything else, including liquor and gas. The co-op is surrounded by a couple of restaurants and several small stores. Another cluster of stores, including a pub and the Union Bay Credit Union (with the island's only ATM), is at the Shingle Spit ferry dock. There is also a small general store, crafts shop, campground and marina at Ford Cove. Store hours on Hornby vary with the season. When I visited in March, no Hornby restaurant served dinner from Monday to Wednesday.

There are many bed and breakfasts on Hornby, as well as lodges and three or four private campgrounds. The two provincial parks are open for day use only. A combined visitor's guide to both Denman and Hornby, including a map of each island, is produced yearly by the Hornby Denman Tourist Services, Hornby Island, BC V0R 1Z0. Contact the office or the Hornby web site at http://hornbyisland.com for more information.

ESPECIALLY FOR WALKERS

While hikers will enjoy climbing Mount Geoffrey, there are plenty of easy and beautiful walks for those less inclined to climbing. Here are a few suggestions:

- The trail at Helliwell Provincial Park (see hike 1, page 82) follows fairly level ground on a cliff edge with spectacular views over the Strait of Georgia. This is the premier walk on the island.
- The High Salal Ranch Trail (see hike 2, page 83) is almost as accessible as Helliwell and offers some of the views that Helliwell offers. If you have to make a choice, choose Helliwell.
- Ford Cove–Shingle Spit Trail (see hike 7, page 88) follows the shoreline and has impressive views across Lambert Channel to Denman Island. There is no strenuous climbing.
- Don't miss Tribune Bay Provincial Park (see Shore and Road Walks, page 90). At the very least, walk the park's spectacular beach.

There are also a great number of shore and road walks outlined at the end of the chapter, all easily accessible.

HIKES

Hiking on Hornby is particularly good because of the large amount of public land. Three trails parallel each other at different heights along the southern slope of Mount Geoffrey (280 m). These trails—the Ford Cove–Shingle Spit Trail nearest the sea, the Bench Trail in the middle and the summit and ridge trails along the top of the bluffs of Mount Geoffrey—can be hiked individually, together or in combination with one of the innumerable other trails that interconnect with them and link them to other parts of the island. You might want to read about all these hikes (hikes 3–7) before deciding which you want to try. Additional suggestions for combinations are made in the descriptions that follow.

In addition to the maps included here, you might like to acquire the laminated *Hiking/biking on Mount Geoffrey* map put out by the Hornby Island Residents and Ratepayers Association ($10) or the free brochure, *Mount Geoffrey Regional Nature Park*, put out by the Regional District of Comox–Strathcona. Commercial maps are also available at the Hornby Co-op.

1. Helliwell Provincial Park ★★★★★

Trail length	6 km loop walk
Time required	90-minute loop
Description	One of the finest walks in the Gulf Islands, through old-growth Douglas fir forest and along weather-sculpted sandstone cliffs with glorious views of the mainland, Lasqueti Island and Texada Island. Consider visiting the park at low tide, so that you can enjoy the tidal pools.
Level	Easy
Access	The well-signed trailhead is at the parking lot at Helliwell Provincial Park, toward the end of St. John's Point Road.
Cautions	No bicycles are allowed in the park. Dogs must be on leash. Stay on the trails: ropes have been used to mark restoration areas beside trails.

This 69-ha park was a gift from John Helliwell to the people of BC in 1966. The best time to visit is late April and early May, when wildflowers decorate the bluffs. A map at the trailhead illustrates the trail system. An interpretive pamphlet produced by Conservancy Hornby Island was also available at the trailhead when I last walked the trail.

After about 5 minutes from the trailhead, you reach a junction where you can choose either fork, as this is the beginning of the loop trail. Turning left at the junction, you walk through forest containing old-growth fir, substantial red cedar, large maple, decorative holly and alder. The forest floor is covered with salal, Oregon grape, red huckleberry and swordferns.

About 10 minutes later, you emerge from the forest at the edge of the water. Just offshore is Flora Islet with its navigational light and dilapidated wooden shacks that were used by fishermen in the 1930s. Flora Islet is part of the park and accessible by canoe or kayak. In the spring, it's covered with wildflowers. It is also one of only two locations in the world where divers have seen the rare six-gill shark, which enjoys the relative shallows around the islet. Much farther east is Lasqueti Island, which is almost dwarfed by Texada behind it.

As you continue right along the shore, you will walk on the edge of spectacular cliffs worn by the wind and waves into sculptural shapes. Somewhere along here, you will see a trail going off into the forest, which leads back to where you started. You can return this way, if you're in a hurry, but I recommend continuing along the cliffs.

When you reach the park boundary on the southwest corner of the park, it's possible to continue along a marked public trail through the "Oak Grove" in the High Salal Ranch development and even as far as Tribune Bay (see hike 2). But you'll most likely want to turn back once this trail leaves the sea. As you return, you can take the trail back to the parking lot—a 5-minute walk through the forest—or if you have the time and energy, retrace your steps along the water and see how different the views are when walking the other way.

2. HIGH SALAL RANCH TRAIL (CONNECTING TO THE HELLIWELL PARK TRAIL) ★★★

Trail length	4 km each way (from access A)
Time required	50 minutes each way (from access A)
Description	A walk through the High Salal Ranch housing development on the west side of Helliwell Provincial Park that eventually follows bluffs overlooking the sea through a forest of Garry oak, arbutus and Douglas fir
Level	Easy
Access	A. Take St. John's Point Road to the High Salal Ranch development (1.7 km from Central Road). You must park at the bottom of the strata development's private road and walk along it to reach the trail. B. A trail from the east side of the outdoor education centre in Tribune Bay Provincial Park quickly leads to the High Salal Ranch road.
Caution	This trail is a public right-of-way through private land. It is important that hikers act responsibly and stay on the marked trail, so this hike remains open to the public. No dogs, bicycles or horses are allowed in High Salal Ranch.

This trail links Tribune Bay and Helliwell Provincial Parks, and is clearly marked with signs for most of the way. Follow the strata road to lot 16 (25 minutes from St. John's Point Road), where the trail turns right toward the water and then left (east) along the bluffs from just beside a private house. The trail continues along the edge of the cliffs for a short distance, through an undisturbed stand of Garry oak and soon joins the western boundary of Helliwell Provincial Park (see hike 1).

3. Coltsfoot ★★

Trail length	3 km each way
Time required	45 minutes each way
Description	Old logging roads connect Strachan Road with the firehall on Central Road.
Level	Easy
Access	A. Behind and to the left of the firehall off Central Road B. From the end of Strachan Road, about 2 km from Central Road
Caution	In the winter and spring, parts of the trail may be washed out by Chasm and Beulah Creeks.

Coltsfoot is a former forestry road through a previously logged area that has filled in with alder and ferns. Near the firehall, it passes by the rear of the Ministry of Highways yard. There are innumerable trails that connect the Crown land, Mount Geoffrey Regional Nature Park and the new provincial park on Mount Geoffrey. If you decide to combine Coltsfoot with some of the other trails, carry a compass and check the trail offshoots with those shown on the map, to ensure that you end up where you want to be—or just enjoy the luck of the draw. Chances are, if you end up some distance from your intended destination, someone will give you a ride to where you need to go. I found following Spasm Chasm (west off Coltsfoot) and then turning left (southwest) on Logging Railroad an enjoyable way to join Northwind (right) and then climb to Cliff Trail.

4. Cliff Trail from Lea Smith Road ★★★★★

Trail length	About 4 km each way, depending on how far you choose to hike along the bluffs
Time required	About 2 to 3 hours return
Description	The most beautiful hike on Mt. Geoffrey, this is a short, steep climb to spectacular western views. The trail leads into the Mount Geoffrey Regional Nature Park.
Level	Moderate, except for a very steep beginning
Access	The trailhead is well marked at the end of Lea Smith Road (off Central Road). At the trailhead, you'll also find a full-colour map showing all the trails in this area.
Caution	Take great care as you proceed along the bluffs, as the trail is badly eroded in many places.

Note: Much of this trail is the same as hike 5.

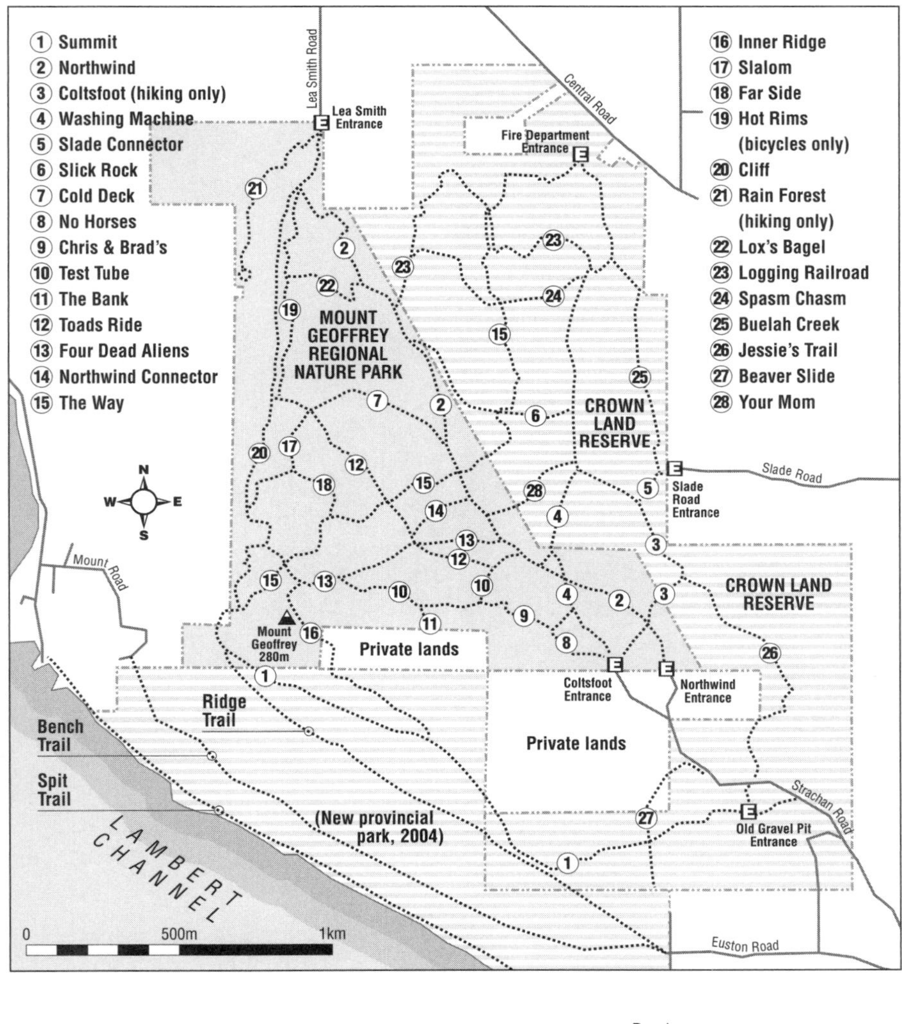

Mount Geoffrey Trails

This hike has everything—lovely forest, spectacular views, rugged cliffs and rockfaces. It also follows a real foot trail rather than an old logging road. The trail from the end of Lea Smith Road climbs very steeply and you soon find yourself high above your starting place, which is still visible far below through the trees. The trail zigzags up the mountain but is well established and clearly marked. Regional park signs identify almost every major trail that leaves Cliff Trail (but not always correctly).

It climbs first through a pretty forest of fir, cedar, alder and some maple, with an undergrowth of salal. In some more open parts of the trail, you cross moss-covered

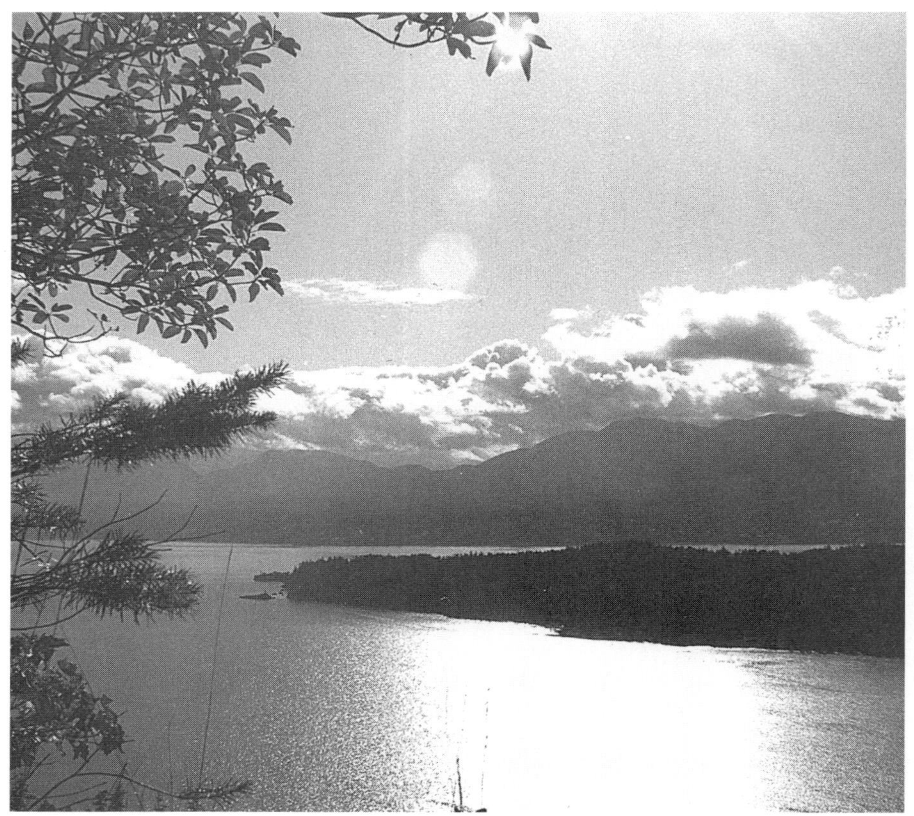

The Cliff Trail on Mount Geoffrey boasts unparalleled views of Denman Island on the far side of Lambert Channel and the peaks of Vancouver Island beyond.

rocks. After 15 minutes or so of climbing, you begin to see views west toward Denman Island and the mountains of Vancouver Island.

There are many picnic spots on the edge of the bluffs, with wide-angle views down to Shingle Spit by the ferry dock, and out to Denman and Vancouver Islands. You can continue along the edge of the bluffs for an hour or more. After that, the trail goes deeper into the forest and begins to descend. You'll pass a short trail leading east to Mount Geoffrey's peak, which is unnamed but marked by a large cairn. It's not worth the effort to reach the peak, however, as the views are obscured by the surrounding forest and you'll have to retrace your steps to regain the main trail. Farther along, the Cliff Trail merges with both the Summit Trail and the Ridge Trail. However, as the Ridge Trail is less obvious, you will probably find yourself on the Summit Trail, which goes away from the ridge before joining the Bench Trail (see hike 6). Nevertheless, both of these trails eventually merge with the Bench Trail, allowing you to combine hikes 4 and 6.

5. Cliff Trail from Strachan Road to Northwind Trail ★★★★★

Trail length	About 8 km in total, depending on route chosen
Time required	2.5 hours
Description	An uphill climb along an old logging road leads to gorgeous views west from a cliff edge.
Level	Moderate
Access	From Central Road, proceed about 1.7 km along Strachan Road until you see a regional park sign announcing the Northwind Trail entrance. Turn right and continue until you see the yellow steel posts placed to stop cars at the trailhead. The trail leads into the Mount Geoffrey Regional Nature Park.

Note: Much of this trail is the same as hike 4.

The logging-road trail climbs steadily to the northwest. This part of the hike is not very exciting. The forest has been thoroughly logged and now contains a mixture of spindly alder and young fir. However, the well-packed trail, covered with fir needles and grass, is a pleasant enough place to stroll. Many other trails feed into it and most are identified, should you want to take an alternative route to Cliff Trail. I took Cold Deck, which brought me about midway along Cliff Trail.

If you continue along Northwind, it will take you about an hour to reach the edge of the bluffs. You are now on Cliff Trail, which continues left (south) for quite some way and is very close to the edge of the bluffs in many places, so walk carefully. There are numerous offshoots along the way, so you can vary your return to the trailhead, if you like. For more information about Cliff Trail, see hike 4.

6. Bench Trail ★★★★

Trail length	3 km each way
Time required	1 hour each way
Description	This gently climbing trail through mixed forest provides superb views west to Denman and Vancouver Islands.
Level	Easy
Access	A. A sign marks the trailhead at the top end of Mount Road (1 km from Shingle Spit Road). B. From the end of Euston Road. This access is not recommended if you want to combine the Bench and Shingle Spit Trails to make a round trip.

From Mount Road, the trail heads southeast. It soon reaches the edge of a ridge and follows the bluffs east, providing wonderful views of Denman Island and the mountains on Vancouver Island. Below, you can see Shingle Spit to your immediate right and Ford Cove to the left in the distance.

The trail climbs steeply, in places, but is not difficult. You will pass arbutus and several large fir trees, as well as alder and a surprising number of maple. After a while, the trail leaves the edge of the bluffs, returning at a couple of viewpoints.

After about 50 minutes of hiking, you will reach the end of the trail, at Euston Road. About 200 m before the end of the trail, another trail goes off to the left and leads to other trails on Mount Geoffrey.

If you are combining this hike with the Ford Cove–Shingle Spit Trail (hike 7), a 4.3 km road walk connects the two. Walk along Euston Road to Marylebone Road and then to Strachan—a distance of about 1.4 km. Continue right (southeast) on Strachan to Central Road and then turn right again (southwest) down the hill. This last bit of road has views of rolling farmland edged by the sea and of Denman Island in the distance.

Before taking the Ford Cove–Shingle Spit Trail portion of this hike, explore the wonderful sandstone shore around Ford Cove (behind the shop). In Ford Cove, you can buy food and refreshments. To begin the Ford Cove–Shingle Spit Trail, retrace your steps up Central Road for about 200 m, where you'll find the unmarked trailhead on the left (west) side of the road. See cautions in hike 7 before taking this trail.

7. Ford Cove/Shingle Spit Trail ★★★

Trail length	2.5 km each way
Time required	45 minutes each way
Description	This picturesque, mainly forested trail runs between a spectacular conglomerate rockface on one side and bluffs overlooking the sea on the other.
Level	Easy
Access	A. Off Central Road about 200 m from Ford Cove Marina, you'll see the narrow trailhead on the west side of the road. B. The trail enters the woods east of the ferry dock.
Cautions	Several areas along this trail are subject to winter and spring washouts and can be difficult to cross. Until recently, this was private land, and there's still a house to the south of the trail at its west end. Respect the landowner's privacy.

Note: As mentioned above, this trail makes a good round trip with the Bench Trail (hike 6).

Starting from the Ford Cove trailhead (access A), you'll pass through an area of short shrubs, as the trail follows a bluff overlooking the water.

Until the 1950s, this hiking trail was a passable road. When it was washed out, the Ministry of Highways refused to rebuild it, thus cutting out a crucial link in a round-Hornby road.

Most of the trail passes through mixed young forest—alder, maple, cedar and fir, punctuated with the occasional grove of arbutus. To the north is the escarpment of Mount Geoffrey; to the south is the sea. Although the old roadbed can still be seen for much of the way, it has filled in with young trees in many places. Elsewhere, large boulders of conglomerate have fallen onto the roadbed from the cliffs above. Don't miss the interesting rock formations along the shore that are visible from time to time through the trees. If you hike this trail during the wet months, you'll be treated to a gushing waterfall tumbling around moss-covered rocks down to the sea.

In less than an hour, you emerge behind the pub and restaurant at Shingle Spit. This is a good spot to stop for an ice-cream cone or something more substantial. The setting is so pleasant, you might make this your final hike of the day.

SHORE AND ROAD WALKS

There are many beautiful beach walks on Hornby with ample access points. The following are a few of the best:

Shingle Beach: From the ferry, you can walk north along sandy Shingle Beach for some distance at low tide. The oyster beds are privately leased and the oysters should not be touched.

Phipps Point: Turn off Shingle Spit Road just where Central Road begins. (The beach-access road looks like a westerly extension of Central Road.) The view is toward Denman Island.

Collishaw Point: Take Savoie Road (off Central Road, about 3 km north of the ferry) to its end. From here, a trail descends to the rocky beach. You can walk right (northeast) as far as Collishaw Point. The oyster beds are privately leased and the oysters should not be touched.

Galleon Beach: Take Sollans Road (off Central Road between the Community Hall and the school) to its end (at Gunpowder Road), where you will find a small community park. From here you can walk north to Grassy Point, where there's another beach access and small park. It's possible to combine road and beach walks between these accesses.

Tralee Point: Take Ostby Road (off Central Road, near Tribune Bay Provincial Park) to Fowler Road. At the end of Fowler Road, a trail goes down to the beach. Herons nest in the nearby treetops, and if you're here in the spring, you'll hear their noisy chatter. At low tide, you can walk along the beach for quite some way. Much of it is made up of sandstone boulders. There are petroglyphs visible on the rocks near Tralee Point to the north.

Whaling Station Bay: There are several beach accesses off St. John's Point Road. The soft, sandy beach is surrounded by summer cottages. This beach is said to have the warmest water around Hornby.

Tribune Bay: Off St. John's Point road, 95-ha Tribune Bay Provincial Park gives you access to perhaps the loveliest and longest sand beach in the Gulf Islands. At low tide, you can walk far out into the bay to investigate tidal pools. You can scramble over the rugged sandstone boulders that line both sides of the bay and find rocks from which to launch yourself into the pleasantly warm water. While dogs are not allowed on the beach, they are allowed on leash on the short trails through the park's woods, one of which leads to an old lodge. The lodge was part of a resort that operated here from 1928 until the early 1970s. Since 1978, when the property became a park, the lodge has been used for the school district's outdoor education program. To the east of this building, a trail leads northwest to the High Salal Ranch development and, ultimately, to Helliwell Park (see hikes 1 and 2). You can also access Tribune Bay by following Salt Spray Road (beside the co-op) to its end, beside the Tribune Bay Campsite.

Little Tribune Bay 1: Take Seawright Road (off Central Road, toward the south end of Little Tribune Beach). This access is a narrow, wooded path with houses on either side. There are rock steps down to the beach at the end of the path. (Watch out for the board joining the steps to the beach; it's quite slippery when wet.) At low tide, you can walk along the beach all around Little Tribune Bay. The beach is rocky, with great slabs of sandstone, so wear appropriate footwear. From here, you can walk south to Dunlop Point and then along sandy Sandpiper Beach to Downes Point, where you will find another petroglyph. *Caution:* Be sure to check for a red-tide warning before eating any oysters or clams from this beach.

Little Tribune Bay 2: Take Little Tribune Road, a gravel road toward the middle of Little Tribune Bay. The road ends at an open area on the beach, which is very popular with skinny-dippers. There's an outhouse in this small community park area.

There are many pleasant roads to explore on Hornby.

Seawright Road (near Little Tribune Bay)**:** You might use the beach access here to combine some beachcombing with a road walk.

Whaling Station Bay (off St. John's Point Road in the northeast)**:** The roads here pass interesting homes, many of them summer retreats. Again, you can use one of the many beach accesses to create a combined road-and-beach walk.

Central Road from Strachan Road to Ford Cove: This has been designated as a "heritage road" in Hornby's official community plan. As you come down the hill toward Ford Cove, you will enjoy excellent views of the beautiful farmland below and the sea beyond. From Ford Cove, you can continue along one of the loveliest sculptured sandstone shorelines in the Gulf Islands to Heron Rocks and Norman Point.

Central Road from the bakery to the co-op: You can walk this 4-km route mostly on a multi-use trail that parallels the road.

HERON ROCKS

South along the sandstone beach from Ford Cove is the area known as Heron Rocks, where you'll find some of the most spectacular weathered sandstone formations in the Gulf Islands. At low tide, you can walk for hours over the sandstone, examining the weird hoodoo-like formations and the tidal pools.

Early morning is a wonderful time to be here, with the sun rising on the sea, eagles perched on the high points of the rock islands just offshore and, especially in the spring and fall, sea lions barking on the points below and many waterfowl swimming by. Continue walking to the small island off Norman Point, which is accessible at low tide. It has great views south to Vancouver Island.

On the way, you pass the Heron Rocks Camping Co-op, owned by Hilary and Harrison Brown until 1967, when the Browns turned the running of the campground over to the campers.

In 1989, Hilary Brown founded the non-profit Heron Rocks Friendship Centre to protect and preserve the land, flora and fauna of Heron Rocks; promote environmental responsibility and sustainable practices; promote cross-cultural exchanges and educate in methods of conflict resolution. The centre organizes workshops, seminars, retreats, small conferences, informal gatherings and public events oriented toward social change, global understanding and environmental responsibility. Recently, the centre has made a special effort to provide educational and other opportunities for youth.

AND IF YOU PADDLE . . .

If you bring your kayak, try to go out at high tide; if you don't, Hornby's shallow, rocky shoreline will force you to paddle quite far from shore. Here are three routes to try:

Whaling Station Bay: Put in here and paddle along Helliwell's rocky shoreline to the opening of Tribune Bay. On the way back, stop at Flora Islet and enjoy the flowers for which it's named. In the spring, the island is covered with blue-eyed Mary and sea blush. Be aware that there are no places to land along Helliwell Provincial Park's shoreline and that strong southeast winds can start up suddenly and blow against these bluffs.

Ford Cove: Start here and paddle to the mouth of Tribune Bay. If you're here in spring, you'll likely have one or more sea lions for company. They frequent a rocky islet just offshore. The highlight of this paddle is Heron Rocks with their fascinatingly weathered shapes.

Phipps Point: Launch here and paddle past Shingle Spit, the ferry terminal and, perhaps, as far as Ford Cove. The logs on Shingle Spit are a good place for lunch. There's lots of activity to watch, with Vancouver Island's Beaufort Range as a backdrop. Give the ferry lots of space if you happen to arrive when it does.

Lasqueti ISLAND

Engaging Lasqueti Island lies midway between Vancouver Island and the mainland, and that's the way its 367 permanent residents like it: alluring and almost out of reach. A magnet for draft dodgers in the 1960s, Lasqueti's artistic and close-knit community still enjoys a rustic lifestyle and is known for its self-reliance. Serviced by a private, passenger-only ferry from French Creek on Vancouver Island, all the cars on the island have been brought over by barge. By choice, none of the homes are on the electricity grid and islanders rely on alternative energy sources for power. Although Lasqueti is difficult to reach, has no public transportation, limited accommodation and no campgrounds, it's worth the trip. The roads are tranquil and, in places, the scenery is breathtaking. If you go, I suggest taking a bicycle. Despite covering 68 square km, Lasqueti has few public trails and is not a great place to hike. Nevertheless, its roads are good to walk or bicycle along and it's a great place to kayak. Everything from crafts to organic fruit can be purchased from businesses in False Bay.

HISTORY

In times past, the Pentlatch summered on Lasqueti. The first non-Native settler arrived in 1860 but settlement proceeded very slowly. The first farmers raised sheep, which were taken to market in Nanaimo. Farmers tried to raise cattle in the 1960s but had little success. Logging began in 1898 and reached its height in the 1950s. Around the same time, the Lasqueti Fishing Company, which still exists today, began to build and operate seiners. These days, islanders support themselves through a variety of activities including shellfish farming, growing produce and working for a local company that makes buttons and other accessories from deadwood. While Lasqueti's permanent population has not changed much since the 1980s, it attracts a large summer population whose cottages can be seen all around the island.

GETTING THERE

Lasqueti's ferry leaves French Creek (3 km north of Parksville) two or three times a day during the summer (except Tuesdays) and covers the 17-km trip to False Bay in about an hour. The ferry takes no cars, but for an extra fee, you can bring your bike, canoe or kayak. (See Resources, page 235.) The ferry crossing can be quite rough.

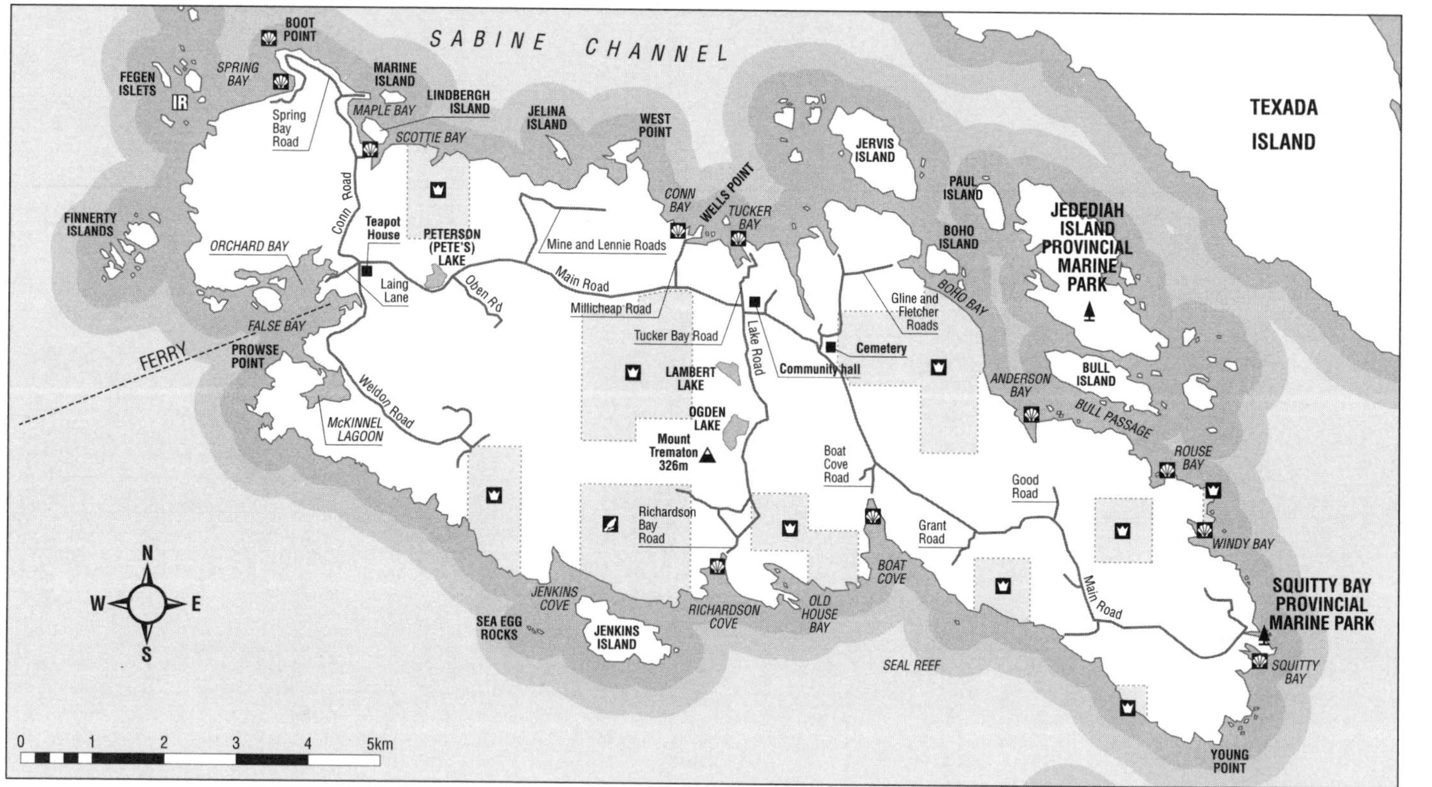

Lasqueti Island

SERVICES AND ACCOMMODATION

Near the False Bay dock (where you will find a public telephone) is a small complex with a hotel that was not operating at time of writing. Across the road is a grocery store that has takeout food, and a little farther along Main Road, there is a bakery that also has takeout and serves pizza on Friday nights. At the corner of Main and Conn Roads is the Teapot House, a house built in the 1930s that is now used to host community events once a month, except in the summer.

Lasqueti has only a couple of bed and breakfasts, and at time of writing, there was no public or private camping on the island, although residents did not object to people setting up tents on some of the beaches, such as those on Spring and Conn Bays. There is no public washroom on Lasqueti, although there is a pit toilet and water pump at Squitty Bay Provincial Marine Park and another outhouse at the top of the False Bay hill.

BEACH AND ROAD WALKS

Although much of Lasqueti is Crown land, little of it can be reached without trespassing on private land. The only parkland is Squitty Bay Provincial Marine Park at the southeastern end of the island.

With the permission of property owners, residents enjoy many trails that cross private land. If you wish to use these trails, find out who owns the land and request their permission. For visitors unwilling to go to this bother, walking on Lasqueti will be restricted to walking along the island's extensive and charming rural roads. With the exception of the road from the end of the dock at False Bay to the top of the hill (300 m), none of the roads are paved, which makes them soft to the feet but dusty in the summer and often muddy the rest of the year. The roads are also fairly hilly, so don't despair if you seem to be climbing a lot; you'll soon be walking downhill.

At the far end of Lasqueti, Squitty Bay shelters old boats from the strait.

Conn Bay feels remote and isolated, snug in a corner of larger Tucker Bay, offering views of the little islands in Sabine Channel and hulking Texada beyond.

Main Road runs the length of the island, from the ferry terminal to Squitty Bay Provincial Marine Park (18 km). For convenience, the description of Main Road has been divided into three sections: Main Road from the ferry to Conn Road (1.2 km), Main Road from Conn Road to Tucker Bay Road (6.3 km) and Main Road from Lake Road to Squitty Bay (10.5 km). Worthwhile detours are also given, two of which are treated separately as they come up along the way: Conn Road to Spring Bay (5 km) and Lake Road to Richardson Cove (4.5 km).

It might be best to start with the road around False Bay and the closest detours, rather than the long hike to Squitty Bay. If you decide to come just for the day, try the walk along the beach from Boot Point to Spring Bay (see Conn Road to Spring Bay, page 97), which can easily be done between ferries. Use this information to plan an outing that suits your energy level and the time you have available:

Main Road from the ferry terminal to Conn Road (1.2 km one way): Main Road climbs steadily to its intersection with Conn Road. Just past the hotel, you will see Weldon Road on your right. It parallels the coast and provides views of McKinnel (a.k.a. Johnson) Lagoon, which stretches inland from the sea for some distance.

A bit farther down Main Road after Weldon Road, you'll see a lot on the right, which is managed by the regional district and has an outhouse and a picnic table. No open fires or camping are allowed here. The lot you'll see on the left is the church parking lot; the church can be found hidden behind some trees at its end. Not far from here is the island's post office and its arts centre.

Slightly less than 1 km from the ferry is Laing Lane, on the left. Walk down this short road to a beach access that offers ocean views, a beach for swimming and the opportunity to collect clams and oysters from the large tidal flats.

Opposite Laing Lane is the island's excellent bakery. Next, you'll see a gift shop, the school, the fire hall, the recycling centre and, at Conn Road, the Teapot House. The building's name comes from the shape of its two chimneys: one looks like a teapot and the other like a sugar bowl (the sign of a bootlegger). At time of writing, it was difficult to see the building from the road through the thick foliage.

Conn Road to Spring Bay (5 km): Conn Road heads north toward the sea. After a couple of kilometres, where it nears Scottie Bay, its name becomes Spring Bay Road.

At this point, you'll see a cluster of signs where a roadway heads right. This leads to the Lasqueti Fish Company on Scottie Bay. There is public access to the beach farther along and to the north of the boatyard. The dock is private, however, and you should ask permission if you want to use it.

Returning to Spring Bay Road and continuing north, you'll soon see a road heading off to the right, alongside some mailboxes. This short road leads to the beach along Maple Bay, just north of Lindbergh Island. It is one of Lasqueti's few public beach accesses and it's a good one. You can walk north along the beach toward Marine Island, for some way.

Continuing along Spring Bay Road for 1 km or so, you'll find another road going off to the right. It leads to Boot Point, where there is another public beach access. From here, at low tide, you can walk left (northwest) all the way to Spring Bay.

The next road off Spring Bay Road is called Nichols Road, which leads to Spring Bay beach, where you can beachcomb, swim, enjoy the views of Texada Island, picnic and examine rock formations left over from the ice age. From here you can return to Main Road the way you came, or at low tide, walk around Spring Bay Point to Boot Point, where you can regain Spring Bay Road.

Main Road from Conn Road to Tucker Bay Road (6.3 km one way): About 1 km from the Teapot House, you'll pass Peterson Lake, which is the source of False Bay's water supply. Half a kilometre farther is Oben Road on the right (south). I don't recommend that you take this forested road.

After 1 km or so, you'll see a sign for Mine and Lennie Roads, heading off on the left (north). This is another detour that is not worth taking. Somewhat over 2 km farther down Main Road, however, Millicheap Road goes off to the left (north) for about 1 km and takes you down to a public beach access on Conn Bay. Here, there is a trail leading onto a peninsula consisting of moss-covered rocks and windswept arbutus trees. This rugged peninsula is a very pretty place to walk and, perhaps, picnic. The trails here are probably sheep trails and you could meet one of the island's feral sheep, as I did.

Back on Main Road, the next road on the left (north) is Tucker Bay Road. It descends less than 1 km to Tucker Bay. On the way to the bay, you'll pass a covered steam donkey left over from an old logging operation. At the end of the road, there is public access to the water, near an old house. The coast is quite rugged. If you walk out to the point at the mouth of the bay, you will have good views of Texada and Jervis Islands, and it's possible to swim here.

A Tale of Two Settlements

There's little in Tucker Bay today to suggest what it looked like in the past. In the early part of the 20th century, Tucker Bay was the dominant community centre on Lasqueti. A dock was built there in 1913, and steamship service and mail delivery began. Up until then, the mailman had to row over 25 nautical miles (46 km) to Nanaimo to pick up the mail and then deliver it personally to each recipient. A post office was built in Tucker Bay to receive the mail, and a school and store followed. But when a salmon cannery opened in False Bay in 1916, the population began to shift. Soon there weren't enough students to keep the Tucker Bay school open and a new one opened in False Bay.

Tucker Bay's bad luck continued when, after a steamship hit a rock in Tucker Bay in 1923, the Union Steamship Company cancelled the service. Mail was then brought from Pender Harbour by small boat. However, the final blow for the community came in 1926 when the Tucker Bay store mysteriously burned down and the post office was moved to a private home. The next year, False Bay acquired both steamship service and the mail contract. A new post office opened there, and with the school, store and steamship service, its position as the island's centre became permanent.

Lake Road to Richardson Cove (4.5 km, one way): Lake Road runs right (south) off Main Road, just beyond Tucker Bay Road. This narrow country road rises past farms that look as though they've been here for generations. The road passes several ponds and moss-covered rock outcroppings, as well as Lambert Lake and Ogden Lake. There is no public access to either lake but near Ogden Lake you get a good view of Mount Trematon, a rugged land form named after Trematon Castle in Cornwall, England. At 326 m, Mount Trematon is the highest point on Lasqueti and offers panoramic views of the Strait of Georgia from Campbell River in the north to Vancouver in the south. Although it is on private land, you can request permission to climb it from the owner, who lives at the end of Lake Road, 500 m beyond the turnoff to Richardson Bay Road. (You'll find references to Richardson Bay on Lasqueti. However, the official marine charts refer to this small bay as Richardson Cove.) The trail to the top of the mountain goes west off Lake Road, just before the entrance to the farm.

Richardson Bay Road descends steeply for 1 km, past a large farm, to the very small bay, surrounded by sheer cliffs. There is public access to the beach but little walking. When you're through exploring, you must return to Main Road the same way you've come.

Main Road from Lake Road to Squitty Bay (10.5 km one way): Continuing east along Main Road from Lake Road, you almost immediately pass a seasonal waterfall on your right and, soon after, the island's community hall.

Lasqueti's cemetery is on Main Road, about 2 km from Lake Road, just past Gline and Fletcher Roads. The land for the cemetery was donated and the two donors are buried here, along with about 50 others.

Boat Cove Road goes off to the right after another 500 m. Take the 5-minute walk down the road to a lovely cove, where you can dig clams at low tide along an extensive beach. The access is at the end of the road, just left of the Darwin farm. The swimming here is good and there's a fine view of Vancouver Island. Do not disturb the creek that empties into Boat Cove; part of a salmon-enhancement program conducted since 1952, it is a spawning stream for coho and chum.

Continuing along Main Road, you will pass several side roads over the final 7 km to Squitty Bay. None of these roads have access to the water.

Squitty Bay Road runs off Main Road into the provincial marine park. The 13-ha park has a pump for drinking water, at the head of the bay, and picnic tables and an outhouse near the government dock. There are views of the nearby cormorant-covered rocks at the mouth of Squitty Bay. Nearby is a 5.7-ha piece of land, obtained by the Nature Trust of British Columbia in 1987, which contains Rocky Mountain juniper and is fenced to protect the natural flora from animals. Walk through it to its outer point, which provides a magnificent 270-degree view of Texada Island and Sabine Channel on the left, of Thormanby Island to Mount Baker on the mainland straight ahead, and of Vancouver Island on the right. There are a couple of short trails in the provincial marine park, as well as a pleasant rocky area overlooking Little Squitty Bay to your right as you enter the park.

If you wish to explore further, you can continue walking beyond the park along Main Road, which winds away from the shoreline. The road descends into a relatively new subdivision and finally ends a couple of kilometres from Squitty Bay, some distance from the water.

AND IF YOU PADDLE . . .

Lasqueti's indented shoreline is ideal for paddling. You can bring your boat on the passenger ferry and put it into the water as soon as you disembark. You can then explore Lasqueti's shoreline, as well as some of the nearby islands. Be aware that, except for False Bay and Bull Passage, Lasqueti is quite exposed and subject to strong wind, and Sabine Channel has quite strong currents that create steep seas. Check the marine forecast before leaving and consult your tide and current tables. Novice paddlers should not venture outside of Bull Passage or False Bay without a guide.

Here are some suggestions:

Tour Jedediah Island Provincial Marine Park (see pages 223–225).

Circumnavigate Lasqueti, using the many pieces of Crown land to rest, including the Finnerty Islands, Jervis Island and the islets to its west, and Paul Island. (Much of the Crown land on Lasqueti's own shore is cliff and inappropriate for camping.) Stop at one of Lasqueti's beach accesses or government docks—at Spring Bay, Scottie Bay, Tucker Bay, Anderson Bay, Rouse Bay, Windy Bay, Squitty Bay, Boat Cove and Richardson Cove—and explore some of the nearby roads on foot.

Mayne ISLAND

AT 21 SQUARE KM, Mayne is one of the smaller Gulf Islands described in this book, but its scenic country roads, sandy beaches, numerous bays and coves make it a major attraction. The majority of Mayne's 880 residents are retired and have time to enjoy the island's quiet pace, bucolic landscape and mild weather. For an island of its size, Mayne has a surprising number of stores and services, including galleries, cafés and a pub. Although there are settlements near Bennett Bay, Georgina Point, Dinner Bay, Horton Bay and Gallagher Bay, most businesses are concentrated around Miners Bay and toward nearby Village Bay, where the ferry docks. Mayne has fewer parks and hiking trails than most of its neighbours but has some pleasant and worthwhile walks. Wildflower enthusiasts will be enthralled by the profusion of blooms in the spring and early summer and birdwatchers by the plethora of bird species that visit or live on the island.

HISTORY

Archaeological evidence shows that First Nations people had a presence on Mayne more than 5,000 years ago. In 1794, Captain George Vancouver's crew camped on Georgina Point, leaving a coin and knife that would be discovered by settlers more than 100 years later.

The large bay at the northwest corner of the island became known as Miners Bay following the 1858 Fraser River gold rush, when prospectors heading from Victoria to the mainland would frequently stop and camp along its protected shores. A couple of years later, a community developed in Miners Bay. Historic buildings from the 1890s still stand in this area, including the Springwater Lodge, the original jail (now the museum) and the Church of St. Mary Magdalene.

Good agricultural land attracted settlers, and by the 1890s, several farms were thriving. There were many orchards on the island at the time and the Mayne Island King apple was one of the first varieties developed in BC. In the 1930s, a third of the island's residents were Japanese, who collectively grew 50 tonnes of tomatoes each year. These settlers were displaced during the internment of Japanese Canadians during World War II but their contribution to the island's heritage is now honoured with an exquisite memorial garden at Dinner Bay.

Miner's Bay Pub is the perfect place to relax after a long day's hike and watch the sun set over the boat traffic in Active Pass.

GETTING THERE

Each day, there are several sailings to Mayne from Swartz Bay (near Victoria) and two sailings from Tsawwassen (near Vancouver). There is also almost daily service between Mayne and Galiano, Pender, Salt Spring and Saturna Islands. For more information, obtain a Southern Gulf Islands schedule or contact BC Ferries. Harbour Air and Seair Seaplanes fly to Mayne from Vancouver (see Resources, page 235).

SERVICES AND ACCOMMODATION

Most of Mayne's stores and services are on Fernhill and Village Bay Roads in Miners Bay. Mayne has no bank but there is an ATM at the general store in Miners Bay. There are bed and breakfasts, lodges, inns and resorts, as well as a few restaurants and cafés. At time of writing, only limited private camping was available. The island also has a taxi service and a health centre.

The Mayne Island Community Chamber of Commerce (Box 2, Mayne Island, BC V0N 2J0 or www.mayneislandchamber.ca) provides a tourist information brochure, including a good map of the island and lists of accommodation and services. You may be able to obtain additional information on hiking and local natural history events from the Mayne Island Naturalists Club, the island's parks and recreation commission or from www.mayneisland.com.

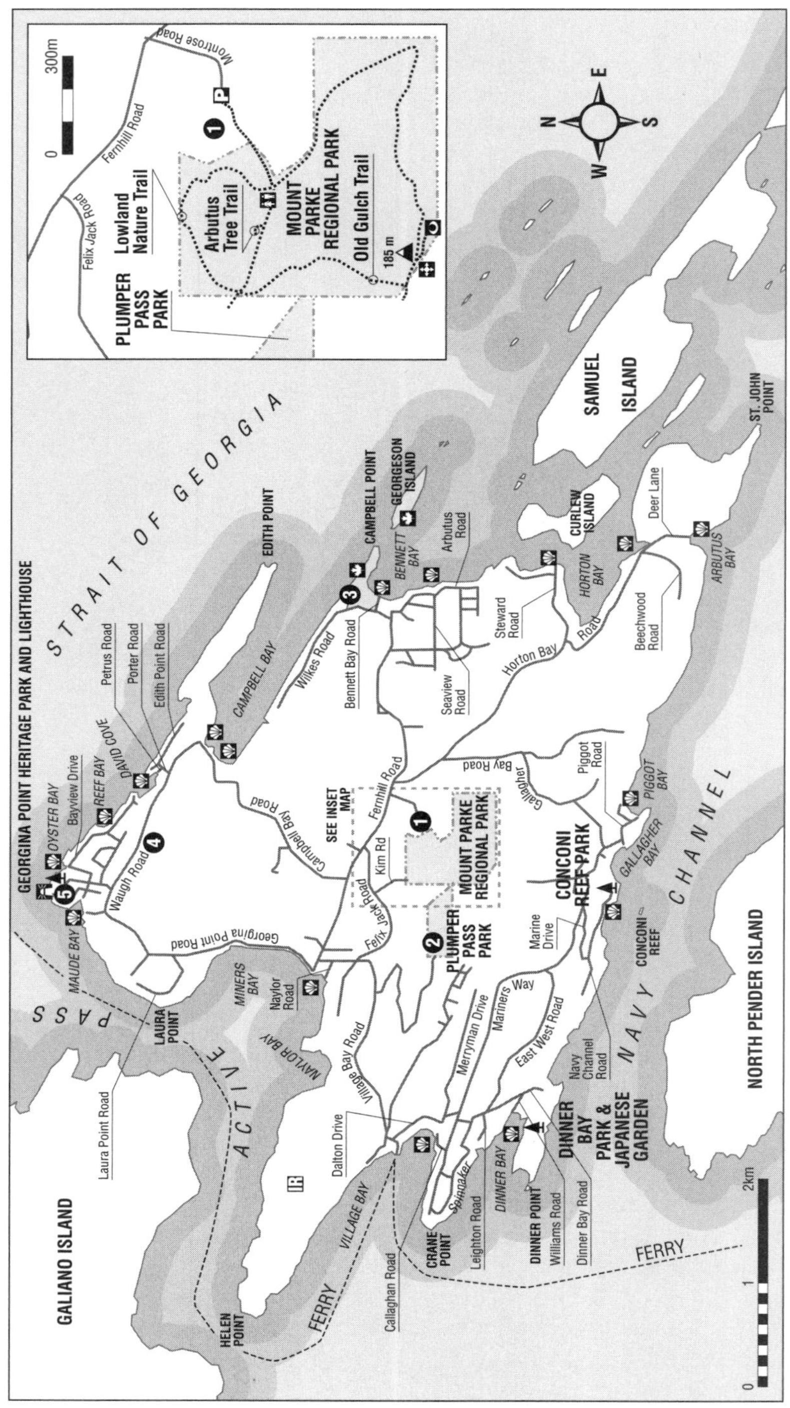
Mayne Island
GALIANO ISLAND
NORTH PENDER ISLAND
SAMUEL ISLAND
CURLEW ISLAND
GEORGESON ISLAND
STRAIT OF GEORGIA
ACTIVE PASS
NAVY CHANNEL
GEORGINA POINT HERITAGE PARK AND LIGHTHOUSE
MOUNT PARKE REGIONAL PARK
PLUMPER PASS PARK
CONCONI REEF PARK
DINNER BAY PARK & JAPANESE GARDEN
SEE INSET MAP
MAUDE BAY
OYSTER BAY
REEF BAY
DAVID COVE
CAMPBELL BAY
BENNETT BAY
HORTON BAY
ARBUTUS BAY
PIGGOT BAY
GALLAGHER BAY
MINERS BAY
NAYLOR BAY
VILLAGE BAY
DINNER BAY
LAURA POINT
HELEN POINT
CRANE POINT
DINNER POINT
CONCONI REEF
EDITH POINT
CAMPBELL POINT
ST. JOHN POINT
Bayview Drive
Petrus Road
Porter Road
Edith Point Road
Waugh Road
Georgina Point Road
Campbell Bay Road
Wilkes Road
Bennett Bay Road
Fernhill Road
Kim Rd
Felix Jack Road
Seaview Road
Steward Road
Arbutus Road
Horton Bay Road
Deer Lane
Beechwood Road
Gallagher Bay Road
Piggot Road
Marine Drive
Mariners Way
Merryman Drive
East West Road
Navy Channel Road
Naylor Road
Village Bay Road
Laura Point Road
Dalton Drive
Spinnaker
Leighton Road
Williams Road
Dinner Bay Road
Callaghan Road
FERRY
0 1 2km
Lowland Nature Trail
Arbutus Tree Trail
Old Gulch Trail
185 m
Montrose Road
0 300m
Roads
Trails
Park boundary
Gulf Islands National Park Reserve
Beach access
Indian Reserve
Lighthouse
Viewpoint
Peak
Parking
Sign
Outhouse
See text
N E S W

ESPECIALLY FOR WALKERS

Mayne Island's gentle terrain offers numerous places for easy walking, many of them in stunning locations along the shore. In addition to the many Shore and Road Walks suggested below, try the following:

- Campbell Point–Bennett Bay Trails, part of the new Gulf Islands National Park Reserve (see hike 3, page 105)
- Georgina Point Heritage Park (see hike 5, page 106)
- Japanese Garden, Dinner Bay (see page 107)

HIKES

Most land on Mayne is privately owned. The island has one regional park, a heritage park, and Bennett Bay and Campbell Point form part of the new Gulf Islands National Park Reserve. However, Mayne has no provincial parks or Crown land. The island has a growing number of short trails and small parks established by the volunteer-run parks and recreation commission. Future development should increase public parkland, as provincial law requires that developers allocate five percent of their land to public use.

1. MOUNT PARKE REGIONAL PARK ★★★★

Trail length	About 5 km in total
Time required	90 minutes to 2 hours for both trails
Description	A woodland loop trail and a second, steeper trail leads to a ridge with panoramic views.
Level	Easy to moderate
Elevation	185 m at the Halliday Lookout (The summit of Mount Parke is 255 m but is on private land.)
Access	The parking area at the end of Montrose Road (off Fernhill Road)

The trails in this 47-ha regional park have something for everyone. From the parking lot, a 300-m trail leads to a junction where three trails lead deeper into the park. There's also an outhouse at this junction and a plaque commemorating Mary Jeffrey, who bequeathed much of this property to the island in 1992.

The trail to the left leads to a splendid viewpoint. The first half of the trail is relatively flat but then it climbs steeply through an arbutus and Douglas fir forest. Near the top, you will see signs for the Halliday Lookout, named after one of Mayne Island's first parks and recreation commissioners. On a clear day, you will have terrific views of Saturna Island to the southeast, Navy Channel and the Pender Islands to the south, Vancouver Island to the southwest, and Prevost and Salt Spring Islands to the west.

In the spring, wildflowers adorn the edge of the bluff. Stay on the trails at all times, as the moss and lichen are very fragile and slow to recover from any disruption.

In addition to its fantastic 180-degree views, Mount Parke is rich in flora and fauna—red cedar, red alder, arbutus, Douglas fir, giant swordfern, Oregon grape and, in spring, blue-eyed Mary, early saxifrage and spring gold. CRD

From here, you can return the way you came or continue along the 600-metre Old Gulch Trail, which hooks up with the lower loop trail.

The other two paths that start near the outhouse form a 1.3 km loop called the Lowland Nature Trail. Starting on the right-hand trail, you pass through a mature cedar forest with an understory of swordfern and step moss, and then through arbutus and Douglas fir. Just before the end of the trail, a side trail takes you to a very large arbutus, which is definitely worth the detour. The loop takes about half an hour.

2. Plumper Pass Park ★★

Trail length	1.7 km loop
Time required	30–60 minutes
Description	A loop trail through mature second-growth forest on the north slope of Mount Parke and parallel to the summit ridge
Level	Moderate
Access	From the end of Kim Road, an access trail heads south for 270 m to the loop trail.
Caution	The trail is steep in parts, climbing 135 m.

Following my visit to the island, the Mayne Island Parks and Recreation Commission completed this loop trail in Plumper Pass Park, west of Mount Parke. The access trail from Kim Road goes through heavy underbrush for about 100 m and then heads south on an old skid road for another 170 m, to the beginning of the loop trail. Going left, you proceed up a steep switchback for 150 m and then traverse the Mount Parke slope for 500 m, still gaining in elevation. After you pass a trail that leads to Mount Parke Road, a private road in the nearby strata development, you begin to descend. Around the halfway point, the trail veers suddenly to the east and follows a berm. At the foot of the berm is a large, beautiful pond. The last 300 m of the loop trail is on an old logging road.

3. CAMPBELL POINT–BENNETT BAY TRAILS (GULF ISLANDS NATIONAL PARK RESERVE) ★★★

Trail length	3 km in total
Time required	40 minutes for both trails
Description	Forest trails along the shore with an opportunity to walk the beach in Bennett Bay
Level	Easy
Access	The end of Bennett Bay Road or from the end of Wilkes Road

Part of the recently created Gulf Islands National Park Reserve, this park consists of 4.5 ha on the Campbell Point peninsula, 5.8 ha along Bennett Bay and the 6.5-ha Georgeson Island offshore.

Campbell Point contains arbutus and Douglas fir. The terrain is relatively flat and there are views of Edith Point to the north and Georgeson Island offshore to the east. Rocky Mountain juniper thrives on the outside edge of the peninsula. The main trail proceeds down the centre of the peninsula.

Although some walkers return along unofficial paths at the cliff edge, Parks Canada is discouraging this because of problems with erosion and public safety. At time of writing, park officials were considering ways to give visitors a loop option along the beach, perhaps using a staircase to join the beach and main trail.

The Bennett Bay section of the park contains the former owner's house, guest cabin and small barn beside a large, lush, green field. A trail proceeds east down to the beach, where you can continue south for a short way. Another trail passes behind the buildings and leads south to Bennett Bay Road.

Bennett Bay, Campbell Point and nearby Georgeson Island form part of the recently established Gulf Islands National Park Reserve. Parks Canada

4. Chu-an Park and Viewpoint ★★

Trail length	1.2 km in total
Time required	30 minutes round trip
Description	A short, steep walk to a viewpoint
Level	Moderate
Access	Opposite 537 Waugh Road, 600 m east of Georgina Point Road

Look carefully or you'll miss the trailhead for this 0.6-ha local park because its sign is not visible from the road. "Chu-an" means "looking out over the sea," and this is possible from the viewpoint at the top. This trail is contained in a 3-m strip of land provided by a developer and ends up at a gravel viewpoint that is barely 2 m wide, although the park allows room for expansion. From here, you can see Roberts Bank on the mainland. The trail is steep, climbing about 150 m in a short distance, so don't try it if you don't like climbs.

5. Georgina Point Heritage Park ★★★

Trail length	1 km in total
Time required	30–60 minutes
Description	Beach access, picnic area and grasslands along the seashore
Level	Easy
Access	The end of Georgina Point Road
Facilities	Washroom facilities, picnic tables, garbage cans

The site of the Active Pass Light Station, this federal land is leased to the Mayne Island Parks and Recreation Commission on a month-to-month basis.

There is good walking on the rocks in front of the lighthouse and through the grounds. This is a great spot to watch boats negotiating the turbulent opening to Active Pass. You can see right across to the mainland, and at low tide, you can walk east along the beach for quite some distance. It is also an excellent place for viewing wildlife, including seals, orcas if you're lucky, and seabirds. The park is open from dawn to dusk and is an excellent picnic spot.

SHORE AND ROAD WALKS

Active Pass: You can access the fascinating Active Pass shoreline at Miners Bay, from the end of Naylor Road. The beach walk is short but is a good location to use your binoculars to examine the distant Galiano shore, check the prowess of the anglers mooching for salmon or watch the constant boat traffic through one of the busiest bits of water on the West Coast.

JAPANESE GARDEN

The Japanese garden at Dinner Park is a must-see. To commemorate the Japanese settlers who were integral to Mayne's development, locals created this beautiful garden on 2 ha of land that once belonged to a Japanese Canadian family. The garden has a waterfall, ponds, Japanese lanterns, a large variety of plants, including traditional Japanese cherry trees, and a reconstructed charcoal kiln.

Although the idea for the garden dates back to the 1980s, it wasn't until 1999 that its construction began. It was dedicated by Lt.-Gov. Iona Campagnolo on May 29, 2002.

The construction of the garden and the ongoing maintenance is the work of volunteers and many of the plants were gifts. A donation box has been installed to help cover expenses. There are many trails through the garden, as well as lovely spots to sit, contemplate the surroundings or meditate.

The narrowest place in the channel is at Helen Point, where the tidal flow sweeps through the narrow passageway north toward Georgina Point at up to 8 knots, creating a problem for navigation. When this fast-moving water meets wind coming from the opposite direction, dangerous rip tides result. The combination of the swirling water and the heavy boat traffic has resulted in many accidents over the years.

A highlight of being in Active Pass, especially in the spring, is the wildlife viewing. Seals, sea lions, porpoises and, occasionally, killer whales visit the waters of this narrow channel. At different times of the year, there are high concentrations of bald eagles, gulls, cormorants, loons and many species of duck.

There are public beaches at Campbell Bay, Bennett Bay, Arbutus Bay (local name), Piggot Bay, Conconi Reef Park, Dinner Bay (the last abuts a small community park), Village Bay, Oyster Bay and David Cove.

Campbell Bay: By far the deepest bay on Mayne. At low tide, you can walk along the beach for a long way. Although the peninsula leading to Edith Point is private land, you are free to explore the foreshore. You can access this beach by a narrow, tunnel-like path through the trees. To find this access, follow the fence of the large farm opposite 327 Campbell Bay Road.

Bennett Bay: The longest beach walk on Mayne is along this sandy beach, where you can easily spend an hour or more beachcombing. The public access point is at the end of Bennett Bay Road. From the beach, you have good views of Georgeson Island and part of Curlew Island just offshore.

Arbutus Bay (local name): A 300-m trail on Deer Lane (500 m south of Horton Bay Road, on Beechwood Drive) leads to a pristine, secluded, rocky beach on Navy Channel. It is a perfect spot to watch wildlife. The trail descends very steeply for its last 50 m.

Piggot Bay: This driftwood-littered sand beach on Piggot Bay (Plumper Sound) can be walked for some distance (20 minutes or so at high tide but much more at low tide). The access is at the end of Piggot Road (off Gallagher Bay Road).

Conconi Reef Park: Although the walking here is somewhat limited, this sandy beach at the end of Navy Channel Road (off Marine Drive) is a peaceful spot with views of the Pender Islands and the navigational beacon on a nearby reef.

Dinner Bay: You can access the beach at Dinner Bay Community Park at the end of Williams Road, using steps that begin just beyond the washrooms. Although the beaches do not provide much space for walking, you can walk the nearby 600-m trail that connects the corner of Dinner Bay Road and Leighton Lane with the Japanese garden. Named the Ed Williams Memorial Trail, after one of Mayne's first parks and recreation commissioners, it goes through woods and along the shoreline at Dinner Bay Park before reaching the stunning Japanese garden.

Village Bay: You can access this bay by using a trail that begins opposite Merryman Drive, where it intersects with Dalton Drive. There are two trails: the right-hand one leads to a beach on Village Bay, which is also accessible from the end of Callaghan Road (off Mariners Way), and the left-hand one leads to Mariners Way.

Oyster Bay: This small beach on the north tip of the island at the end of Bayview Drive has beautiful rock formations and terrific driftwood.

David Cove: This attractive beach at the end of Petrus Road (left off Porter Road from Waugh Road) is too small to afford much walking.

The road walks on Mayne are pleasant but unspectacular. You might try Edith Point Road (right off Porter Road from Waugh Road) and the roads around the Georgina Point Lighthouse. Georgina Point Road from Miners Bay follows the shore for some distance, is very pretty and offers great views of Active Pass. You will also find the Church of St. Mary Magdalene. One of the prettiest churches in the Gulf Islands, St. Mary's was consecrated in 1898 and its wooden steeple is a familiar sight to boats travelling through Active Pass. You will enjoy walking its pleasant grounds and having a look at its charming interior. The 180-kg sandstone baptismal font was brought from Saturna Island by rowboat.

AND IF YOU PADDLE . . .

Mayne Island has more bays than many of the larger islands and many of these are suitable places for beginners. Only experienced paddlers, however, should even consider going into Active Pass or in the passages between Mayne and Saturna Islands without a guide, and then only at slack tide after consulting tide and current tables. Ferry traffic is quite heavy to Mayne Island, so watch for these large boats and their wash if paddling in or near Village Bay.

Here are a few paddling suggestions:

Georgina Point Heritage Park: On a calm day, you can explore the Strait of Georgia shoreline. From here, you can paddle as far as Edith Point and around into cavernous Campbell Bay.

Horton Bay: Put in from the dock or the accessible shoreline at the end of Horton Bay Road. From here, you can explore Curlew Island and continue north along the Mayne shoreline to Bennett Bay, Campbell Point and Georgeson Island (Gulf Islands National Park Reserve). The south shore of Georgeson has fantastic sandstone formations, but as there is virtually nowhere to land, you're best to restrict your visit to the water. An alternative launch site is at the end of Steward Road (known locally as Spud Point) where you can paddle either north to Bennett Bay or south along the shore of Curlew Island and east into Horton Bay.

Village Bay: The access is at the end of Callaghan Road (off Mariners Way). From here, you can paddle south to Dinner Bay. Be sure to avoid the ferries in Village Bay. Always clearly point your boat away from them, so that they cannot mistake your intentions.

North & South Pender ISLANDS

LOCATED JUST WEST OF SATURNA and east of Salt Spring, "the Penders" cover 24 square km. A bridge connects the more rugged south island to the gentler north island. Only 159 of the Penders' 1,935 year-round residents live on South Pender and the majority of its services, including pubs, restaurants and a grocery store are on North Pender. With beautiful bays and coves, and more public beach accesses for their size than any other Gulf Island, boaters and hikers alike enjoy these islands. Although there are only a couple of lengthy (half-day or longer) hikes on the Penders, their parks, roads and shores provide plenty of opportunities for pleasant walking and exploration.

HISTORY

Until 1902, when the federal government dredged a canal between them, the Penders were a single island joined by a narrow isthmus. Prior to the creation of the waterway, residents used to drag their boats across the narrow bit of land separating Port Browning and Bedwell Harbour to avoid the long, and at times dangerous, trip around the south island. It wasn't until 1955 that a bridge was built to span the canal. In the mid-1980s, the largest archaeological excavation in the Gulf Islands took place here and artifacts dating back 5,000 years were found in the midden.

Until steamship service began at the turn of the 20th century, islanders transported all their goods by sailing sloop. The first wharf on North Pender was built at Port Washington in 1891 and this was followed some years later by a second wharf in Hope Bay. Early settlers sold their produce in the Nanaimo market and the products of North Pender's farms and apple orchards were sold in Victoria. Logging was an important early industry, although other enterprises such as the herring saltery and fish-processing plant run by Japanese residents at Hyashi Cove, and a commercial brickyard at Bricky Bay were also lucrative. A plant in Shingle Bay produced lubricating oil and fertilizer from herring and dogfish.

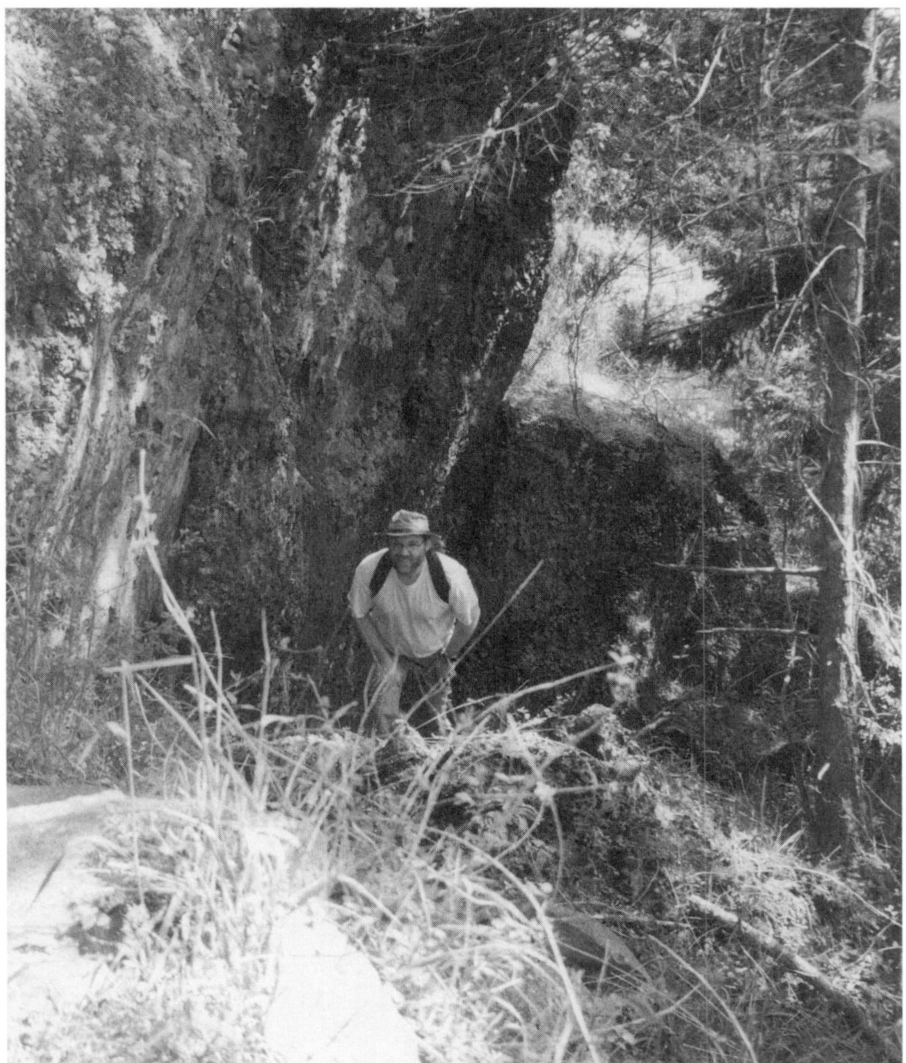

The rocky terrain, beautiful vegetation and expansive views at the top of Castle Rock make the tough climb worthwhile.

GETTING THERE

Ferries connect Otter Bay on North Pender with Swartz Bay (near Victoria) and with Tsawwassen (near Vancouver). Ferries also connect the Penders with Mayne, Saturna, Galiano and Salt Spring Islands. Reservations are recommended on Fridays and Saturdays in the summer. For more information, obtain a Southern Gulf Islands schedule or contact BC Ferries. You can also reach the Penders by water taxi and float plane (see Resources, page 235).

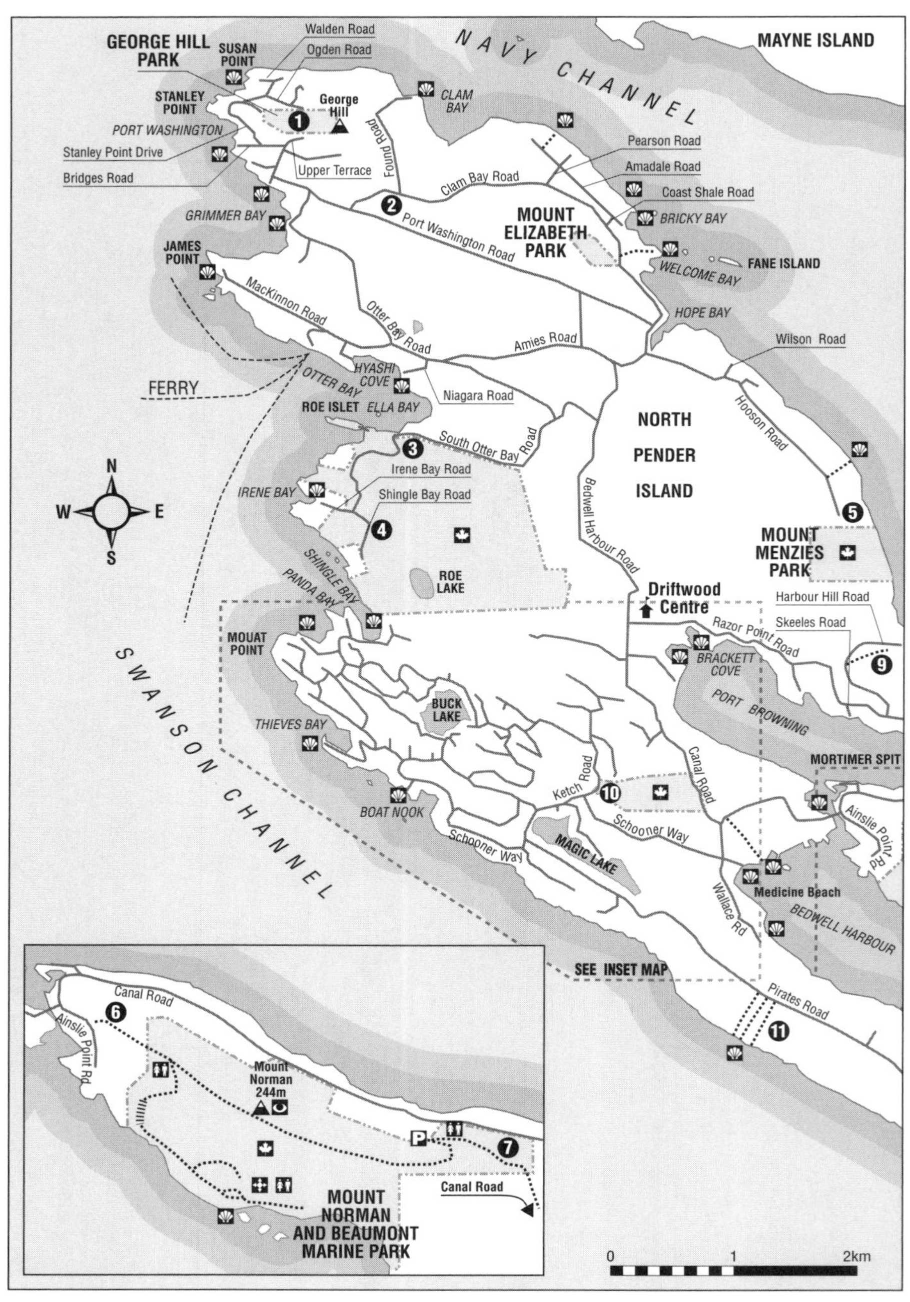

Pender Islands

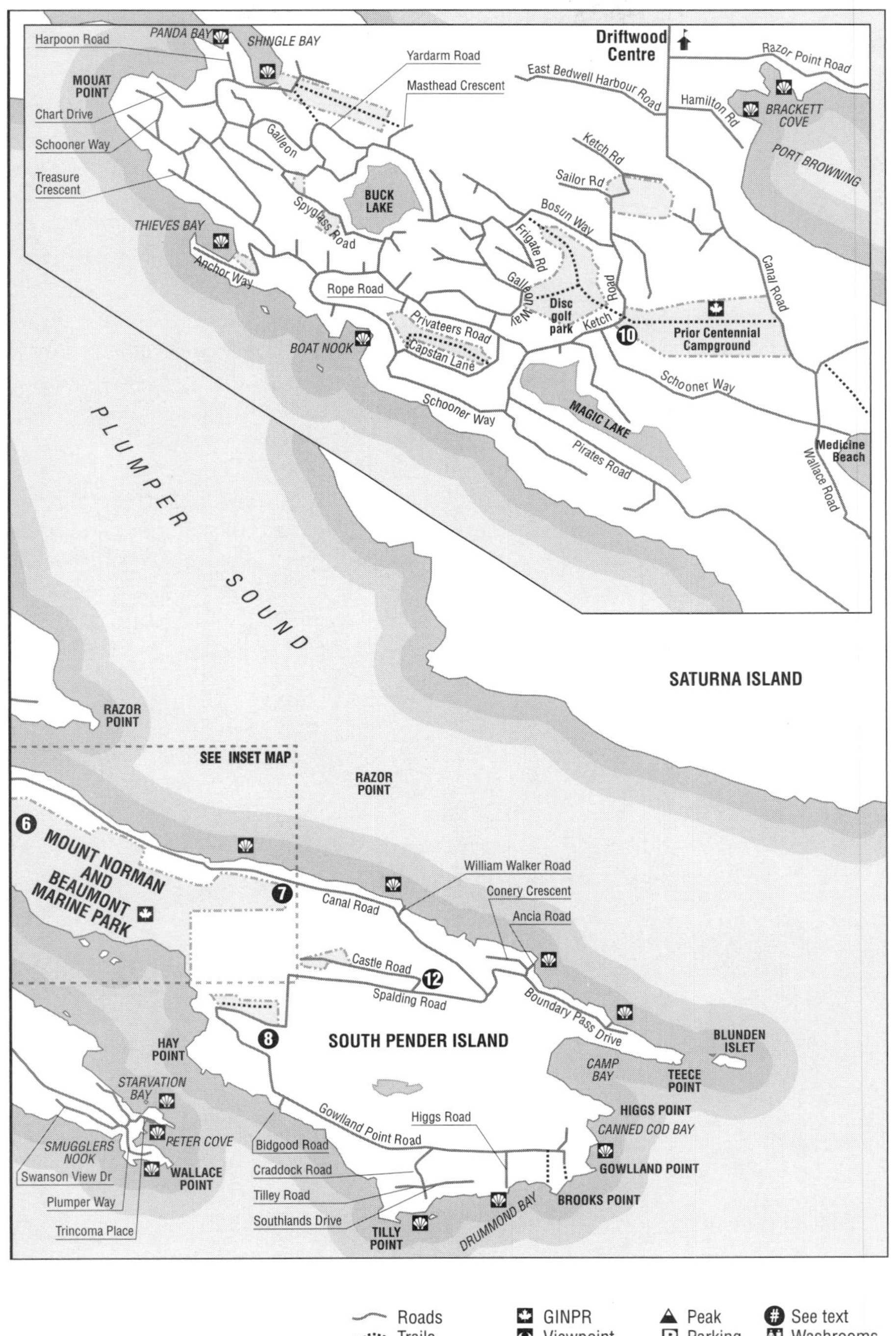

Harpoon Road
PANDA BAY
SHINGLE BAY
Driftwood Centre
Razor Point Road
Yardarm Road
Masthead Crescent
East Bedwell Harbour Road
MOUAT POINT
Chart Drive
Schooner Way
Treasure Crescent
Hamilton Rd
BRACKETT COVE
PORT BROWNING
Galleon
Ketch Rd
Sailor Rd
BUCK LAKE
Spyglass Road
Bosun Way
THIEVES BAY
Frigate Rd
Anchor Way
Canal Road
Galleon Way
Ketch Road
Rope Road
Disc golf park
Privateers Road
Capstan Lane
BOAT NOOK
Prior Centennial Campground
Schooner Way
Schooner Way
MAGIC LAKE
Medicine Beach
Pirates Road
Wallace Road
PLUMPER SOUND
SATURNA ISLAND
RAZOR POINT
SEE INSET MAP
RAZOR POINT
MOUNT NORMAN AND BEAUMONT MARINE PARK
William Walker Road
Conery Crescent
Canal Road
Ancia Road
Castle Road
Spalding Road
Boundary Pass Drive
BLUNDEN ISLET
SOUTH PENDER ISLAND
HAY POINT
CAMP BAY
TEECE POINT
STARVATION BAY
HIGGS POINT
CANNED COD BAY
Higgs Road
Gowlland Point Road
SMUGGLERS NOOK
PETER COVE
Bidgood Road
GOWLLAND POINT
Swanson View Dr
WALLACE POINT
Craddock Road
Plumper Way
Tilley Road
BROOKS POINT
DRUMMOND BAY
Southlands Drive
Trincoma Place
TILLY POINT
Roads
Trails
Park boundary
GINPR
Viewpoint
Beach access
Peak
Parking
Sign
See text
Washrooms
Shopping

SERVICES AND ACCOMMODATION

Most of the islands' services are on North Pender. The Driftwood Centre on Bedwell Harbour Road has most of the island's businesses, including a bakery, grocery store, gas station, restaurant, pharmacy, laundromat, bookstore and liquor store. You'll also find pubs in the marinas at Poets Cove (Bedwell Harbour) and Port Browning. Other restaurants and many bed and breakfasts are scattered throughout the two islands.

Camping is available in the Gulf Islands National Park Reserve's Prior Centennial Campground from mid-March to the end of October. There is also year-round camping (water access or walk-in only) at Beaumont Marine Park. In the summer, the Lions Club staffs an information centre about 250 m from the ferry. There is also a walking/hiking club on the island. For more information, ask at local stores, consult the monthly *Pender Post* or check the Pender Island Parks Commission's web site at www.crd.bc.ca/penderparks. Biking is not permitted on the islands' trails.

ESPECIALLY FOR WALKERS

Because of their relatively flat topography, the Penders, especially North Pender, are excellent for walking and bicycling. At time of writing, the Parks Commission listed 68 parks. Most of these are shown on the map and many are described below. As many of these parks are so small that exploring them takes only a few minutes, in addition to road and short off-shore walks, I have added information on short strolls, in the walk section near the end of this chapter.

In addition to these walks, don't miss:

- Roe Islet (see hike 3, page 115)
- the Enchanted Forest Park (see hike 8, page 120) with its interpretive signs

HIKES

I am greatly indebted to Parks Commissioner Newell Smith, whose detailed comments on the following descriptions have added to their accuracy.

1. George Hill Park ★★★

Trail length	2 km each way
Time required	About 60 minutes round trip
Description	A steep but beautiful walk through mixed forest to spectacular views
Elevation	183 m
Level	Moderate to strenuous
Access	The trailhead is on the south corner of Walden Road and Ogden Road

This well-constructed, steep trail climbs 130 m to 180-degree views. Benches are provided at the two viewpoints. The climb to this fantastic spot is well worth the effort.

2. Found Road to Beach ★★★

Trail length	1.5 km each way
Time required	40 minutes round trip, plus time to explore the shoreline
Description	An up-and-down hike through mixed forest to a rocky beach that you can walk for some distance
Level	Moderate
Access	Off Clam Bay Road, 500 m from Port Washington Road
Facilities	At time of writing, the Parks Commission was planning to install a toilet, a bike rack and interpretive signs.

The name for this trail probably derives from the difficulty you may have finding it. The small trailhead sign is tucked between the western boundary of Clam Bay Farm and the private property at 2218 Clam Bay Road.

This great trail descends, ascends and finally descends again about 70 m to the water. According to the parks commission, you pass through five ecological zones on the way down to the shoreline. Once on the beach, you can walk southeast all the way to Bricky Bay during summertime low tides.

3. Roesland (Gulf Islands National Park Reserve) ★★★★

Trail length	600 m
Time required	About 30 minutes, but you could easily spend a relaxing day here
Description	A short walk through a former seaside resort, part of which is on a beautiful islet connected to the main island by a bridge
Level	Easy
Access	On the west side of South Otter Bay Road, 1.6 km from its intersection with Otter Bay Road (about 3.5 km from the ferry terminal)
Facilities	Signboard, outhouse
Caution	This property contains a very sensitive ecosystem, so be sure to stay on the trails. Also, respect the privacy of the people who live here.

This former resort was popular from the 1920s until relatively recently. Many of the old and now dilapidated cottages, as well as the historic general store, provide a kind of outdoor museum. Parks Canada suggests that you walk between the cottages, instead of beside the residential property, on your way to Roe Islet, which is connected to the rest of the resort by a short bridge. The original Roe house, on the left as you walk toward the water, is being restored by the Pender Islands Museum Society and will house its office, archives and, eventually, a few exhibits. For me, the highlight of this little park is Roe Islet, a real gem with its old-growth Douglas fir, spring wildflowers, beautiful moss-covered rock and many short paths.

4. Roe Lake Trails (Gulf Islands National Park Reserve) ★★★

Trail length	6 km or more, depending on route taken
Time required	75 minutes to circle the lake and return to the trailhead but more hiking on other trails is possible
Description	A trail through second-growth forest and around a lily-filled lake
Level	Easy
Accesses	A. 300 m along Shingle Bay Road (off South Otter Bay Road) on left (east) side. This is the official Parks Canada access and is marked with a signboard and map. B. 1 km past Roesland (hike 3), on the east side of South Otter Bay Road (2.5 km from the intersection of Otter Bay and South Otter Bay Roads)
Cautions	Watch for ticks, especially near the south end of the lake. There will be major trail realignments in this area, so check for maps on signboards and follow trail signs carefully.

From access A, walk south for 5–10 minutes to the junction marked by a small channel of the lake containing a graduated black-and-white ruler (used to measure the water level). The trail straight ahead descends to the end of Galleon Way (near Shingle Bay); it is quite steep and intersects many other trails that lead elsewhere.

The trail to the left will take you clockwise around the lake. After you have circled the lake, look for another trail to the left that will take you back to the access trail. If you miss this trail, you can retrace your steps or continue to access B off South Otter Bay Road. From here, it's a 300-m walk, to the left, back to where you started.

From access B, walk 300 m until you reach a gate. Continue through the gate and walk uphill for about 5 minutes, until you see a trail going off to the right beside a hydro pole. (I suggest that you not continue on the trail straight ahead as it climbs for about 15–20 minutes to reach a communications tower with no views.)

Soon after turning at the hydro pole, you will reach another junction. Continue going straight for 5 minutes to reach Roe Lake and then continue along the trail to circle the lake in a clockwise direction. There are several offshoot trails but most of these dead-end at the lakeshore.

You'll find many other old logging roads in this part of the park. These roads go off in other directions and you might like to explore them as well. At the south end of the lake, you will see the well-defined track heading to the end of Galleon Way near Shingle Bay, in the Magic Lake area.

5. Mount Menzies Area Trails ★★★

Trail length	2 km or more, depending on trails taken
Time required	Up to 2.5 hours (30 minutes to complete the short local park trail, 1 hour or more to explore the bluff trail and up to 1 hour to explore Loretta's Wood Nature Reserve)
Description	One trail climbs 80 m to a ridge with no view, a second leads to a cliff edge with spectacular views and the third (through Loretta's Wood Nature Reserve) connects with the first trail.
Elevation	195 m
Level	Moderate
Access	End of Hooson Road. The local park trail is on the south side of the cul-de-sac, the bluff trail is on the east side and the access to Loretta's Wood Nature Reserve is from lot 16 of the subdivision.
Caution	This area is ecologically sensitive, so stay on the trails.

The loop trail through the local park affords a pleasant walk through mature forest rising about 80 m to a ridge. Stop at the bench, as this is the boundary of the local park.

The old skid road to the bluff starts at the end of the cul-de-sac and climbs east through salal on a 28-ha piece of land acquired as part of the Gulf Islands National Park Reserve. Continue until you reach a well-established connecting trail and then head left down a steep incline. You will soon find another trail heading off to the left. This one will take you up a rock face to the top of a 140-m bluff. From here, you have panoramic views of Plumper Sound across to Samuel and Saturna Islands to the north and Blunden Islet to the east. It will take you about 20 minutes to walk from the end of Hooson Road to the viewpoint. Respect the adjacent pieces of private land that are linked to this piece of land by old logging roads.

At time of writing, the 40-ha Loretta's Wood Nature Reserve, owned by the Islands Trust Fund, was the Penders' newest park, and trails were being built to link it with the local park and the National Park Reserve land. The walk is mainly through forest.

6. Mount Norman and Beaumont Marine Park (Gulf Islands National Park Reserve) ★★★★

Trail length	Up to 6 km, depending on route taken
Time required	Up to 2 hours return if climbing to the summit and descending to the beach
Description	A hike up to a viewpoint with panoramic views, followed by a descent through Douglas fir and western red cedar forest to a campground near the beach
Elevation	244 m
Level	Moderate
Accesses	A. Immediately after crossing the bridge from North to South Pender, turn right onto Ainslie Point Road. The trailhead is about 500 m from the bridge, on the left side of the road. B. 2.5 km past the Pender Islands bridge, there's a parking area off Canal Road on the right.
Facilities	Outhouses
Cautions	From access A, follow an easement across private property into the park. Respect the owner's rights and stick to the trail.

Note: From access B, the trail for hike 7 heads southeast from the parking lot near the outhouses. If you have the energy, you may wish to combine these hikes.

From access A, it's a 30-minute climb to the summit and another 30-minute steep descent to the campground. A grassy roadway leads to the park boundary, marked by an outhouse. Soon after, the trail to Beaumont Marine Park branches off to the right. To reach the summit, continue until you see a signed, second trail. Turn right.

The summit trail ends at a well-constructed boardwalk leading to a viewing platform. The view from the top makes the whole climb worthwhile. Here you can sit on a bench, enjoy a drink or a picnic lunch and get a panoramic view of the nearby Gulf Islands, the San Juan Islands in the distance and, on a clear day, the Olympic Mountains in Washington and the Sooke Hills on Vancouver Island.

From access B, it's a longer (3 km) but more interesting hike through open second-growth forest and heavy salal to the top of Mount Norman. From the summit, you can continue down toward Ainslie Point Road and then take the trail that descends to Beaumont Marine Park.

The trail to the campground descends steeply but takes you to what is arguably the loveliest part of the Penders and then continues along the shore to the campground.

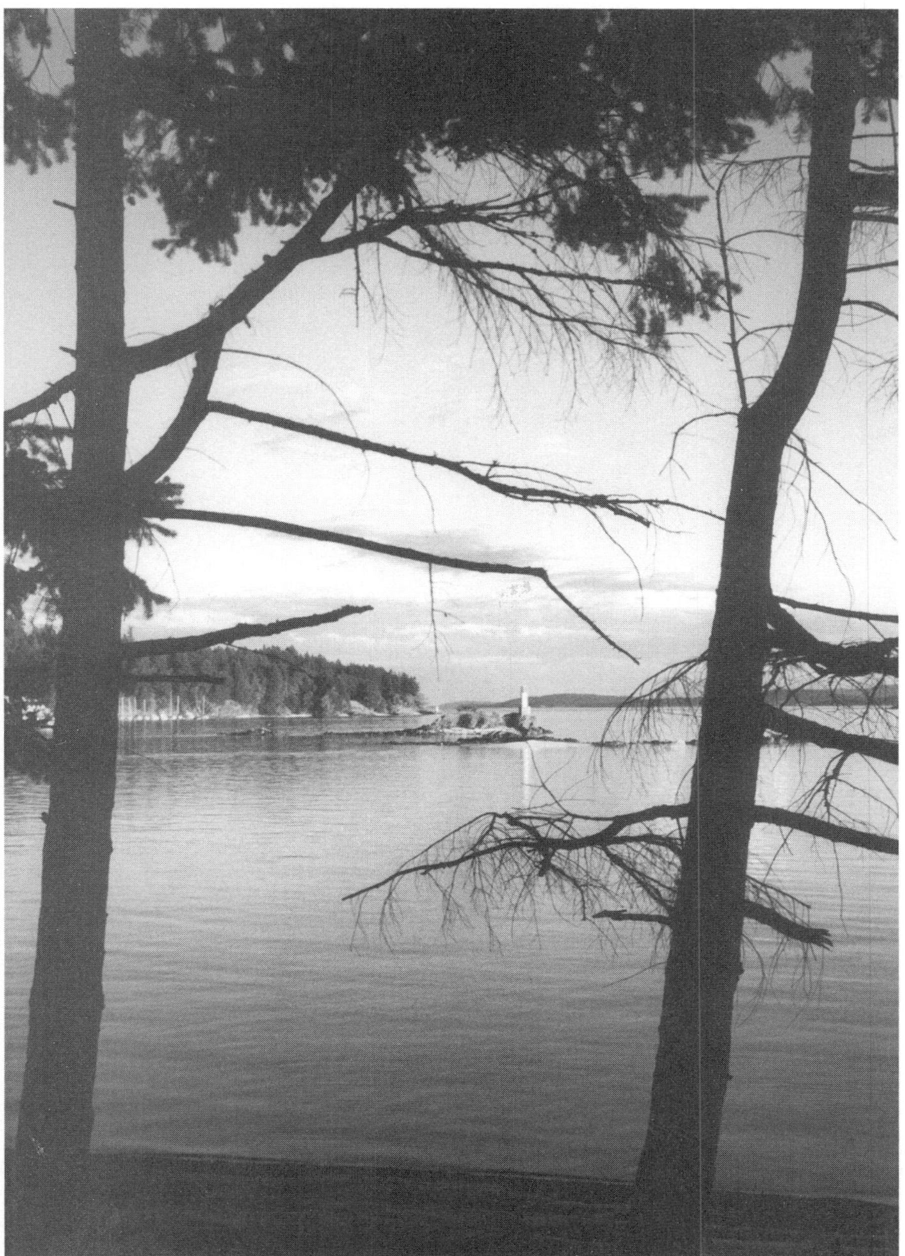

A view of Skull Islet from Beaumont Marine Park. With its lush coastal Douglas fir–arbutus habitat and intriguing views across to North Pender, the trail in Beaumont Marine Park along the Bedwell Harbour shoreline is one of the most beautiful places in the Gulf Islands.

7. William Walker Trail ★★

Trail length	5 km
Time required	One hour each way
Description	The trail crosses a managed-forest woodlot and includes a short loop along the beach using two beach accesses.
Level	Moderate
Accesses	A. From the Gulf Islands National Park Reserve parking lot off Canal Road (2.5 km from the bridge) B. From the trailhead along Canal Road (4 km east of the bridge)

Note: You can combine this hike with hike 6.

From access A, the trail heads southeast. It passes an osprey's nest and offers some glimpses of the sea before heading into the woodlot, where it parallels logging roads. This is mature forest and there is at least one huge old-growth fir to admire; however, the trail is otherwise not very interesting until it comes out at Canal Road. Here you cross the road to a beach access. Continue left (west) along the beach about 1 km to another beach access, where you return to the road, passing the historic Walker house. At this point, you can loop back to the William Walker Trailhead 1 km left (east) along the road or you can walk right (west) along the road 3.5 km to the National Park Reserve parking area, where you started.

8. Enchanted Forest Park ★★★

Trail length	2 km each way
Time required	40 minutes if you return by the road
Description	Trail containing interpretive signs and leading to a view
Level	Easy
Access	On the right (north) side of Spalding Road just before it becomes Gowlland Point Road
Facilities	Benches, bike rack, interpretive signs

This interpretive trail identifies and provides aboriginal uses for plants such as electrified cat's tail moss, goose-necked moss, slough sedge, Menzies tree moss, swordfern, wild rose, stinging nettle and vanilla leaf. The trail meanders through this 4-ha park, passing through wetland and ending at a seasonal waterfall. You can go back the way you came or turn south and take a shortcut by returning the much shorter distance along the road.

ROAD WALKS AND SHORT OFF-ROAD WALKS

There are many quiet, pleasant roads on the Penders. The areas around Hope Bay and Port Washington in the north are particularly scenic and historic. The area around Gowlland Point in the south is also an enjoyable place to walk. Below are off-road walks that shouldn't take more than 30 minutes:

9. Gardom Pond Trail: Park near the end of Harbour Hill Road and walk up the paved road in the subdivision. The trail, marked with a signboard containing a map, goes off to the left (east). It ends at a viewpoint above Gardom Pond. If you turn right at the sign, another trail leads to a bench and a view over Port Browning.

10. Heart Trail/Heart Trail Extension: The access to this trail is on the east side of Ketch Road just north of the firehall. This trail connects the Magic Lake area with Prior Centennial Park (now part of the National Park Reserve). Once in the park, you can explore several short trails that branch off the Heart Trail. This trail was built by the Pender Island Parks and Recreation Commission with the help of the First Open Heart Society of BC, in appreciation of continued community support. A link trail connects the Heart Trail with Disc Golf Park.

11. Oaks Bluff: The access to this trail is on the south side of Pirates Road about halfway to Wallace Point. This steep, 20-minute trail in a 5-ha park starts from Pirates Road and continues to the bluffs. It offers two spectacular views: the first of the Bedwell Harbour marina and the second of Swanson Channel and the Sooke Hills on Vancouver Island in the distance. The strategically placed benches are perfect for enjoying the magnificent views.

12. Castle Road Trail: This steep trail leading to Spalding Hill has fine views and beautiful rock faces. Allow about 45 minutes to climb the hill and return to the trailhead. This is one of the best sites in the Gulf Islands for viewing turkey vultures and bald eagles, and how they interact. This trail can be very hot in the summer.

In addition to these walks, there are a number of short strolls you can take on the Penders. Most of the following trails will take only about 5 minutes round trip, though a few will take up to 15–20 minutes. Most of the trails in the Magic Lake area, and some of the others listed here, are short community link trails. There is a picnic area and a swimming spot at Magic Lake that you may want to visit. Most walks with a viewpoint require some climbing.

NORTH PENDER

Grover Sergeant Cairn: The boardwalk to the cairn is on Clam Bay Road, just west of Pearson Road. Walk on a wheelchair-accessible boardwalk to a memorial to Grover Sergeant, who crashed his plane on this site while training during World War II.

Mount Elizabeth Park: This 350-m trail (20 minutes return) is off Clam Bay Road just north of Hope Bay. The walk was named after Elizabeth Auchterlonie, a member of one of North Pender's pioneer families. The park is a good example of a pristine swordfern environment. There is an outhouse and map here.

Wilson Road viewpoint: Park at the corner of Hooson Road and walk down Wilson Road to the trail, which has a viewpoint looking north over Plumper Sound and little islets. It's possible to reach the rocky beach here but be careful not to trespass on the adjacent private property.

Seawest Trail viewpoint: This trail begins 1.5 km from the end of Hooson Road on the left (north) side. The trail climbs to a viewpoint 75 m above the shoreline, where you have good views of Mayne Island, the Coast Mountains and Saturna Island.

Skeeles Road viewpoint: Skeeles Road is a gravel lane off Razor Point Road, leading to a single house. The trail parallels the road and leads to a viewpoint above a beach (no beach access) complete with a bench for enjoying it. The view is south over Port Browning to Mortimer Spit.

Masthead Crescent to Shingle Bay Park: This trail, which is at the end of Masthead Crescent, in the Magic Lake area, leads to Shingle Bay Park, crossing Galleon Way in the process. If you take Galleon Way to its end, you will find a trail leading up to Roe Lake in the National Park Reserve. This is a favourite walk with locals.

Schooner Way to Chart Drive: You will find this trail at the end of Chart Drive, in the Magic Lake area. It connects Chart Drive to Schooner Way.

Yardarm Road to Shingle Bay: This steep trail links the middle of Yardarm Road, in the Magic Lake area, with Shingle Bay Park.

Schooner Way at Reef Road (viewpoint): There's a bench at this viewpoint in the Magic Lake area.

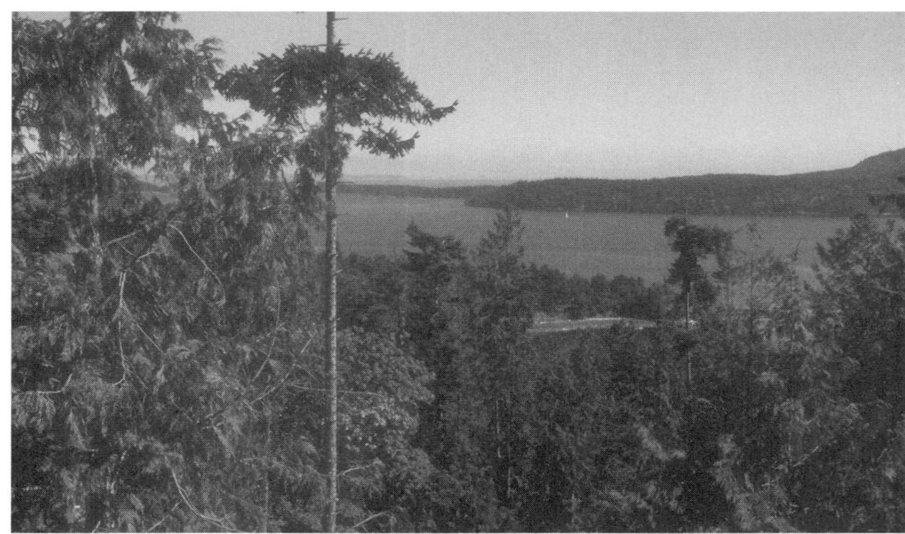

The expansive view from Mount Norman includes the Gulf and San Juan Islands as well as mountains in both Washington State and on Vancouver Island. Richard Blier

Bosun Way–Galleon Way Trail: Access this Magic Lake community trail from Bosun Way, Galleon Way or Schooner Way. This trail will take you about 20 minutes to complete.

Galleon Way to Disc Golf Park: Trails at the east end of Galleon Way, in the Magic Lake area, lead to Disc Golf Park and connect with other trails leading to the firehall and Prior Centennial Park (now part of the National Park Reserve).

Capstan Lane Park: Access the trails off Capstan Lane or Rope Road in the Magic Lake area. Two trails link both roads, passing through a fine wetland area.

Lively Peak Park: This is near Sailor Road, in the Magic Lake area. A steep trail leads off to the left of a skid road to a viewpoint and benches from which to enjoy it. You will need about 15 minutes to complete this trail.

Abbott Hill Park: This trail, off the west side of Spyglass Road, returns farther along the road. This steep, rough trail with rock faces was named for surveyor Mel Abbott, who developed Magic Lake Estates, which was completed in 1974.

Compass Crescent/Starboard Crescent/Tiller Crescent: Two short, steep trails leading to Buck Lake.

Buck Lake Link Trail: This trail, which links Spyglass Road to Privateers Road and Privateers Road to Schooner Way, takes about 15 minutes to walk. The trail passes two small waterfalls.

Mumford Road Viewpoint: This appealing trail leads down to the shoreline of Pender Canal, providing good views of Mortimer Spit and the Penders' bridge. This is a great place to see river otters.

Swanson View Drive: This viewpoint, at the end of the road, looks toward Turn Point on Stuart Island.

Plumper Way Viewpoint: The viewpoint is at the end of Plumper Way. There's no beach access (it's very steep) but there is a bench at this excellent viewpoint looking toward Turn Point on Stuart Island.

SOUTH PENDER

Bridge Trail: Access this trail off Ainslie Point Road. The trail, which is near the mailboxes, leads to a viewpoint overlooking the canal area and the bridge. There is no beach access.

Lilias Spalding Heritage Park: This park is toward the end of Castle Road (off Spalding Road). Stroll through history at this homestead site of one of South Pender's pioneer families. Lilias MacKay and Arthur Spalding married in 1889 and Lilias continued to live here until about 1938, six years after Arthur's death. This 4-ha park contains many heritage trees and shrubs, as well as the ruins of a farm building. This park is undergoing further restoration and development.

Southlands Drive–Tilley Road Viewpoint: The trail, which is at the intersection of Southlands Drive and Tilley Road, leads to a bench and a somewhat obscured view over Tilley Point.

Craddock–Gowlland Loop Trail: This trail, which connects Gowlland Point Road and Craddock Road, is somewhat overgrown and passes through prickly gorse thickets.

BEACH ACCESSES

There are also a number of places on the Penders where you can reach the shore. The Parks Commission has provided a bench and other amenities at most of the following beach accesses. On most beaches, you can walk only a short distance.

NORTH PENDER

Walden Road: Just past Stanley Point Road. A short trail leads to stairs to a pebble beach.

Found Road: See hike 2.

Bridges Road: 200 m west of Stanley Point Drive. Steps lead to a shell and sand beach.

Tracy Road: East off Armadale Road, just northwest of Pearson Road. Tracy Road is no more than a lane to a house. The 5-minute trail leads to a lookout platform.

Bricky Bay: At the south end of Armadale Road. Steps lead down to a rocky beach that can be walked, for some way, at very low tide.

Welcome Bay: Just north of Hope Bay, off Clam Bay Road. Walk 5 minutes to stairs down to a pebble beach.

Zolob Road: Off Otter Bay Road, just south of Port Washington Road. A short trail leads to stairs to a sandy beach.

Otter Bay Road: Percival Cove, just south of Port Washington, north of 1211 Otter Bay Road. Low-tide access only.

MacKinnon Road: At the end of MacKinnon Road. Stairs lead to a small, ecologically sensitive beach.

Niagara Road: Park at Pender Lions Info Centre (2332 Otter Bay Road) and walk to end of narrow Niagara Road, where steep stairs descend to the best sand beach on the Penders.

Irene Bay: At end of Irene Bay Road, 3 km down South Otter Bay Road from its intersection with Otter Bay Road.

Shingle Bay: Off Galleon Way. This short trail leading to stairs to a sandy beach is part of the Masthead Crescent Trail.

Panda Bay: End of Harpoon Road (off Galleon Way), in Magic Lake Estates. A short trail leads to stairs to a mixed sand and gravel beach.

Thieves Bay: Two trails lead from Anchor Way to the sandy beach at Thieves Bay.

Boat Nook: Off Schooner Way, just west of Capstan Lane, in Magic Lake area.

Wallace Road: Off Wallace Road, just north of Schooner Way. Steep steps and a ramp provide access to the corner of Medicine Beach on Bedwell Harbour, which has a short loop trail. The adjacent 8 ha of marshland is owned by the Islands Trust Fund.

Starvation Bay: End of Bedwell Drive. Take steps to a sand, shell and gravel beach.

Peter Cove (North): At end of Trincoma Place. Steps lead down to a sandy beach.

Peter Cove (South): Beside 7946 Plumper Way, a narrow roadway leads to a sandy beach where you could easily launch a small boat.

SOUTH PENDER

Fawn Creek Park: Off Ainslie Point Road, south of the Bridge Trail. A 10-minute loop trail passes through beautiful mature forest (large cedars and firs) and gives access to a muddy beach.

Mortimer Spit: Near the bridge on Canal Road. This gravel road allows easy car access to this beach and mud flats, and the site is a favourite launch site for kayakers. There's also an outhouse.

Canal Road: Between 9858 and 9864 Canal Road, about 3 km east of the bridge. A rope handrail at the end of this steep descent will help you reach the flat, rocky shore, which can be walked for some distance at low tide.

William Walker Road: Opposite Walker Trail, leading to the Gulf Islands National Park Reserve's parking area for accessing Mount Norman, about 4 km east of the bridge. Steps lead down to this sand and rock beach.

Ancia Road: Off Conery Crescent. A wide path leads to two long flights of very steep stairs to a rocky beach with a beautiful view across Plumper Sound to Mount Warburton Pike on Saturna Island.

Boundary Pass: Opposite 9930 Boundary Pass Drive (near the end of the road). A short trail leads to a bench and then stairs descending to the beach. At low tide, you can walk to a small rocky islet with tide pools.

Bidgood Road: Off Gowlland Point Road. A steep, 5-minute trail leads to steps and a handrail that permit access to this pebble beach.

Craddock Road: End of Craddock Road. Stairs lead to a pebble beach.

Higgs Road: You can access the beach here at low tide. Bring your picnic lunch.

Gowlland Point: At end of Gowlland Point Road. Stairs lead to a pebble and sand beach.

AND IF YOU PADDLE . . .

The Penders are well endowed with deep bays that provide interesting exploration. You can launch from the marinas in Hyashi Cove, Port Browning or Bedwell Harbour. You can also launch from government docks at Port Washington in Grimmer Bay and at Hope Bay, both of which are worth visiting to see a bit of historic North Pender. Be aware that there are strong currents in many places around the islands and watch for turbulence around the points on South Pender and around Blunden Islet. Watch for ferries and their wash, if paddling around Otter Bay, in Navy Channel or in Swanson Channel, and for afternoon winds in the summer. Overall, Bedwell Harbour and Port Browning are probably the safest places to explore. You can launch from the following beach accesses:

MacKinnon Road: Near the end of MacKinnon Road, stairs lead down to the beach on the west side of the road. From here, you can paddle north or south along North Pender's fascinating western shoreline.

Niagara Road: At the end of Niagara Road (park at the Lions Club Info Centre on Otter Bay Road), stairs lead to a small beach. From here, you can paddle north or south along North Pender's western shoreline.

Irene Bay: A short path leads from the end of Irene Bay Road to an easy launch site on the beach. Paddle north, avoiding ferries and pleasure boats, to explore Otter Bay, Grimmer Bay and Port Washington. This is very appealing shoreline.

Shingle Bay: This park, near the end of Galleon Way, gives you access to North Pender's western shoreline (see Irene Bay description, above).

Thieves Bay: The park off Anchor Way Road has a boat launch that will give you easy access to North Pender's western shoreline. The most interesting shoreline is to the north, where you'll find Shingle Bay, Irene Bay, Ella Bay, Otter Bay and Grimmer Bay.

Hamilton Beach: Just past the Port Browning Marina Resort on Hamilton Road. This boat launch gives you access to the shoreline of Port Browning. From here, paddle south and under the bridge to explore both shorelines of Bedwell Harbour.

Mortimer Spit: It's possible to drive down to this beach to launch. From here, you can explore Port Browning or go under the bridge to Bedwell Harbour.

Medicine Beach: There's a parking area right behind the beach, at the end of a signed driveway off Wallace Road. Launching at this beach will give you easy access to the fascinating Bedwell Harbour shoreline.

Peter Cove: A lane at the end of Plumper Way leads northeast to a boat launch on the south side of Peter Cove, from where you can explore the southern shore of Bedwell Harbour or the outside southern shore of North Pender. There's a parking space at the top of the lane.

Gowlland Point Road: Launch at the end of Gowlland Point Road and paddle around the beautiful eastern shore of South Pender, north to Teece Point and Blunden Islet, and south to Tilly Point and the entrance to Bedwell Harbour.

Quadra ISLAND

Considered a Discovery Island, as well as a Gulf Island, Quadra is the most northern island described in this book and the second largest (310 square km). Quadra straddles climatic and geological zones, creating a diverse environment that is rich in hiking possibilities. Most of the island's 2,548 residents live on the narrow southern half of the island, where you will find shops, restaurants, accommodation and other services. The north end of the island is mostly Crown land, managed by the Ministry of Forests or forestry companies. In addition to the usual Gulf Island animals—black-tail deer, raccoons, Douglas squirrels, otters, harbour seals and sea lions—Quadra has wolves and cougars. Quadra's mountainous terrain, many lakes, numerous anchorages and long beaches make it a popular destination for outdoor enthusiasts. The island is also home to two well-known resorts: Tsa-Kwa-Luten Lodge and the April Point Resort.

HISTORY

The We Wai Kai Band of the Kwakwaka'wakw Nation have lived at Cape Mudge since the early 1800s, when they overcame and replaced the northern Coast Salish people, who had established a large village there. Geographers in the 19th century thought Quadra and neighbouring Maurelle and Sonora Islands were all one island, which they called Valdes. This caused confusion when another Gulf Island was given the same name in 1859. The matter was clarified when the three islands were correctly mapped and Quadra was renamed after a Spanish naval officer.

Splendid stands of timber and the promise of gold drew loggers and miners to the island in the 1880s. The Lucky Jim Mine, which opened in 1903, yielded tonnes of gold and copper ore. By 1904, Quadra had two post offices, a public school, a hotel, lumber camps and mills, twice-weekly steamer connections, a Methodist mission and a large salmon cannery at Quathiaski Cove. Fishing and logging are still the island's main economic activities but land development and tourism are becoming increasingly important.

GETTING THERE

There are hourly 10-minute ferry sailings from Campbell River to Quathiaski Cove on Quadra Island, daily, from early morning to late night. For more information, obtain a Northern Gulf Islands schedule or contact BC Ferries (see Resources, page 238).

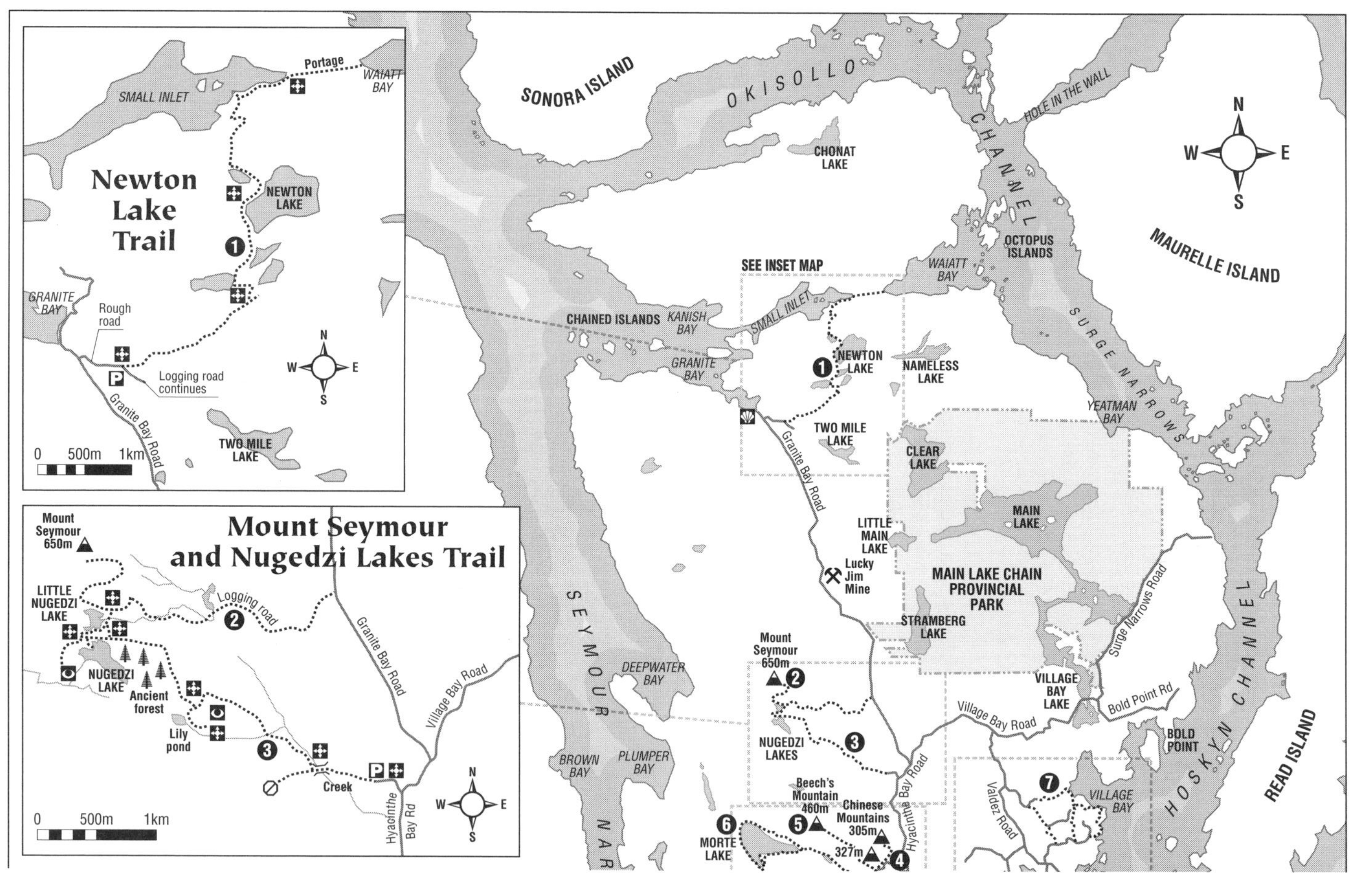
Newton Lake Trail
SMALL INLET
Portage
WAIATT BAY
NEWTON LAKE
GRANITE BAY
Rough road
Logging road continues
Granite Bay Road
TWO MILE LAKE
0 500m 1km
Mount Seymour and Nugedzi Lakes Trail
Mount Seymour 650m
LITTLE NUGEDZI LAKE
Logging road
NUGEDZI LAKE
Ancient forest
Lily pond
Creek
Granite Bay Road
Village Bay Road
Hyacinthe Bay Rd
0 500m 1km
SONORA ISLAND
OKISOLLO CHANNEL
HOLE IN THE WALL
CHONAT LAKE
MAURELLE ISLAND
OCTOPUS ISLANDS
WAIATT BAY
SURGE NARROWS
SEE INSET MAP
CHAINED ISLANDS
KANISH BAY
SMALL INLET
GRANITE BAY
NEWTON LAKE
NAMELESS LAKE
YEATMAN BAY
TWO MILE LAKE
CLEAR LAKE
Granite Bay Road
LITTLE MAIN LAKE
MAIN LAKE
Lucky Jim Mine
MAIN LAKE CHAIN PROVINCIAL PARK
STRAMBERG LAKE
Surge Narrows Road
SEYMOUR NAR
DEEPWATER BAY
Mount Seymour 650m
VILLAGE BAY LAKE
Bold Point Rd
Village Bay Road
NUGEDZI LAKES
BOLD POINT
HOSKYN CHANNEL
READ ISLAND
BROWN BAY
PLUMPER BAY
Hyacinthe Bay Road
Valdez Road
VILLAGE BAY
Beech's Mountain 460m
Chinese Mountains 305m
327m
MORTE LAKE

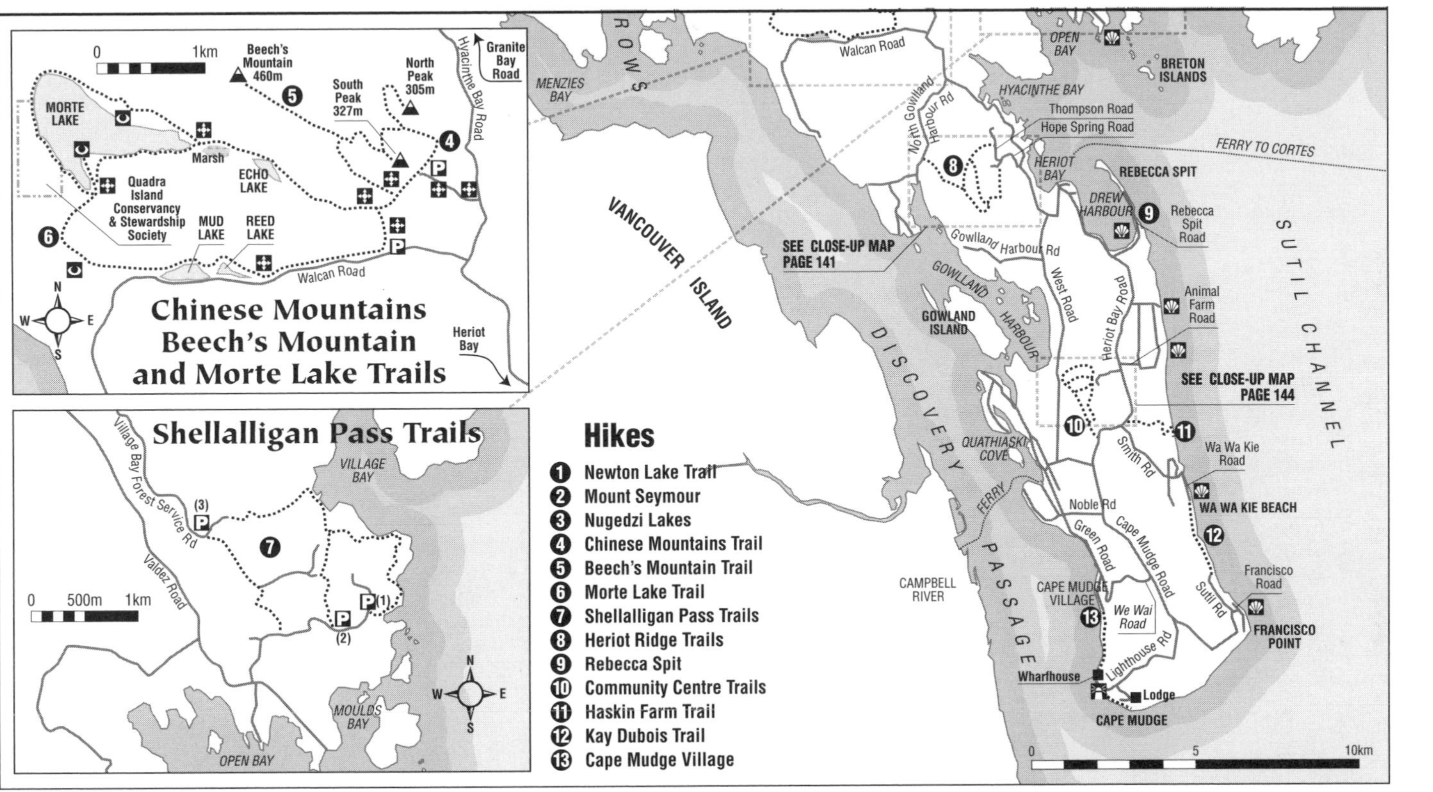

Quadra Island

Roads
Trails
Park boundary
P Parking
Sign
Viewpoint
Peak
No access
Beach access
Lighthouse
See text

SERVICES AND ACCOMMODATION

All of Quadra's services are on the narrow southern end of the island. Most are within a short distance of Quathiaski Cove, mainly in two strip malls: one on Harper Road and another on West Road near Heriot Bay. Quadra has a 24-hour taxi service.

A good range of accommodation is available on Quadra, from several very comfortable resorts to more basic bed and breakfasts. Camping is available at the We Wai Kai Campsite and the Heriot Bay Inn RV Park.

A free map of the island that notes features, accommodation and services is available at most stores. A better map, produced by Discovery Islands Realty, is available for a nominal price at many stores, as is a map by local artist Hilary Stewart, which shows many trails and Crown land. An invaluable resource for hikers is the *Quadra Island Trails* brochure produced by the Trails Committee of the Quadra Island Recreation Society.

For more information on Quadra, check www.quadraisland.ca and www.discoveryislands.ca. You can also contact the Trails Committee of the Quadra Island Recreation Society (QIRS), 970 West Road, PO Box 10, Quathiaski Cove, BC V0P 1N0; tel: 250-285-3243; www.quadrarec.bc.ca.

ESPECIALLY FOR WALKERS

Although there are many challenging hikes on Quadra, there are also some relatively easy trails. In addition to the Shore and Road Walks on page 147, try one or more of the following:

- Rebecca Spit (see hike 9, page 142)
- Community Centre Trails (see hike 10, page 144)
- Kay Dubois Trail (see hike 12, page 146). If doing this one, be sure to start from the end of Wa Wa Kie Road and omit the steep climb at the end to Sutil Road.
- Cape Mudge Village (see hike 13, page 146). The trails around the lighthouse at Cape Mudge are particularly scenic.

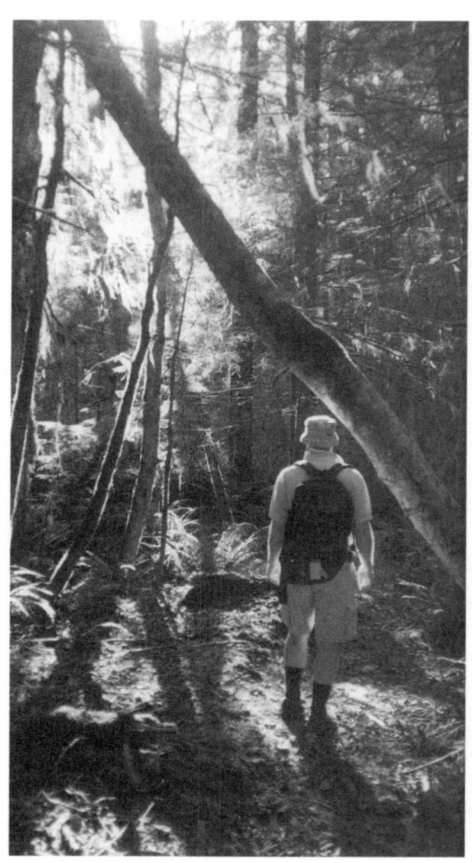

The trail linking Small Inlet and Waiatt Bay is lush and cool.

HIKES

Hiking on Quadra can be strenuous and tricky. There are countless trails, including many unmarked trails on old logging roads. Many of these trails are threatened by the tremendous amount of logging activity taking place, or slated to take place, on Crown land. Because of the dangers of hiking in areas where there is active logging or poorly marked trails, I have restricted the hikes in this chapter to well-established trails maintained by the Trails Committee of the Quadra Island Recreation Society, whose volunteers have signed the trails beautifully, spending time and money to make the trails accessible to the public. Some of the hikes and walks in this chapter can be grouped together to make a longer day out, which is indicated in the text.

These trails may be quite wet from fall to spring, particularly the areas around Waiatt Bay (hike 1) and the Nugedzi Lakes (hike 2). If you decide to try roads and hikes that aren't outlined below, check with locals before setting out.

1. NEWTON LAKE ★★★/ NEWTON LAKE TO WAIATT BAY ★★★★

Trail length	6.4 km to Newton Lake return; 12.8 km to Waiatt Bay return
Time required	2 hours to Newton Lake return; 4.5 hours to Small Inlet and Waiatt Bay return
Description	A pleasant hike to a pretty lake. If continuing on to Waiatt Bay, you will descend steeply through mature forest.
Level	Moderate
Access	From Heriot Bay, it's about 20 km to the trail-head. Take Hyacinthe Bay Road and turn left at Granite Bay Road. Continue for about 10 km to within 200 m of Granite Bay. Just after you cross a one-lane bridge, take the unsigned road on the right and drive carefully (it's rough) for about 600 m, to the sign indicating the trail-head.
Cautions	The hike from Newton Lake to Waiatt Bay is on private land owned by the Merrill and Ring logging company. Permission to hike in this area has been granted informally and could be rescinded if the land is not respected. Stay on the trail, light no fires, do not camp and do nothing to disturb the land or the midden at Waiatt Bay. The descent to Small Inlet is very steep in places.

Newton Lake. The hike to Newton Lake heads first east and then north along an old, often rocky, logging road. In spring, the ground along the first part of the hike is often quite wet. The trail soon crosses a little wooden bridge over a stream, which parallels the logging road for a while. You hike steadily uphill for about 1 km through alder and small, feathery hemlock. After about 1.6 km (15–20 minutes), you pass the first of three small lakes and the hike becomes more interesting.

After about 2.5 km, you reach Newton Lake, touted locally for its emerald colour. The rest of the trail follows the west shore of the lake, ending at a rocky knoll that is a great swimming spot. At this point, you will have walked 3.2 km. From here, you can return or continue another 3.2 km to Waiatt Bay.

To Waiatt Bay via Small Inlet. A faded sign just past the Newton Lake knoll points you right (east) to a trail leading across a creek (over a jumble of logs) and then down (north) to Small Inlet. (A side trail to the east takes you to another fine picnic rock on Newton Lake.) The first part of the trail is difficult to find, but once you're on it, you'll find it flagged here and there with red survey tape.

The trail follows the east side of the creek, which tumbles down through the canyon to meet the sea below. About 10 minutes after leaving Newton Lake, you will see a seasonal waterfall. You walk through lovely open rain forest, past the charred stumps of old-growth trees that were logged many years ago. The trail winds its way right down to the bottom and ends 1.6 km (45 minutes) from Newton Lake, at the aptly named Small Inlet.

From a rocky knoll jutting out into the water, you can look at the small islets in front of you and beyond them through the mouth of the inlet to the mountains on Vancouver Island. The trail continues another 600 m (10 minutes) through the boggy terrain to a small spring-fed pool of water behind the head of the inlet. This area, lush with ferns, still contains some large trees. From the pool, the trail doubles as a portage to Waiatt Bay, another 800 m (10 minutes) away.

This part of the trail passes old-growth stumps with the springboard notches carved by the hand loggers who felled them still visible. At Waiatt Bay, there is a view of the Octopus Islands and Maurelle Island behind them.

Waiatt Bay was the site of a large Native summer settlement. You can see the shell midden in the badly eroding banks. Great care should be taken here, as the site is deteriorating. Do not dig into the bank or camp on it.

Granite Bay 100 Years Ago

It's hard to imagine, looking at the few houses in Granite Bay today, that this was once a bustling little harbour, with its own store, post office, hotel, school and even a floating brothel. Between 1900 and 1916, a timber company that employed up to 500 men had a logging camp and booming ground here. Many of the loggers were Scandinavian migrants or from Eastern Canada. In the summer, these men were joined by Kwagiulth workers, who had a summer camp in the area. Taking advantage of how difficult it was to enforce the law in such an isolated spot, the men entertained themselves with drinking, gambling and prostitution.

2. MOUNT SEYMOUR ★★★★

Trail length	10 km return; up to 15 km if combined with hike 3
Time required	Up to 3 hours; up to 6 hours if combined with hike 3
Description	The first two-thirds of this hike follows an old logging road that climbs the mountain. The last third is on a trail with expansive views and lovely vegetation.
Level	Strenuous
Elevation	650 m; elevation gain: 475 m
Accesses	A. On the left (west) side of Granite Bay Road, about 2 km from its junction with Village Bay Road (see map). Just beyond the entrance to the trail (an old logging road), there's a small parking space on the shoulder of Granite Bay Road. B. From the Nugedzi Lakes trails on the east side of Little Nugedzi Lake (see hike 3)
Cautions	Even though the last part of this trail is well marked with cairns, red flagging and occasional red metal diamonds, it crosses mossy rocks and is easy to lose. Try to keep a cairn or flag in view ahead of you at all times.

From access A, you climb quickly and soon link up with a rocky logging road, which heads alternately south and west, is occasionally marked with flagging tape and is easy to follow. The trail forks after 25 minutes and again after 45 minutes; go left both times, following the wooden trail signs.

After about 50 minutes of walking up the logging road, you reach the junction of the Nugedzi Lakes trails (left) and the trail to the summit of Mount Seymour (right). If you are planning to combine the two hikes, I suggest you see the summit first and then continue with the Nugedzi Lakes trails on the way back. The climb to the summit takes only about 30 minutes but it is complicated, changing directions repeatedly. Fortunately, it is well marked and you can usually spot a cairn or a flag ahead of you.

After about 10 minutes on the summit trail, you'll have a view over Nugedzi Lake. Soon you will see Brown Bay and other points on Vancouver Island. When you emerge on the summit, note where you came from so that you won't have trouble finding your way back. The view from the summit looks northeast to Bute Inlet and Estero Peak. You can also see Cortes Island to the east.

3. Nugedzi Lakes ★★★★★

Trail length	10 km return, including side trips; up to 15 km if combined with Mount Seymour
Time required	4 hours; 6 hours if combined with Mount Seymour
Description	From access B (the main access), it's a hard, boring climb up a stony logging road for about 2 km, followed by a delightful hike through some old-growth forest and around two lovely lakes with good viewpoints. From access A, it may be a little less arduous but it's still a slog.
Level	Strenuous
Elevation	510 m
Accesses	A. On the left (west) side of Granite Bay Road about 2 km from its junction with Village Bay Road (see map). Just beyond the entrance to the trail (an old logging road), there's a small parking space on the shoulder of Granite Bay Road. The trail meets the nicest part of the Nugedzi Lakes trails at the east end of the boardwalk at Little Nugedzi Lake. B. The parking area is 100 m up the Old Plumper Bay Road, a rough gravel road running left (west) off Hyacinthe Bay Road, 3.1 km north of Walcan Road (a.k.a. Missing Links Road). Look for the sign, Nugedzi Lakes.
Caution	Fires prohibited.

Note: If you want to hike to the Nugedzi Lakes only, I recommend you start at access B (described below). If you plan to combine this outing with hike 2, I recommend you start at access A, climb Mount Seymour, follow the Nugedzi Lakes trails and end your hike at access B. From here, it is a 3-km road walk along Hyacinthe Bay Road and Granite Bay Road, to your starting point.

The Nugedzi Lakes were named in 1992 to honour Billy Assu (1867–1965), chief of the We Wai Kai Band at Cape Mudge for many years. Nugedzi means "big mountain" in the Kwa-kwa-la language. The well-marked trail was developed co-operatively by the Quadra Island Recreation Society and Fletcher Challenge (now TimberWest).

Using access B, walk 700 m past the designated parking area on the gravel road. After crossing a creek bed, turn right onto another old logging road. This part of the hike is up a steep, stony gully. Don't be put off, as the last part of the hike is magnificent and makes the slog worthwhile.

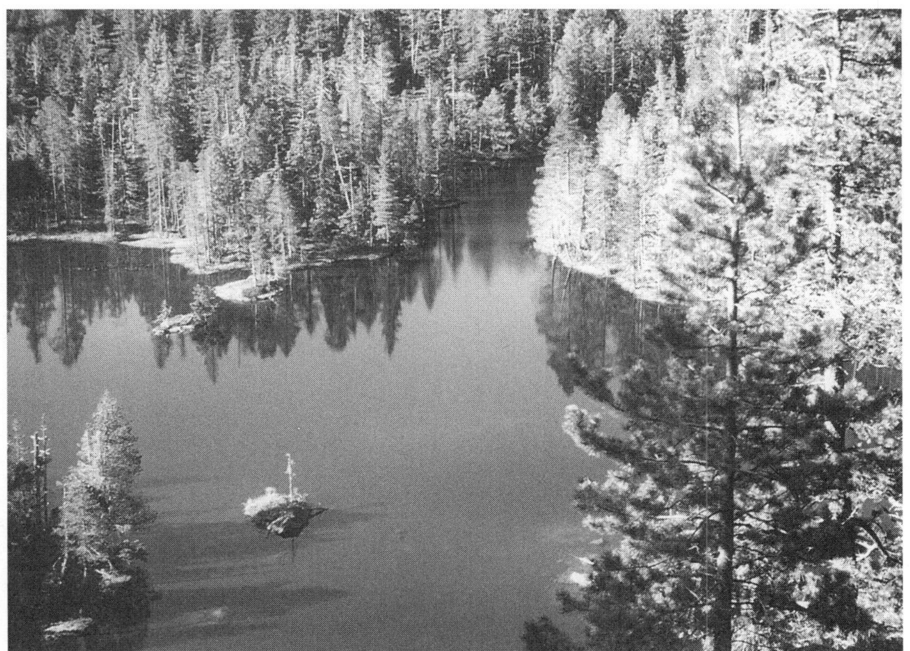

Glimpsed from the trail to Mount Seymour, Nugedzi Lake reflects the surrounding forest in its calm waters.

About 2 km from the parking area, you will see a cairn on your left. At this point, the logging road ends and an excellent foot trail heads off to the left (south). From here, the hike is very pleasant.

About 5 minutes farther, you will find signposts at a small bridge, directing you south to a lily pond, a viewpoint and the Chinese Mountains. It's worth doing the 20-minute detour to see the pond and view but leave the Chinese Mountains for another day. It takes about 5 minutes to reach the pond, and from here, a sign will direct you another 5 minutes to the spot overlooking the Breton Islands, Read Island and Rebecca Spit.

Return to the bridge and continue toward Nugedzi Lake. From here, the trail passes through an ancient forest that includes about half a dozen old-growth giants, as well as diverse vegetation that includes several varieties of wild mushrooms.

About 1.5 km (20 minutes) from the bridge, you'll see a sign for Nugedzi Lake, Little Nugedzi Lake and Seymour Narrows Lookover. Be sure to visit them all.

Nugedzi Lake is very pretty. There's a huge rock on the lake's edge that is perfect for a picnic, and swimmers will find the water irresistible—if the weather and time of year are right. I once braved it in October and it was, well, quite refreshing.

Another 15 minutes takes you to the viewpoint looking southwest toward Seymour Narrows. You can descend to a second, lower viewpoint, which offers a good view of Brown Bay on Vancouver Island.

When you've had enough of the viewpoints, return the way you came and take the turnoff for Little Nugedzi Lake. Much of the trail to the lake is on a boardwalk over marshy ground. Despite the wetness, there are many small pine trees and quite a lot of kinnikinnick. The lake is exquisite, like something constructed for a Japanese garden, with little grassy islands dotting the lake's surface. It will take you only 15 minutes to walk this part of the trail but you'll probably want to linger here.

If you're going to access A, or decide from here that you want to combine this hike with Mount Seymour, you'll find the trail at the south end of the boardwalk at Little Nugedzi Lake. Otherwise, retrace your route to access B.

4. Chinese Mountains ★★★★

Trail length	Up to 5 km, depending on routes chosen; 16 km if combined with Morte Lake trails, 7 km if combined with Beech's Mountain Trail
Time required	2–3 hours; 5–6 hours if combined with the Morte Lake trails; 4 hours if combined with Beech's Mountain Trail
Description	A fairly steep climb along ridges and over rocky knolls to two separate peaks offering excellent views
Level	Strenuous
Elevation	South Peak 327 m; North Peak 305 m
Access	A. From a parking area on a road that goes left (west) off Hyacinthe Bay Road 600 m north of Walcan Road (a.k.a. Missing Links Road) B. From a short connector trail that intercepts the Morte Lake Trail (see hike 6) shortly past its trailhead. This is not recommended unless you are combining this hike with a circumnavigation of Morte Lake.
Cautions	The trail is very steep and rugged in parts. In many places, it crosses mossy, rocky knolls, where the route may not be easy to discern. Cairns mark the trail but it is still easy to get lost. Take a compass, do not hike alone and make sure to leave yourself lots of time.

Note: The trails to the north and south peaks of the Chinese Mountains (sometimes called China Mountain) are linked and you can hike them following a somewhat circular route. Since the South Chinese Mountain Trail and Beech's Mountain Trail (see hike 5) share the same path for some distance, you may wish to combine these hikes.

From the parking lot (access A), take the South Chinese Mountain Trail on the left (southwest) side of the parking lot. This is a lovely hike, first through hemlock and fir forest and then along moss-covered rock bluffs. The trail heads south and west and soon opens up with views of mountains and Rebecca Spit to the southeast. For a while, the trail follows a stream bed. It will take you about 35 minutes to reach the well-signed junction of Beech's Mountain Trail and the South Chinese Mountain Trail. If combining the hikes, I recommend taking the Beech's Mountain Trail first (see hike 5) and then returning to hike the Chinese Mountains.

From this junction, it's at least 25 minutes to the south peak (3 km from the parking lot). Here there are panoramic views of Read and Cortes Islands and the Coast Mountains to the east, and of Campbell River and the Vancouver Island ranges to the southwest.

You can descend by a second trail, leading northwest, that branches off from the trail just below the south peak. You will have walked about 1 km (about 15 minutes) by the time you reach the junction with the trail to the north peak. From here, it's another 500 m (20 minutes) of climbing to the north peak, which I recommend you skip. The views are not as good as those at the south peak and the trail is a bit tricky to find in places, especially on the way back. The parking lot is about 1 km (15 minutes) from the junction of the trails to the two peaks.

5. BEECH'S MOUNTAIN TRAIL ★★★★

Trail length	3–4 km each way; 7 km if combined with hike 4
Time required	2 hours return; 4 hours if combined with hike 4
Description	A climb through beautiful forest and over mossy rock bluffs to a spectacular 180-degree view
Level	Strenuous
Elevation	460 m; elevation gain: 345 m
Access	Follow the trail on the southwest side of the Chinese Mountains parking area (see hike 3) to the signed junction of the Beech's Mountain trail.
Cautions	Even though the trail is marked with cairns and flagging, it crosses rocky bluffs and is easy to lose. Try to keep a cairn or flag in view ahead of you at all times.

This is a lovely hike, first through hemlock and fir forest and then along moss-covered bluffs. The trail heads south and west and soon opens up with views of mountains to the south and Rebecca Spit to the east. For a while, the trail follows a stream bed. It will take about 35 minutes to reach the well-signed junction of the Beech's Mountain Trail and the South Chinese Mountain Trail. Turn left.

More views soon open up, looking west to Brown Bay on Vancouver Island and south to snow-capped mountains. The hike is a steady uphill climb until the last

From up here, hikers get a splendid view of Quadra Island and the maze of waterways that surround it and other nearby islands.

60 m, which are dramatic and fast. The spectacular 180-degree view to the east is worth the effort. Turkey vultures soar on the updrafts above, below is Rebecca Spit and, in the distance, are the Breton Islands and Cortes Island.

On your way back, you can hike the Chinese Mountains (hike 4) before returning to the parking area.

6. Morte Lake ★★

Trail length	10.5 km including all trails; 16 km if combined with hike 4
Time required	3 hours; 5–6 hours if combined with hike 4
Description	A rocky trail that crosses streams, passes lakes and follows a ridge with several fine viewpoints above Morte Lake
Level	Moderate
Access	On the right, 800 m along Walcan Road (a.k.a. Missing Links Road). Walcan Road runs left (west) off Hyacinthe Bay Road (watch for the Walcan Seafood sign).
Caution	Much of this trail follows a humdrum, rocky logging road that is not very pleasant to walk along. In places, the trail crosses rocky outcrops, where cairns mark the trail.

After about 5 minutes, you reach the signed junction for the Chinese Mountains trail (on the right). Another 10 minutes or so farther along is Little Morte Lake (a.k.a. Echo Lake) with a great echo that's well worth trying. Fifteen minutes past this lake is a signed junction that gives you a choice of circumnavigating Morte Lake (3.6 km) clockwise or counter-clockwise. I recommend continuing straight ahead and walking counter-clockwise around the lake. This route will take you up some steep slopes as it follows the north and west side of the lake but then it ambles nicely along the south shore of the lake back to the junction. There are several nice spots along here to picnic and swim.

Cairns like this one mark many of Quadra's hikes.

Although the trail map shows an alternative trail back to Walcan Road that passes a couple of small lakes, I recommend that you stick with circling Morte Lake and retrace your route to the parking area.

7. SHELLALLIGAN PASS TRAILS ★★★

Trail length	Up to 15 km of trails (including 9 km on logging roads), depending on route taken
Time required	Up to 4–5 hours, depending on your speed, how long you might want to spend on the beaches and how much of the trail system you want to hike
Description	Two loop trails through ferny woods, descending to the sea where you scramble up and down over the rocky shoreline
Level	Moderate to strenuous
Accesses	A. Follow Village Bay Road 2.3 km east from Granite Bay Road to Valdez Road. Turn right (south) and continue 4 km to the signed trail turnoff (on the left). From here, drive 1.5 km to parking area 2 or 1.8 km to parking area 1. B. Take Village Bay Road to Village Bay Forest Service Road (500 m beyond Valdez Road). Turn right. You'll see the sign for the trail 2.4 km along this road. Park here (parking area 3) and walk the remaining 200 m to the trailhead.

These trails are well flagged and you-are-here maps are provided at the trailheads at the three parking areas and at the junction of the two loops. You could do either loop or both.

Starting from parking area 1 (access A), the trail descends quickly to the nearby beach, where the trail follows the rocky terrain above the shore. Be aware that the trail can be slippery and strenuous in places. Leaving the beach, the trail then climbs steeply inland (about 60 m) for another 10–15 minutes, eventually reaching a junction of the two loop trails. If you want to complete the first loop, turn left and head to parking area 2 (about 15 minutes away). From here, it's another 5 minutes to parking area 1. This last bit of trail passes ferny woods and then goes through a recently replanted woodlot. This loop would take you about an hour to walk but allow more to enjoy the beaches and views.

I suggest continuing straight ahead on the second loop. The trail descends quickly (about 40 m) to a bay where there is an oyster farm. It continues along the shore for about 5 minutes and then heads up and inland, climbing through beautiful ferny woods beside a seasonal stream to parking area 3 (just off the Village Bay Forest Service Road). From here, turn left on the forest service road and walk about 200 m, until you see a trail beginning on the left. This will take you back to the woodlot logging road, where you will turn left to return to the parking area.

8. Heriot Ridge Trails (Hope Spring Trail, Heriot Ridge Trail, Thompson Trail, Gowlland Harbour Trail) ★★★

Trail length	12 km, depending on route taken
Time required	2–3 hours
Description	A beautiful trail that crosses a variety of terrains and ecosystems—wetland, fern- and moss-covered rocky outcrops, and mixed forest, including old-growth trees
Level	Moderate
Accesses	A. The end of Hope Spring Road. The signed access is just inside and on the right-hand side of the driveway to 855 Hope Spring Road. B. The signed access is on the left near the end of Thompson Road, which runs off Hope Spring Road (see map, page 141)

These trails were built by the Quadra Island Trails Committee, volunteers and Katimavik students. They offer viewpoints and pass by old-growth Douglas fir. The trails are well signed and flagged whenever there is any possibility that you might miss a step.

Beginning at the Hope Spring Road trailhead, the Hope Spring Trail follows a stream and passes lovely moss- and fern-covered rock outcrops. After 15 minutes of walking, you reach the first two viewpoints (elevation about 250 m) and the junction

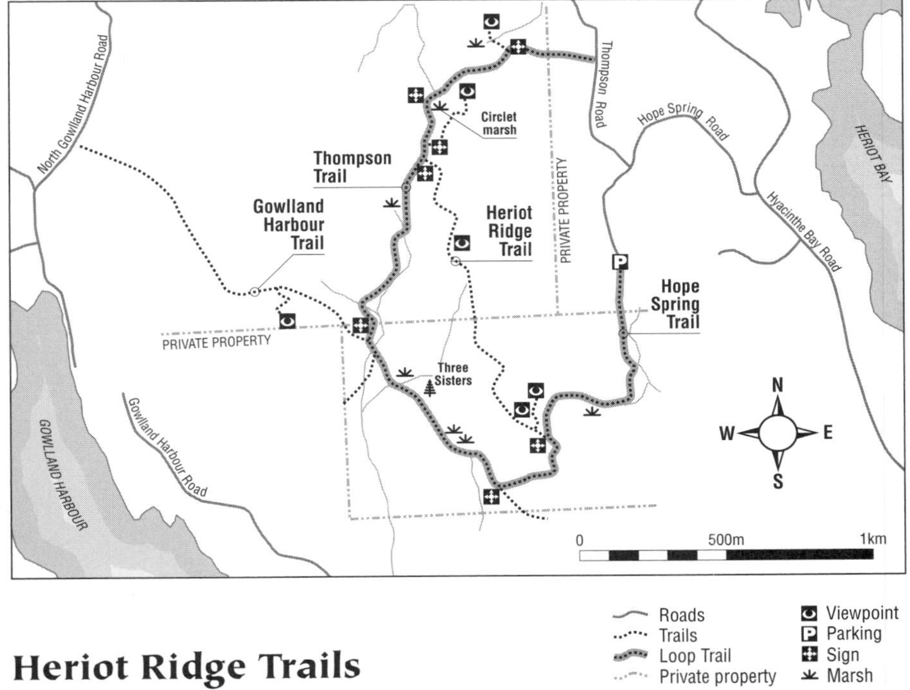

Heriot Ridge Trails

of the Heriot Ridge Route (see the description below). Ignore this trail for now (you can follow it back here later if you want) and allow yourself time to enjoy the views. One looks east to Rebecca Spit and the Breton Islands and southwest to Campbell River on Vancouver Island. The other viewpoint provides a panoramic vista of a Campbell River pulp mill.

From here, the Hope Spring Trail passes through a wet area containing skunk cabbage, in the spring, and becomes the Gowlland Harbour Trail. Look for a stand of old-growth Douglas fir with three huge, fire-blackened trees called the Three Sisters to the right of the trail.

A short distance from the Three Sisters, the Gowlland Harbour Trail heads off left (northwest) and the main trail (right) becomes the Thompson Trail. If you want, you can follow the Gowlland Harbour Trail for another 2 km (25 minutes) to where it meets North Gowlland Harbour Road but you will want to retrace your steps to the main trail to get back to where you parked. (Otherwise you are looking at a 5.6-km walk along North Gowlland Road, Hyacinthe Road and Hope Spring Road to return to your vehicle.)

Continuing on the Thompson Trail you will soon come to another junction, this time with the Heriot Ridge Route (the other end of which you passed near the two viewpoints at the beginning of the hike). You can elect to take this route back (see description below) or continue another 2 km on the Thompson Trail to Thompson Road, from where it's an 800-m walk to the trailhead on Hope Spring Road.

If you elect to stay on the Thompson Trail, you should give yourself an additional 40 minutes to see the two remaining viewpoints (see map). The trail to the first viewpoint (on the right) rises steeply to about 240 m above sea level. It looks east from a rocky ridge to Drew Harbour and Rebecca Spit on the right, and Read Island on the left. Take time to explore the ridge, as the view opens up as you walk farther along it. This detour will take at least 20 minutes. The next viewpoint (on the left) is somewhat lower (about 200 m) and you have to climb a steep rock outcropping to reach it. Here you look northeast to the Breton Islands and Read Island.

Heriot Ridge Route. If you prefer not to walk along the roads, you might try this rugged route. Although well marked, the trail can be a bit of an adventure, passing over a moss-covered ridge and through thick salal. As the vegetation can easily obscure the trail, to avoid getting lost retrace your steps if you do not see a flag or cairn ahead of you. If all goes well, it will take you about half an hour to return to the two viewpoints near the beginning of the hike.

9. Rebecca Spit Provincial Marine Park ★★★★

Trail length	2–4 km return, depending on whether you use the park entrance or the parking lot as your start-and-end point
Time required	30–60 minutes but you'll want to stay longer
Description	This idyllic spot has great beachcombing, lovely views west across Drew Harbour and east toward Cortes and the snow-topped mainland mountains beyond, and pleasant trails through mature second-growth forest.
Level	Easy
Access	The park entrance is just past the We Wai Kai Campsite on Rebecca Spit Road, which is off Heriot Bay Road (see map, page 129).

The spit is just over 2 km long. You can hike from the park entrance down the centre of the spit or drive to a parking/picnic area partway along the spit. Here you will find an easy path, which follows the inner Drew Harbour shore and then continues around the outer Sutil Channel shore. For a short stretch at the spit's narrowest point, the two paths combine. You can also walk around the spit along the beach.

Rebecca Spit is a magical place. The sounds of grebes, ducks, scoters, mergansers, herons, gulls and other waterfowl are often the only thing you'll hear. In the summer, pleasure boats bob at anchor in expansive Drew Harbour. Fishing boats head out or return in their search for fish. The light is particularly pleasant here, as the spit is narrow and well-separated from the land around it. Whether you wind in and out of the second-growth forest or beachcomb along the shore, you will inevitably spend much longer than the hour or so it takes to walk all the trails.

A BRIEF HISTORY OF REBECCA SPIT

Archaeologists believe that, in the late 18th century, a major battle was fought at Rebecca Spit between the Coast Salish and the Kwagiulth. A few grass-covered trenches are all that remain of the extensive Coast Salish fortifications.

The spit was named, in about 1864, after a British trading schooner. It was a We Wai Kai reserve until the government traded it for nearby land, during World War I, so that the spit could be used for military purposes. For many years after the war, the land belonged to the Clandening family, whose members allowed Quadra islanders to use it. In 1946, an earthquake reduced the total area of the spit by more than a third. The land was obtained by the province and made into a park in 1959.

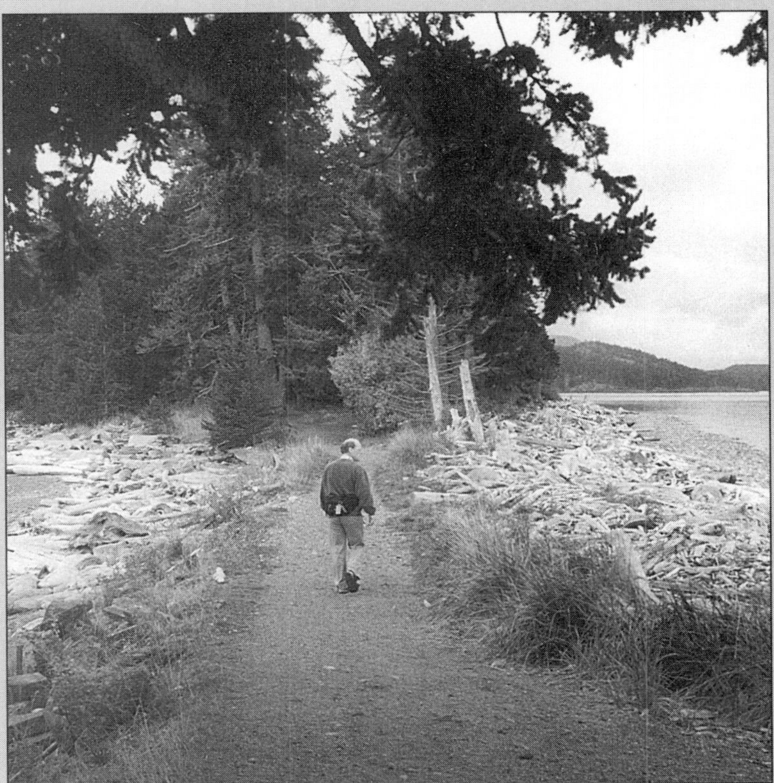

The trail at Rebecca Spit parallels the shoreline of Drew Harbour to the light on the point and then returns along the open water of Sutil Passage.

10. Community Centre Trails (Blenkin Memorial Park) ★	
Trail length	Over 10 km
Time required	2 hours or more
Description	Hikers share these short trails with equestrians and cyclists
Level	Easy
Access	These trails start from the Community Centre on West Road and link with Heriot Bay Road at Animal Farm Road (at Smokey's Bike Shop) and again just west of Smith Road. The trails also have accesses on West Road.

Note: This hike can be combined with the Haskin Farm Trail (hike 11).

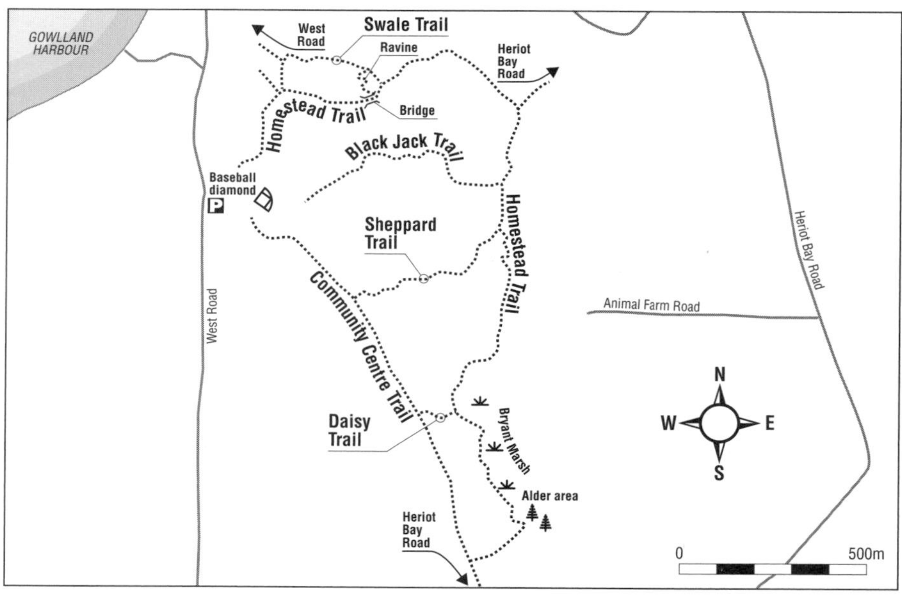

Community Centre Trails

Blenkin Memorial Park was established in 1962, after islanders raised the money to acquire this 16-ha area in memory of John and Mary Blenkin and their two daughters, who were killed in a car crash. The park is on the original homestead of "Black Jack" Bryant and his family.

The park has several trails, with the longest being the Homestead Trail and the Community Centre Trail. The original Bryant home was near the junction of these trails (reportedly near where the large maple tree stands today) and the marsh here was once drained to make way for the family's garden.

The woodsy trails are pleasant and serve an important community function. I found some sections quite soggy, especially on the southeast side. There are picnic tables in a couple of spots and a number of bridges over the seasonal creeks that cross the property.

- The Homestead Trail starts on the north side of the Community Centre and loops around the property until it merges with the Community Centre Trail at the southeast part of its loop. Several trails run off it. Of these, I found the Swale Trail (at the north end of the park) particularly enjoyable with its mixed forest and old stumps sprouting little gardens.
- The Community Centre Trail runs east from the Community Centre and joins with Heriot Bay Road.
- Two trails link the Homestead Trail with West Road: an unnamed trail comes out across the street from 1015 West Road while one end of the Swale Trail comes out opposite 1033 West Road.
- The Black Jack Trail starts at the ballpark and heads north to meet the Homestead Trail.
- The Sheppard Trail (named after Mary Sheppard, Black Jack's wife) and the Daisy trail (named after their daughter) run roughly north-south linking the Homestead Trail with the Community Centre Trail.

11. Haskin Farm Trail ★

Trail length	1.5 km each way
Time required	About 30 minutes each way
Description	This trail follows bridlepaths down to a beach.
Level	Easy
Access	The signed trailhead is on the northeast side of Heriot Bay Road at the intersection of Smith Road. (There is also an unsigned linking trail from the end of Fir Drive.)
Caution	The trail is very easy for its first two-thirds but then drops steeply to the ocean for the final 10 minutes.

Note: This hike can be combined with the Community Centre Trails (hike 10) and the Kay Dubois Trail (hike 12).

This well-established trail proceeds east from Heriot Bay Road down to the beach. After about 500 m, the trail branches off in several directions but the paths all seem to merge again farther on. The trail narrows and crosses a grassy meadow before entering into the forest again. After crossing an old logging road, the trail snakes its way down an escarpment to the beach.

From the beach, there is a beautiful view of Marina and Cortes Islands to the east and the mountains on the mainland behind them. You can return the way you came or walk for about 1 km south along the beach or along a path through the salal, parallel to the beach, until you reach the access off Wa Wa Kie Road. From here, you can continue walking south down Wa Wa Kie Road and take the Kay Dubois Trail (see hike 12) or you can follow nearby Smith Road back up to Heriot Bay Road.

You can also walk north for quite some distance parallel to the beach on a well-used path through the salal. The sound of the water, the fresh sea air and the lovely vistas through the trees make this a very pleasant walk.

12. Kay Dubois Trail ★★★

Trail length	2 km each way
Time required	40 minutes each way
Description	This beautiful path through mature rain forest connects Wa Wa Kie Road to Sutil Road.
Level	Easy
Accesses	A. At the end of Wa Wa Kie Road B. At the end of Sutil Road
Caution	The trail descends steeply from Sutil Road.

Note: This hike can be combined with the Haskin Farm Trail (hike 11) and Francisco Point (hike 13).

The trail is named to honour the memory of a popular, long-time resident of Wa Wa Kie Road. For most of its length, this path follows the southeast coast. As you walk through this splendid second-growth forest, you'll see stumps left over from early logging days.

The path through the alder and fir trees is a rich, soft bed of humus covered by fir needles, with only a few exposed roots to trip you up. Along the way, you glimpse the sea through the trees, only a few short steps away at any time.

If you want to extend this hike, you can walk south along Sutil Road to Francisco Road and then follow the rocky beach to Francisco Point.

13. Cape Mudge Village–Lighthouse–Francisco Point ★★★

Trail length	About 6 km each way (2.5 km if you go only as far as Tsa-Kwa-Luten lodge)
Time required	2 hours each way
Description	A pleasant walk along a trail, past a lighthouse and local lodge, and along a rocky beach

Level	Easy
Access	To the right of the hydrant at the southern end of Green Road in Cape Mudge Village
Cautions	Much of this hike is on land owned by the Cape Mudge Band. Official permission to use these trails should be obtained from the band council (250-285-3316). Watch your footing on the rocky beach between the lodge and Francisco Point.

Walk for 1 km along the trail, until you reach the Tsa-Kwa-Luten Wharfhouse. Another 500 m along a driveway takes you to the Cape Mudge Lighthouse. The trail then winds around behind the lighthouse and follows the shore for another 1 km to the Tsa-Kwa-Luten Lodge. You may choose to return from this point or continue past the lodge and down to the rocky beach, where you can continue on to Francisco Point.

Cormorants, gulls, ducks and herons can be viewed around the offshore rocks. Past the lodge, there are impressive sand cliffs above the beach. You will enjoy expansive views south and west to Campbell River and the Vancouver Island mountains beyond.

SHORE AND ROAD WALKS

It is possible to walk all around the southern end of Quadra by a combination of trail and beach. The total distance from Cape Mudge Village (on the west side of the island) to just north of Wa Wa Kie Beach (on the east side) is about 15 km but you might choose to do only one or more sections of it. This walk would include hikes 11 to 13, using beach and roads as connections. Be very careful to walk beaches only at low tide.

Green Road: Just south of the Quathiaski Cove ferry dock, down to Cape Mudge Village, is a very pleasant walk. The road offers glimpses of the ocean through large trees and the village is picturesque. While there, you might visit the United Church, Quadra's first church (dedicated in 1932) as well as the Kwagiulth Museum and Cultural Centre. The museum contains an intriguing potlatch collection, including some of the artifacts taken by the federal government in 1922, when it enforced its law banning the potlatch. There are also a number of petroglyphs in the grounds around the museum, which were taken from Cape Mudge beaches. For more information, contact the Kwagiulth Museum and Cultural Centre, Box 8, Quathiaski Cove, Quadra Island, BC V0P 1N0; tel.: 250-285-3733.

Wa Wa Kie Road (at the foot of Smith Road)**:** The houses along this pleasant road are interesting and distinctive, and there are glimpses of the sea between the houses all along the walk. This walk can be combined with the walk along the beach north of Wa Wa Kie Road, with the Haskin Farm Trail (hike 11) or with the Kay Dubois Trail (hike 12).

In summer, the cool promise of Morte Lake is a strong draw for hikers following the trail around it.

Granite Bay: The quiet roads in this area are interesting to explore. You can drive or walk down to the dock to look at the boats—some of which are quite old—by turning into the road opposite the access to the Newton Lake trail (hike 1).

AND IF YOU PADDLE . . .

Quadra has the finest lakes in the Gulf Islands. If you hike many of the trails described in this chapter, you will see several of these lakes; however, you will miss some of the loveliest. These are the lakes in Main Lake Chain Provincial Park (off Village Bay Road)—Village Bay Lake, Main Lake and Little Main Lake—which, together, form the largest freshwater lake system on the Gulf Islands.

I strongly recommend spending a day or two exploring these lakes by canoe or kayak. There are a number of excellent places for picnics and several campsites. If the weather's fine, you might like to swim at one of the beaches or off a rocky ledge. If you're feeling ambitious, there's a 2.6-km, water-access-only hike along the Yeatman Portage: a steep, old logging road that links the northeast corner of Main Lake with Yeatman Bay.

If you want to paddle in the ocean, keep in mind that Quadra is surrounded by some of the most treacherous passages on the West Coast, with strong currents affecting most of its coastline. In some channels, these currents reach between 11 and 16 knots, and during tide changes, there are whirlpools and rapids in Seymour Narrows, Hoskyn Channel, Surge (a.k.a. Beazley) Narrows and parts of Okisollo Channel. In addition, winds and waves can pound the southeast side of the island. Except in protected harbours, novice and intermediate kayakers would be wise to head out with a guide. Here are a few of the more benign paddles:

Rebecca Spit: Launch at the boat ramp and paddle around Drew Harbour or along the Quadra shoreline. When it's calm, the Breton Islands east of Open Bay are fun to paddle around. If you have a few days, you might like to venture up the coast through Surge Narrows (at slack current only) to the gorgeous Octopus Islands at the mouth of Waiatt Bay. This is one of the most beautiful places I've ever camped.

Granite Bay: Put in here and paddle out to the Chained Islands. When you reach the last one, you'll see the turbulent water in Seymour Narrows. On the way back to Granite Bay, you might like to paddle into Small Inlet. At the head of the inlet, you can take the portage trail, with or without your boat, from Small Inlet to Waiatt Bay and, on foot, continue up to Newton Lake.

Valdez Road: You can easily launch your boat from the rocky beach at the end of this road. From here, you can paddle south around Open Bay to Hyacinthe Bay, Heriot Bay and, finally, Drew Harbour and Rebecca Spit. Alternatively, you can paddle out to the Breton Islands offshore or north to Village Bay and Bold Bluff Point at the south end of Hoskyn Channel between Quadra and Read Islands.

Salt Spring ISLAND

Salt Spring has everything you could want in a Gulf Island, rolled into one: mountains, lakes, old-growth forest, arbutus and Garry oak groves, farmland, beaches, protected bays and lots of great hiking trails. Most of its shops, eateries and galleries are in Ganges. At 193.5 square km, it is the third largest Gulf Island, but with 9,381 full-time residents, it has about three times the population of Gabriola, the second most-populous island.

Salt Spring Islanders are an eclectic bunch. Many are artists, whose music, writing, films or performances have a worldwide audience. A highlight for many visitors is the extensive crafts and produce market which takes place every Saturday in Ganges from April to mid-October. As well, local and visiting musicians and artists perform and display their work at ArtSpring, the island's beautiful arts centre.

HISTORY

The Tsawout people lived for centuries on Salt Spring and maintain a small, unpopulated reserve on the south coast of the island. Among the first non-aboriginal residents were blacks who fled California and its oppressive laws to come to British Columbia and some of the would-be prospectors who arrived from all over the world to join the 1858 Fraser River gold rush, failed to get rich and ended up on Salt Spring a year later. All the early arrivals acquired unsurveyed land on the island for virtually no money. Most of them established farms—mainly orchards—and sold what they produced on Vancouver Island.

In 1859, Jonathan Begg opened the island's first general store at Fernwood (then called Beggsville), often bartering his groceries, hardware and dry goods for game, furs and other items. Settlements also developed at Beaver Point, Fulford and Burgoyne Bay. In the years that followed, Salt Spring boasted a multicultural population, with immigrants from areas as disparate as the British Isles, Portugal, Scandinavia, Japan and Hawaii.

Salt Spring continues to draw people from afar and now has some of the most expensive real estate in the country. With 48 people per square kilometre, it has also become somewhat urbanized; despite this, islanders voted against becoming a municipality in a 2002 referendum.

With about 7 km of waterfront, moss-covered rocks, and some of the biggest Douglas firs on the island, Ruckle Park is the jewel of Salt Spring. The park receives many day visitors and campers, but once away from the camping and picnic areas, the trails are very quiet. Lynn Thompson

GETTING THERE

Salt Spring has three ferry routes: one travels hourly between Vesuvius Bay (near the north end of the island) and Crofton (an hour south of Nanaimo); a second connects Fulford Harbour (at the south end of the island) and Swartz Bay (near Victoria) every two hours; and the third makes the trip between Long Harbour (5.5 km from Ganges) and Tsawwassen (near Vancouver) twice a day. There are also ferries from Long Harbour to Galiano, Mayne and the Pender Islands once or twice on most days. For more information, obtain a Southern Gulf Islands schedule or contact BC Ferries. You can also get to Salt Spring by floatplane with Harbour Air, Seair Seaplanes, Saltspring Air and Amigo Airways (see Resources, page 235).

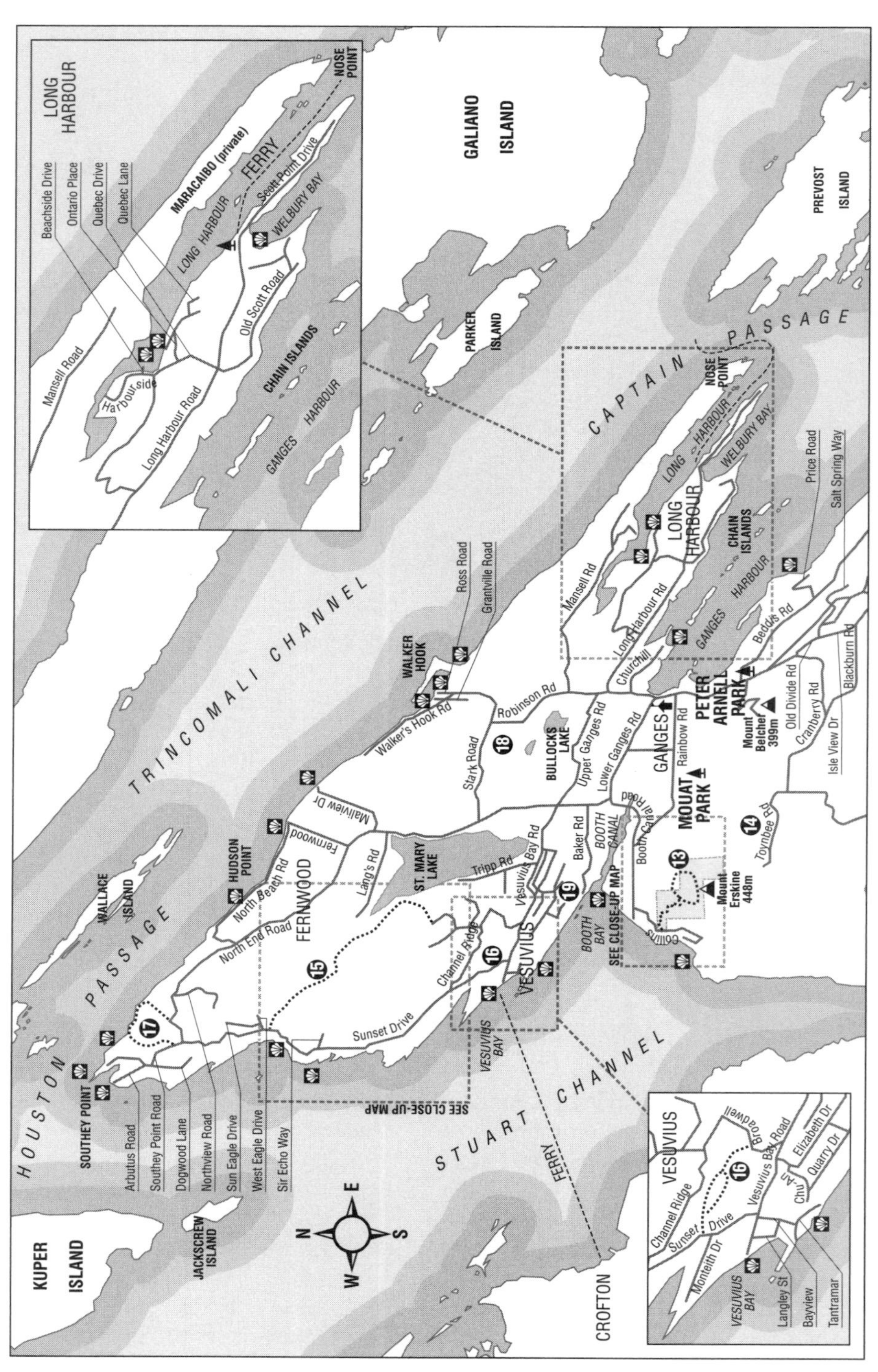

KUPER ISLAND
JACKSCREW ISLAND
WALLACE ISLAND
HOUSTON PASSAGE
TRINCOMALI CHANNEL
GALIANO ISLAND
PARKER ISLAND
PREVOST ISLAND
CAPTAIN PASSAGE
STUART CHANNEL
CROFTON
FERRY
SOUTHEY POINT
Arbutus Road
Southey Point Road
Dogwood Lane
Northview Road
Sun Eagle Drive
West Eagle Drive
Sir Echo Way
SEE CLOSE-UP MAP
HUDSON POINT
North Beach Rd
North End Road
FERNWOOD
Fernwood
Maliview Dr
Lang's Rd
ST. MARY LAKE
Tripp Rd
Sunset Drive
Channel Ridge
VESUVIUS
VESUVIUS BAY
Vesuvius Bay Rd
WALKER HOOK
Walker's Hook Rd
Ross Road
Grantville Road
Stark Road
Robinson Rd
BULLOCKS LAKE
Upper Ganges Rd
Lower Ganges Rd
Baker Rd
BOOTH CANAL
BOOTH BAY
Booth Canal Road
Collins
SEE CLOSE-UP MAP
Mount Erskine 448m
MOUAT PARK
GANGES
Rainbow Rd
PETER ARNELL PARK
Mount Belcher 399m
Toynbee Rd
Old Divide Rd
Cranberry Rd
Isle View Dr
Blackburn Rd
Beddis Rd
Churchill
Long Harbour Rd
Mansell Rd
LONG HARBOUR
GANGES HARBOUR
CHAIN ISLANDS
WELBURY BAY
NOSE POINT
Price Road
Salt Spring Way
LONG HARBOUR
Beachside Drive
Ontario Place
Quebec Drive
Quebec Lane
MARACAIBO (private)
FERRY
Scott Point Drive
WELBURY BAY
Old Scott Road
Mansell Road
Harbourside
Long Harbour Road
CHAIN ISLANDS
GANGES HARBOUR
NOSE POINT
VESUVIUS
Broadwell
Vesuvius Bay Road
Elizabeth Dr
Quarry Dr
Channel Ridge
Sunset Drive
Monteith Dr
VESUVIUS BAY
Langley St
Bayview
Tantramar
N
E
S
W

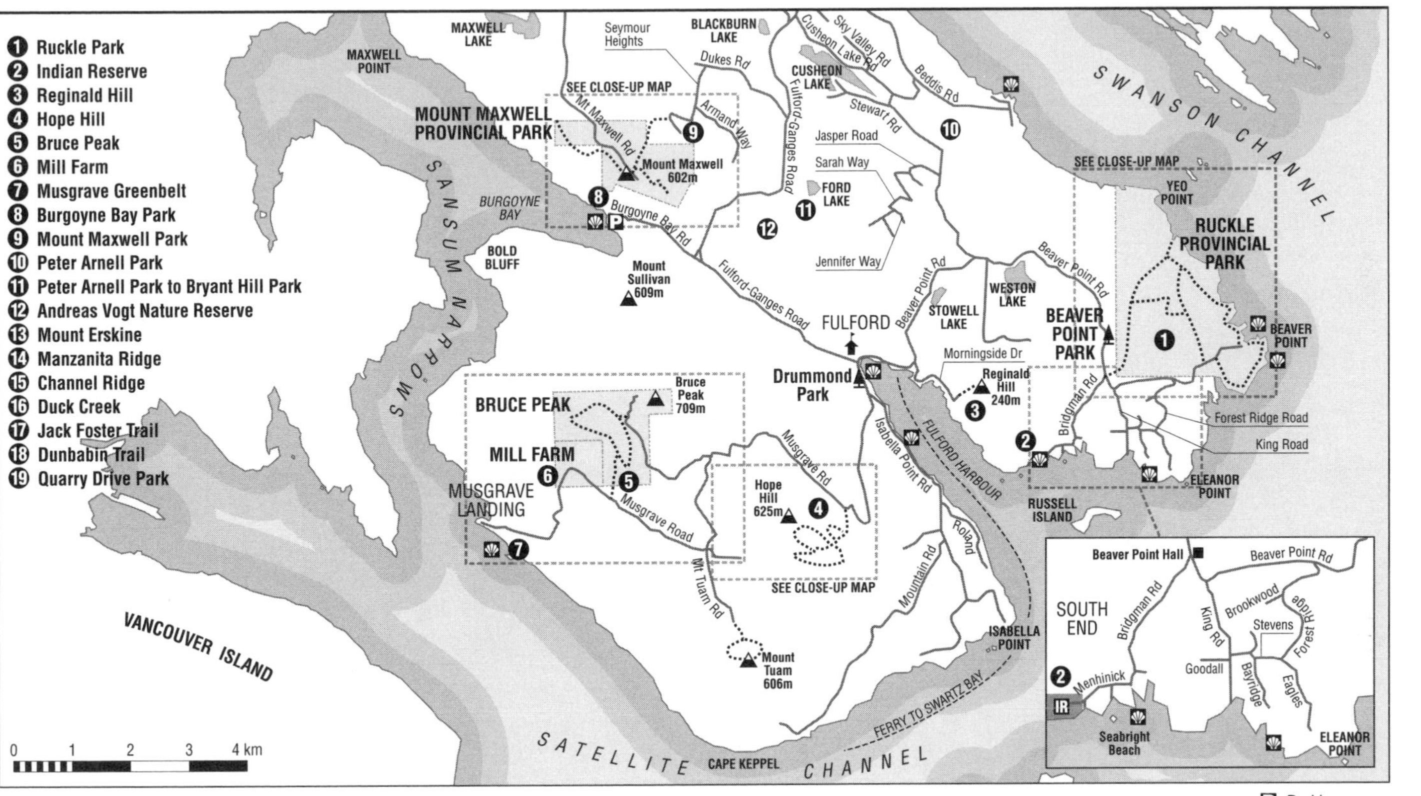

Salt Spring Island

SERVICES AND ACCOMMODATION

Salt Spring's numerous bed and breakfasts range from comfy-casual to luxurious. The island also has a hotel, a number of resorts and inns, two motels, a hostel, two marinas in Ganges and another in Fulford Harbour, private campgrounds, and RV and walk-in camping at Ruckle Provincial Park.

Most of Salt Spring's services are in Ganges. The much smaller village at Fulford Harbour, 17 km away, has a few basic services. For additional information on Salt Spring, contact the Chamber of Commerce's Visitor Information Centre, 121 Lower Ganges Road, Salt Spring Island, BC V8K 2T1; tel.: 250-537-5252; www.saltspringtoday.com. The island's Information Centre also distributes an annual booklet listing accommodations, activities, services and shopping. Free maps of the island are available at the Information Centre, from stores and from realtors.

ESPECIALLY FOR WALKERS

In addition to the shore and road walks outlined near the end of this chapter, consider trying one or more of the following relatively easy walks:

- the shoreline and forest trails in Ruckle Park, especially those in the picnic and camping areas (see hike 1, below)
- the Indian Reserve (see hike 2, page 157)
- Musgrave Greenbelt (see hike 7, page 165)
- the top of Mount Maxwell from the parking area (see hike 9, page 167)
- Peter Arnell Park (see hike 10, page 168)
- Duck Creek (see hike 16, page 177)
- Dunbabin Trail (see hike 18, page 179)

HIKES

The Salt Spring Trail and Nature Club (Box 203, Ganges PO, Salt Spring Island, BC V8K 2V9) maintains many trails on the island and schedules outings every Tuesday from September to June. The Salt Spring Island Parks, Arts and Recreation Commission (250-537-4448) is also a good source of local hiking information.

1. Ruckle Provincial Park ★★★★★	
Trail length	Over 15 km, including 7 km of shoreline
Time required	A full day if you plan to hike all the trails
Description	A walk along the shore that passes coves and bays and through splendid mixed forest
Level	Easy to moderate
Access	The park is 8.5 km from the Fulford ferry terminal (turn right on Beaver Point Road) or 20 km from Ganges (look for signs just north of Fulford on the Fulford–Ganges Road). You can begin walking the trails from any of the following accesses:

	A. a signed trailhead on the left (north) side of the road shortly after you enter the park B. the farm buildings adjacent to the first parking area you reach after entering the park (described below) C. for a shorter walk you can park near one of the picnic or camping areas (located beyond the farm) and follow one of the connecting trails toward the shore D. behind Beaver Point Hall on Beaver Point Road (about 2 km before you reach the Ruckle Park gate)
Facilities	Camping sites, outhouses, picnic tables, benches, water
Cautions	The Ruckle farm is still active. Keep off the fields and farm roads and respect the residents' privacy. Dogs are best left at home; if you bring one, it must be leashed.

Note: In the following description, the numbers correspond to the numbers on the map on page 156.

Ruckle Park has some of the best hiking in the Gulf Islands and is easy to explore. BC Parks has installed many you-are-here signboards at most of the trail accesses and intersections. While you can hike the park's trails in several directions, I think the route described here is the best.

From behind the historic farm buildings (access B), follow the maple-tree-lined trail along the farm fence down to Grandma's Bay and continue southeast along one of the trails through the stands of arbutus and Garry oak, north to Beaver Point. The higher trail is more level but the trail closer to the shore has better views and offers the chance to see waterfowl, seals, otters and other wildlife.

You will reach the walk-in camping area in about 20–30 minutes. From here, I tend to take the rougher trails near the shore, as much as possible, to avoid the largest camping area and enjoy the views of the water. The camping area ends near Beaver Point—so named because the Hudson's Bay Company Steamer, the *Beaver*, went aground here. Steamships stopped at a wharf in the adjoining bay from 1914 to 1951, and there used to be a general store and post office nearby. Nothing remains of this building, but the area is one of Salt Spring's finest picnic spots.

From Beaver Point, trails lead to the park's picnic area. Walk through this, past the signboard greeting visitors who enter the park from the nearby parking area (1), and follow the trail that continues along the shoreline. This 4.4-km trail crosses many rocky headlands and passes tiny coves and bays, ending at Yeo Point. On the way, you can shorten your hike, or vary your route, by taking one of the alternate trails (described below) into the forest at Bear Point (2) or King's Cove (3).

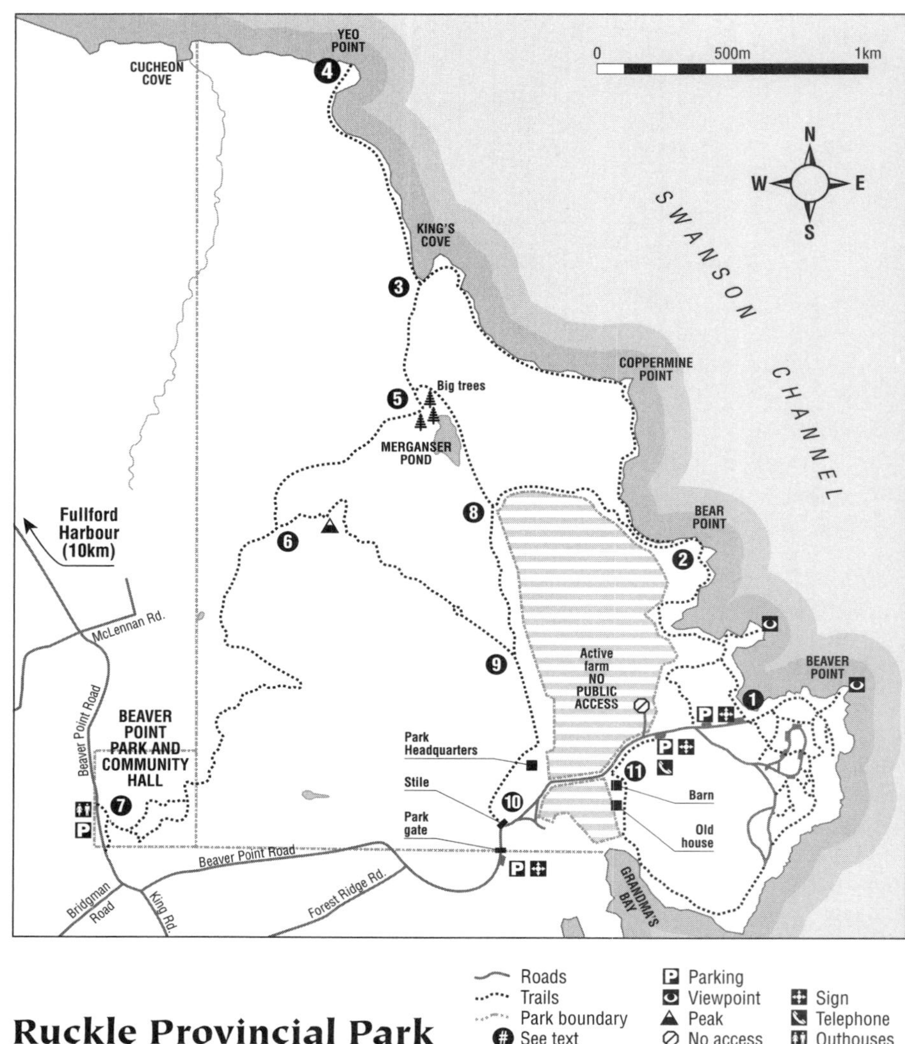

Ruckle Provincial Park

The alternate trail from Bear Point (2), about 1.5 km north of Beaver Point, soon reaches a junction (8). If you turn left (south), the trail will take you to the park's entrance road (near Park Headquarters.) If you go right (north), you will pass Merganser Pond and join a trail (at 5) that links Beaver Point Hall (to the left) and King's Cove (to the right).

King's Cove (3) is named for an 1880s settler, Leon King. Although it was used as a log dump in the 1920s and again in 1946, some of Salt Spring's largest trees still stand nearby. If you take the 3.8-km trail inland from here toward Beaver Point Hall, just past the first trail junction (5), you will find a grove of the largest Douglas firs on

RUCKLE PARK

Ruckle Park gets its name from the Ruckle family who have farmed here ever since Henry Ruckle, an Irish immigrant, arrived on Salt Spring in 1872. About 100 years later, Henry Ruckle's grandson Gordon sold the land to the provincial government but he retained a lifetime tenancy of the buildings and surrounding farmland, which is still being worked. The partly renovated but unoccupied 1870s farmhouse (11) still stands near an orchard that dates back to the 1880s. It is surrounded by other period buildings and equipment retained as a kind of open-air museum.

The Park Headquarters, known locally as the Potato House, has an interesting story. It was built around 1938 for Norman Ruckle (Henry's grandson) and his fiancée. Sadly, the marriage never took place, and for many years, the basement was used to store potatoes—hence the local name for the building. At time of writing, the house was occupied by the farm manager and his family.

Salt Spring, including the one I believe to be the largest—about 8 m in circumference. This tree can be found about 100 m to the southeast of the trail.

You can take the trail to where it emerges behind Beaver Point Hall (7), turn left and walk along Beaver Point Road to the park entrance, or you can follow one of the trails in the park to the left and make your way to Park Headquarters or Bear Point (2).

2. INDIAN RESERVE ★★★★

Trail length	About 1 km each way
Time required	20 minutes each way but you'll want to stay longer
Description	One of the loveliest walks on Salt Spring, passing through mixed forest and along some of the prettiest shoreline on the island
Level	Moderate
Access	At the end of Menhinick Drive (the extension of Bridgman Road, which runs off Beaver Point Road across from Beaver Point Hall)
Cautions	At time of writing, the Tsawout Band allowed visitors; however, be careful to pack out your garbage and do not camp, have a fire or disturb any artifacts you find. Also, respect private property on Wave Hill Farm and in the Reginald Hill Development.

Note: This walk can be combined with hike 3 and/or a walk around Fulford.

The trail in Salt Spring's only Indian Reserve winds through the forest but short side trails lead to secluded, shingle beaches or out to rocky points of land—some of which become islands at high tide. Be sure to take a picnic lunch and enjoy the views of the surrounding islands, boat traffic and the entrance to Fulford Harbour. In the wet season, small streams cross the reserve and cascade into the sea.

Near its end, the trail cuts through the Wave Hill Farm and ends on a road in the Reginald Hill strata development. At time of writing, the owners of the farm allowed hikers to climb over a stile and walk along the edge of the farm property; however, you should check that this is still the case before using this part of the trail.

From Reginald Hill Road, it's an easy walk to Morningside Road and on to Fulford.

3. Reginald Hill ★★★

Trail length	1.5 km each way
Time required	45–60 minutes up, 35–45 minutes down
Description	A very steep, winding ascent through second-growth forest to a lookout with views over the Fulford valley and the San Juan Islands
Level	Strenuous
Elevation	248 m (elevation gain: about 200 m)
Access	Walk through the gate of the Reginald Hill strata development (off the end of Morningside Drive, 1 km from the Fulford ferry terminal). Take the first driveway to the left (100 m beyond the gate) and follow the red metal markers (bearing left) to the trailhead at the edge of an old quarry. There's parking at the end of Morningside Drive. Do not drive into the strata development, as this is a private road and your car could be towed.
Cautions	Much of the surrounding land is private. Please keep to the trail.

Note: This hike can be combined with hike 2 and/or a walk around Fulford.

This trail is in a small public park. Much of the land to the west and south of the park belongs to the strata development, while the land to the east is part of Wave Hill Farm. There's not much of a view until you reach the top. As you near the top, the trail splits and a red arrow directs you to the right. However, both trails meet at the top.

Reginald Hill is not nearly as high as Salt Spring's mountains, so the outlook is more intimate and accessible—perhaps a sparrow's rather than an eagle's view. From here, you have the island's finest view of Fulford Harbour, the nearby Fulford valley and Vancouver Island in the distance. You also can admire Baynes Peak on Mount Maxwell, Bruce Peak (known locally as Mount Bruce) and the San Juan Islands in the east. Return the way you came.

Reginald Hill provides the only public view of the head of Fulford Harbour. From here, you can see how the Fulford Valley cuts a swath through the island to Burgoyne Bay. The snub-nosed peak in the right background is Mount Maxwell, and on the left is Mount Bruce, the island's highest peak. Judy Norget

4. HOPE HILL TRAILS ★★★★

Trail length	7 km
Time required	Half to full day
Description	A hike through fir and cedar forest, and some stands of pine, with excellent views of Fulford Harbour, much of southern Salt Spring, and on a clear day, other southern Gulf Islands, the San Juan Islands, Vancouver, the Coast Mountains and Washington's splendid Mount Baker
Level	Strenuous
Elevation	625 m
Access	On the west side of Musgrave Road, about 3.5 km from Isabella Point Road and 500 m beyond a hairpin bend (about 6 km in total from the Fulford ferry terminal and about 18 km from Ganges)

Cautions	The trails described below and on the map are entirely on Crown land; however, there are a number of off-road motorcycle trails on private property, marked by plastic arrows. Follow only the trails marked with ribbons or red metal markers. There is no public trail to the top of Hope Hill, which is on private property and has no view. Respect the landowner's rights.

Note: In the following description, the numbers correspond to the numbers on the accompanying map.

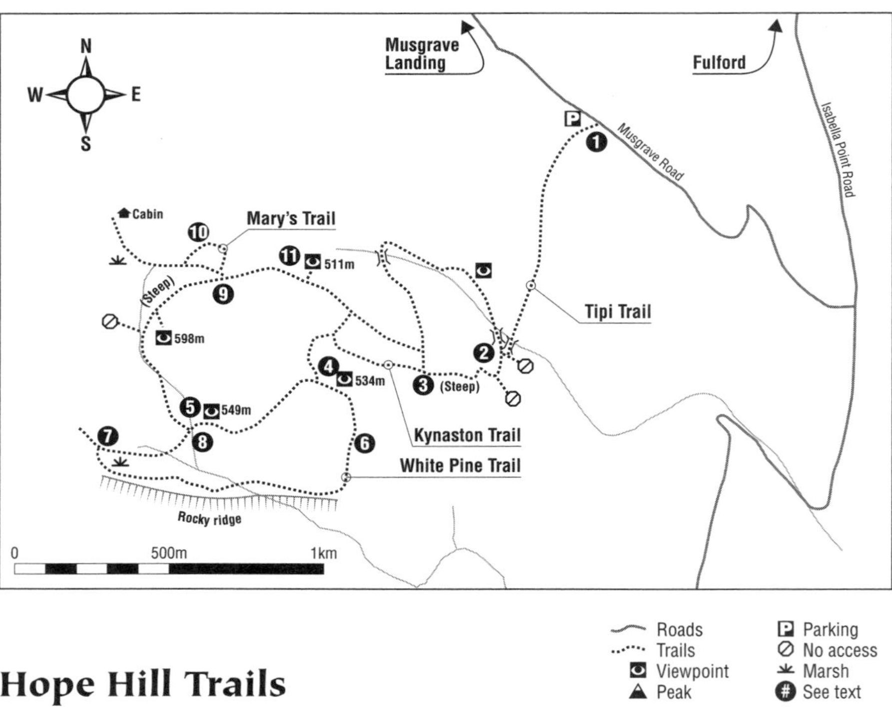

Hope Hill Trails

The trails begin on an old logging road (1). You soon reach a junction (2) marked by a red metal arrow. You can follow either trail, but this description follows the trail to the left and returns down the logging road (on the right).

The trail soon begins to climb steeply. About 25 minutes from the trailhead is a junction (3) with the trail marker on a fallen log. Take the left fork.

Another 10 minutes of steep climbing takes you to the first viewpoint (4). Two trails continue from here, both marked by cairns and ribbons. The shorter trail to the right leads past another, much less interesting viewpoint (5). The second, longer trail, the White Pine Trail (6) on the left, follows a rocky ridge and passes through one of

The top of Hope Hill is a good place to picnic and take in the view of nearby islands. Lynn Thompson

Salt Spring's largest stands of white pine. Both trails emerge on another logging road. If following the White Pine Trail, turn right (at 7) and continue to the junction with the other trail (8), where you turn left. Almost 1 km farther, you will see a short path on the left (9), which leads to a derelict cabin. A little farther along the main trail, look for another short detour on the left; this one leads to the finest view from Hope Hill (11). From here, it's a 45-minute descent down the logging road to the trailhead.

5. Bruce Peak Trails ★★★★	
Trail length	About 6 km
Time required	3–4 hours
Description	A trail through forest with views to the south, east and west. In late spring, look for masses of foxglove in open areas.
Level	Moderate to strenuous, some steep climbs
Elevation	709 m

Access	On the north side of Musgrave Road, 10 km from its junction with Isabella Point Road. Look for a number 1 (as on the accompanying map) on a roadside tree and for red arrows and a red diamond marking the trailhead, which is about 13 km from the Fulford ferry and about 25 km from Ganges.
Cautions	If you dislike rough rocky roads, avoid the 30-minute drive on Musgrave Road to the trailhead. While hiking, stay on the marked trail.

Note: In the following description, the numbers refer to points on the accompanying map (page 163). As you hike, look for the corresponding numbers along the actual trail, which I installed after hearing complaints that people were getting lost on this trail. Hopefully, no one will have removed them. This hike can be combined with hike 6.

From the trailhead (1), the trail climbs steeply for 1 km (30 minutes) to a junction (2). The trail heading left (west) leads to the Mill Farm (see hike 6). To continue to the summit, turn right (east). After 600 m (20 minutes), the trail veers sharply to the north (3). Continuing north, you will have views looking south to Shawnigan Lake and west into Cowichan Bay on Vancouver Island. At the next junction (4), turn right to reach the summit. From here, there are exceptional views east, of the Coast Mountains, Mount Baker, the Gulf and San Juan Islands, and Fulford Harbour below.

You can return the way you came or continue past the last trail junction (4), following an old logging road west through the bush. After 1.6 km (at 6), the trail swerves toward the southeast, eventually leading back to the junction (at 2) from where you can descend to Musgrave Road or take the trail to the right (west) to the Mill Farm Regional Park Reserve (hike 6).

If going to the Mill Farm, you will reach another trail junction (7) after 15–20 minutes. Turn left. Once you're done exploring the CRD park reserve, you can follow Musgrave Road (left from the Mill Farm gate) about 1 km back to your vehicle.

6. The Mill Farm ★★★

Trail length	About 4 km if you follow all the old logging roads
Time required	Plan to spend at least 2 hours in the park reserve; 4 hours if you plan to climb Bruce Peak (see hike 5).
Description	Old roads on a 1919 homestead lead to ponds, viewpoints and old-growth forest.
Level	Moderate

Elevation	About 550 m (elevation gain: about 175 m)
Access	On the north side of Musgrave Road, about 11 km from its junction with Isabella Point Road. Park near the locked gate to the park reserve or 100 m farther along, in a driveway on the opposite side of the road (which is also part of the park).
Caution	If you don't like driving on rough, rocky roads, avoid Musgrave Road.

Note: This hike can be combined with hike 5.

To me, the Mill Farm is a very special place and I encourage you to wander along the many old roads criss-crossing the property and explore the sites where the previous owners had built dwellings. These were usually near some source of water and had viewpoints. In many places, shrubs and plants that these modern-day homesteaders planted still flower. In one spot, you'll even find a couple of palm trees.

Here's the route I usually take: Start at the parking space 100 m beyond the park gate and walk down this driveway to one of the homestead sites. This short walk takes you by a large wetland area and to a knoll that sports daffodils in the spring. Then return the way you came and walk back along the road to the main gate.

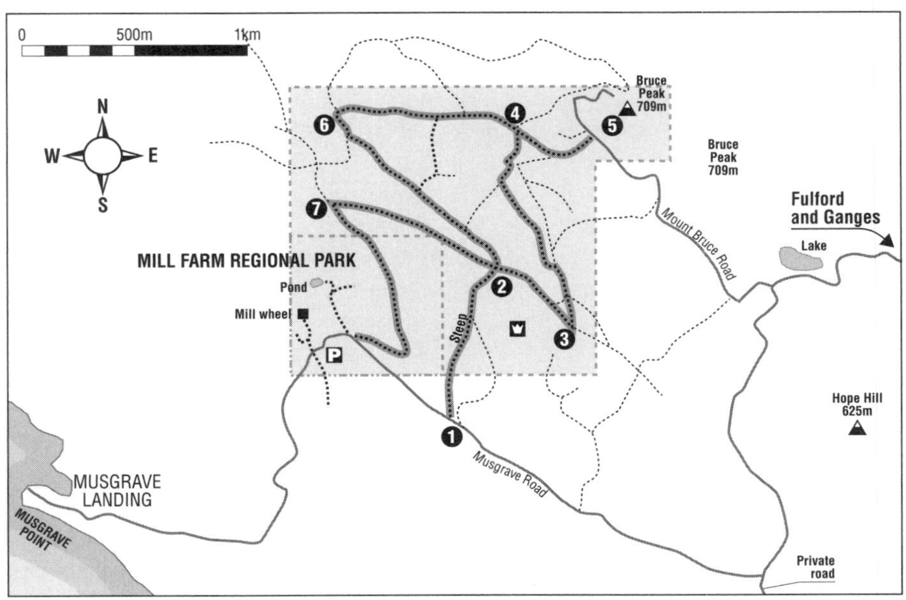

Bruce Peak Trails and Mill Farm

Roads
Trails
Minor trails
Park boundary
Crown land
Peak
Parking
See text

Mill Farm Park reserve

The 65-ha Mill Farm Park Reserve is the site of the 1919 homestead of Arnold Smith, one of three brothers who came to Salt Spring from Lancashire, England. The entrance to Smith's homesite and the remains of his huge, old millwheel is 130 m beyond the park gate.

In 1981, eight people bought the property, planning to build separate homes on the communally owned land. Several cabins were built, although only one couple lived on the property full time. By the early 1990s, some of the owners had changed and there was pressure to sell the land. As soon as it hit the market, it attracted the interest of a logging company interested in the property's 26 ha of old-growth fir. The fledgling Salt Spring Island Conservancy mobilized support to persuade the provincial and regional governments to buy the property and preserve it as a park. More than $150,000 was raised toward the purchase price of $800,000 and the farm became a Capital Regional District (CRD) park reserve in 1996.

Once through the gate, you'll find yourself at the junction of two roads. The one on the left stays on lower ground and eventually leads to a pond and one of the house sites. I recommend taking the road to the right, which climbs about 125 m to the top of the reserve and eventually joins the trail system leading to the top of Bruce Peak (see hike 5). Along the way, you'll pass old house sites with some views looking west to Separation Point and Cowichan Bay on Vancouver Island. About halfway up, an offshoot goes to the right and leads to a house site where a stone worker built a number of rock walls. Just before the gate separating the Mill Farm and the Crown land, you'll pass a spring-fed pond on your right.

From the gate, you can continue to the trails leading to the top of Bruce Peak. In a few minutes, you'll pass a holly tree on your right and soon after that you will reach a lookout that gives you a good view of Cowichan Bay. To the left of this viewpoint is a large Pacific dogwood, which is bedecked with delicate blossoms in the spring. Look for a trail leading off to the right (7). Follow this trail for 15–20 minutes, until you reach a junction (2) of trails leading up Bruce Peak (see hike 5).

If you don't want to climb Bruce Peak, you can return the way you came, exploring some of the other trails on the way. You might try the other road, at the entrance gate to the park reserve, which leads to a pond and to another road that heads back toward the farm site and the remains of the mill. You can also get to this by turning right on Musgrave Road and walking for about 130 m to a driveway on your right. Follow it to the farm site, where you'll also find the remains of old farm equipment, as well as trees, planted by the Smiths, that still bear fruit today.

7. Musgrave Greenbelt ★★

Trail length	2 km
Time required	1 hour or more
Description	A forest walk to a seasonal waterfall, as well as shore access
Level	Easy
Access	The unsigned entrance to the Greenbelt is a driveway on the left (south) side of Musgrave Road, almost at its end, about 13 km from its junction with Isabella Point Road (about 200 m before Musgrave Landing). Park on the grassy fields that make up much of the Crown land.
Cautions	Do not drive along Musgrave Road if you don't like rough, rocky roads.

Notes: The waterfall is on private property. The current owner does not mind hikers visiting the waterfall but the property should be respected; stay on the logging road. Other old roads in this area also cross private property and you should not follow them without permission from the property owners.

Walking in this 34-ha piece of Crown land feels more like exploring than hiking. If you walk straight ahead from where you turned off Musgrave Road, you will be following a roadway leading down to a beach. At very low tides, it is possible to walk left (south) along the shore as far as Cape Keppel, where you can access another trail connecting with Mountain Road. However, be sure that you have lots of time between tides if you decide to attempt it.

If you follow the logging road to the left (east) of where you turned into the Greenbelt, you will soon reach a stream crossing the road (dry in summer, a torrent in winter). Cross the creek and look for a trail almost immediately to your left. This will take you to the seasonal waterfall. This lush spot is very beautiful, although the thick growth of trees keeps out the sun. Return the way you came.

8. Burgoyne Bay Provincial Park ★★★

Trail length	Up to 20 km, depending on route
Time required	Up to a day or more, depending on route
Description	A number of trails follow the shoreline on both sides of Burgoyne Bay, while others climb Mount Sullivan to the south and Mount Maxwell to the north.
Level	Moderate to strenuous
Access	The large parking area at the end of Burgoyne Bay Road

In 1999, the Texada Land Corporation, a logging company, acquired 2,024 ha (about one-tenth of all the land on Salt Spring). This led to wide-scale protests and a massive local drive to protect the land. In 2001, the province, the Land Conservancy of British Columbia and the Capital Regional District (CRD) bought 688.5 ha from the logging company in the Burgoyne Valley, Mount Maxwell, Bruce Peak and Mount Tuam areas. Of the total purchase, 475 ha around Burgoyne Bay were earmarked for a new provincial park. Although legislation for this park had not been passed at time of writing, everyone on Salt Spring considered the park a "done deal."

While islanders have used the hiking trails in this area for many years to access the shoreline of Burgoyne Bay and to climb the nearby mountains, at time of writing, the park was still in its planning stages and an official trail system had yet to be developed. Use the following suggestions to start exploring or ask locals for up-to-date trail information.

From the parking lot, you can follow old logging roads on the north side of the bay for 30–40 minutes before reaching a piece of private property. At this point, either return the way you came or try another logging road in the park. If you try to return along animal trails that follow the shore, be aware that the terrain is treacherous.

Other logging roads from the parking lot lead toward Mount Maxwell Provincial Park above. However, as this involves crossing an ecological reserve, BC Parks would prefer that you access Mount Maxwell from above (see hike 9). Highlights of the higher ground are the many erratics (boulders left behind thousands of years ago

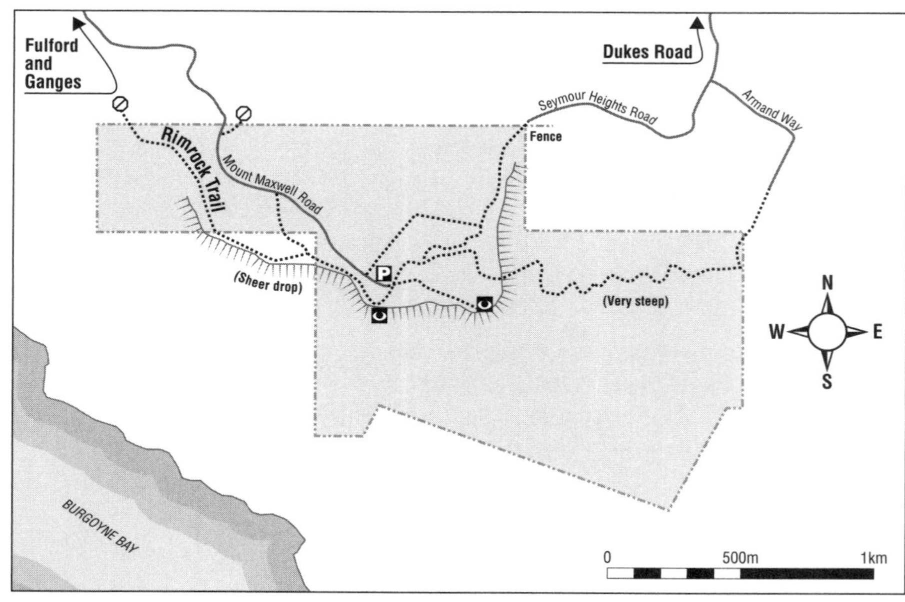

Mount Maxwell Provincial Park

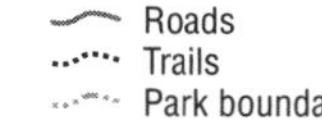

Viewpoint
No access

by glacial action) and the largest arbutus tree on Salt Spring, with several of its branches held up by one of the erratics.

South from the parking lot, trails lead up toward Mount Sullivan and, lower down, along the southern shoreline of the bay. You can walk for up to an hour, alternately along the beach and just above the shoreline, until you reach another piece of private property toward Bold Bluff Point.

9. MOUNT MAXWELL PROVINCIAL PARK ★★★★

Trail length	6–15 km, depending on route chosen
Time required	2 hours or more, depending on route chosen
Description	A steady climb through second-growth fir forest to the summit of Mount Maxwell (known as Baynes Peak), which offers magnificent views
Level	Moderate; some steep sections
Elevation	593 m (elevation gain: 175 m)
Access	A. From the end of Seymour Heights. To get here from the Fulford–Ganges Road, go northwest on Dukes Road (about 6 km from Ganges or 7.5 km from the Fulford ferry terminal) until you reach Seymour Heights (about 1.8 km). The trailhead is on your right at the end of Seymour Heights (another 1.5 km) and is marked with red ribbons and metal markers. There's no parking at the trailhead but you can park at the corner of Armand Way and Seymour Heights (700 m from the trailhead). B. From the end of Armand Way. This trail eventually merges with the trail that starts at access A.
Facilities	Benches, picnic tables, outhouse at the top
Cautions	Beware of the steep drop-offs at the viewpoints.

Many people consider the views from Baynes Peak as Salt Spring's best. Part of a well-signed 199-ha provincial park, it is a popular destination for tourists who can drive up the mountain and enjoy the expansive views from the parking lot at the top. Others walk from the top along the fence-line trail that leads down to what locals call the Rimrock Trail, a beautiful path that passes rock outcrops before descending toward the ecological reserve and Burgoyne Bay. But most hikers take one of the accesses listed above and climb to the summit.

For most of the way, the trail from Seymour Heights (access A) passes through a mainly second-growth Douglas fir forest. The trail from Armand Way (access B) passes through wetter terrain that nourishes giant cedar and swordferns. I prefer the Armand Way access but both are delightful.

From Baynes Peak at the top of Mount Maxwell you can see the full length of beautiful Fulford Valley. Judy Norget

Just before you reach the summit of Mount Maxwell, you will come to a junction. The trail to the right (west) leads up to the parking lot, while the trail to the east descends steeply for about 600 m (10 minutes) to a large, moss-covered bluff from which there is a 180-degree view. To the north, in the far distance, is Vancouver; to the east is Mount Baker and to the south are the Olympic Mountains in Washington state. From the top of Mount Maxwell, you can look over the Fulford Valley all the way to Fulford Harbour, Burgoyne Bay and the boat activity on Sansum Narrows and in Maple Bay on Vancouver Island.

There are many other unmarked trails in the park. Some of these can be confusing, so use your compass if you explore them.

10. Peter Arnell Park ★

Trail length	About 3 km
Time required	45 minutes
Description	A short hike over moss-covered rocky terrain through young forest
Level	Easy
Access	Take Stewart Road south from Cusheon Lake Road for about 1.5 km. The signed trailhead is on your left (east) at a wide bend in the road. The trail comes out again on Stewart Road, about 200 m south, just past the sign for Peter Arnell Park on the west side of the road.

This is a pleasant, if unspectacular, hike in a 13-ha park that commemorates a surveyor who died accidentally and whose family had close connections with Salt Spring. The park extends on both sides of Stewart Road but the main trail is on the east side of the road. The trail crosses moss-covered, rocky terrain. There is a loop at the southeast end of the trail and glimpses of Ganges Harbour to the northeast. When you reach a private driveway, return along the trail the way you came. The sign-posted section of the park on the west side of Stewart Road has little trail but is an access point for hike 11.

11. PETER ARNELL PARK TO BRYANT HILL PARK ★★

Trail length	3.5 km to Bryant Hill Park. There are another 6–8 km of trails within this park.
Time required	75 minutes each way, more if combined with the trails in Bryant Hill Park or with hike 12
Description	Steep climb with some views to a 32-ha park
Level	Strenuous. The trails in the park are of moderate difficulty.
Access	A. From Peter Arnell Park (1.6 km from the junction of Cusheon Lake and Stewart Roads), the trailhead leading to Bryant Hill Park is on the left (south) side B. If you prefer to avoid the steep climb to Bryant Hill Park, you can drive directly there. Take Jasper Road (off Stewart Road) and continue along Jennifer Way to Sarah Way. Proceed almost to the end of Sarah Way, turn right on a gravel driveway, and drive 1 km to its end, where you'll find a small parking area. Beside this, you will see the gate for Bryant Hill Park. C. From the meeting point of Jasper Road and Jennifer Way marked, at time of writing, by rusting diesel tanks

Note: This hike can be combined with hike 12. As the first part of the hike below is steep and not as interesting, I recommend that you take access B and spend more time exploring the trails on the higher ground in the park, the neighbouring Crown land and nearby Andreas Vogt Nature Reserve.

From access A, the first half of the trail is fairly steep but easy to follow, crossing a number of driveways. Look for the red flagging and continue to take the trail facing you, rather than the logging road offshoots you'll cross from time to time.

After about half an hour of walking, just past a green metal bridge, you'll reach a signboard with a map of the trail and the park. This is very close to access C (where

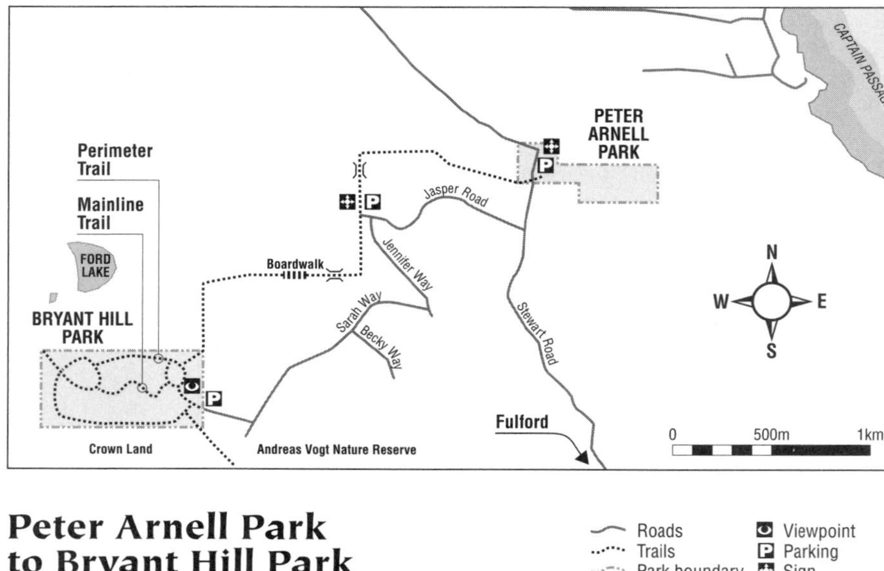

Peter Arnell Park to Bryant Hill Park

Jasper Avenue meets Jennifer Way). Within another 5 minutes, you'll pass a picnic table before reaching a viewpoint over Ganges Harbour to Galiano Island in the distance. Shortly beyond the viewpoint, you will cross a second green metal bridge. At time of writing, the trail from here was overgrown and somewhat difficult to follow. If you have a compass, keep in mind that the trail to the park goes mainly south and west.

Soon after the second bridge, you'll reach a long boardwalk. Follow it to its end and then continue on the trail west. You'll see a little bench in about a minute and the trail starts to descend fairly steeply. It joins an overgrown logging road, but after a few metres, it leaves the road to continue on the left (south). It meets another overgrown logging road but doesn't cross it. Make sure that you don't either. The trail is now heading west and still descending. By the time you have walked about 10 minutes from the boardwalk, you will notice that the trail crosses short wooden bridges over seasonal creeks.

After a few more minutes of walking, you'll cross another overgrown logging road. Don't take it. The trail continues to descend directly ahead of you, in a southwesterly direction. It now switchbacks down a steep hillside. Follow the trail's switchbacks and don't be tempted by animal paths that continue off at their corners.

After this, the trail crosses an area of scrub, continuing south and west. When you reach yet another logging road, turn left (south). A few metres farther, turn right at the cairn. This is the lowest point in the trail's descent. From here, the trail is much easier to find. It now climbs steeply to the park, in a southerly direction.

As you can see on the accompanying map, there are several trails that circle and criss-cross Bryant Hill Park. They have some glimpses of views through the trees.

The Perimeter Trail (about 1.5 km in length)—the one with the most views—circles the park and will take you about 30 minutes to walk. The Mainline Trail (about 500 m long) goes through the middle of the park, following an old logging road, and will take about 15 minutes. You can also link up with the trails in the Andreas Vogt Nature Reserve and the adjacent Crown land (see hike 12).

ROQUEFORT ANYONE?

Bryant Hill Park is unofficially named after Colonel Jasper and Dr. Meta Bryant, a remarkable couple who retired to Salt Spring. During the 1920s, and perhaps right into the 1950s, they kept a herd of goats, making cheese each day and aging it in a cave on their property. With advice from Professor Golding of UBC, they developed a prize-winning Roquefort-type cheese, which they shipped to Spencer's—then Victoria's largest store.

Although they eventually got a phone, the Bryants led a spare lifestyle, relying on a generator for power and using bicycles to get around the island after giving up their car to save gas during the war. Although supposedly retired, Meta still worked in the hospital in the late 1940s. In the 1970s, their deserted goat farm became a hippie commune.

12. ANDREAS VOGT NATURE RESERVE ★★★

Trail length	4 km, more if combined with hike 11
Time required	1–2 hours, more if combined with hike 11
Description	A walk over rocky knolls in Garry oak and arbutus habitat with views of most of Salt Spring's peaks and the San Juan Islands
Level	Moderate
Access	Take Jasper Road (off Stewart Road) and continue along Jennifer Way to Sarah Way. Near the end of Sarah Way, turn right on a gravel road and drive 1 km to the small parking area at its end. Next to the parking area is a gate for Bryant Hill Park (see hike 11). Take the trail to the left (south) of the gate and, after a few minutes, look for flagging on the left, just past a stream bed that marks the trail to the nature reserve.

In 2002, Cordula Vogt and her mother, Oda Nowrath, gave this 29-ha piece of land to the Salt Spring Island Conservancy to preserve, with the hope that future generations will enjoy it as much as they have. It is named for Cordula's late husband.

The loop trail into the property passes a huge cedar and many fine firs on the adjacent piece of Crown land which, unlike the park and the nature reserve, was not logged in the 1980s. The trail soon climbs to the first of many rocky knolls that offer views of islands and mountains in the distance.

Stay on the marked trail, to preserve the vegetation on this beautiful piece of land. You can complete a loop trail, returning to where you started, or carry on to trails in the Crown land that eventually lead to a trail junction in Bryant Hill Park, where you turn right to return to the parking area. At time of writing, the Crown land trails were poorly marked and somewhat confusing, although the island's trailblazers were planning to improve them. Avoid them until this happens (ask locals for an update), unless you have a good sense of direction and lots of time to find your way out of the thick forest.

13. Mount Erskine Trails ★★★

Trail length	2.5 km return
Time required	2.5 hours return
Description	A steep climb through arbutus groves and some Douglas fir to a lookout
Level	Strenuous; some very steep, slippery sections
Elevation	448 m at the summit (The public trail leads to a lower lookout just below the summit, which is on private property.)
Access	A. The east side of Collins Road, 700 m from the point at which Rainbow Road becomes Collins Road. Look for the red diamond sign on a tree on the left (east) side of the road (1). B. The second trailhead (2) is just a bit farther north (closer to Rainbow Road). This trail is a bit less steep.
Cautions	There are slippery sections, ridges and sharp drop-offs. Keep to the trail indicated by the red metal markers. The summit of Mt. Erskine is on private property.

Note: In the following description, the numbers correspond to numbers on the accompanying map. This hike can be combined with hike 14.

From either access, the trail is steep, rocky and slippery. The two trails merge after about 20 minutes of walking (at 3). This part of the trail is called the Jack Fisher Trail, after the local resident who donated the land.

After about 45 minutes of hiking, you will reach a junction (4). Turn right. This is the beginning of a loop and you will return to this junction from the other direction

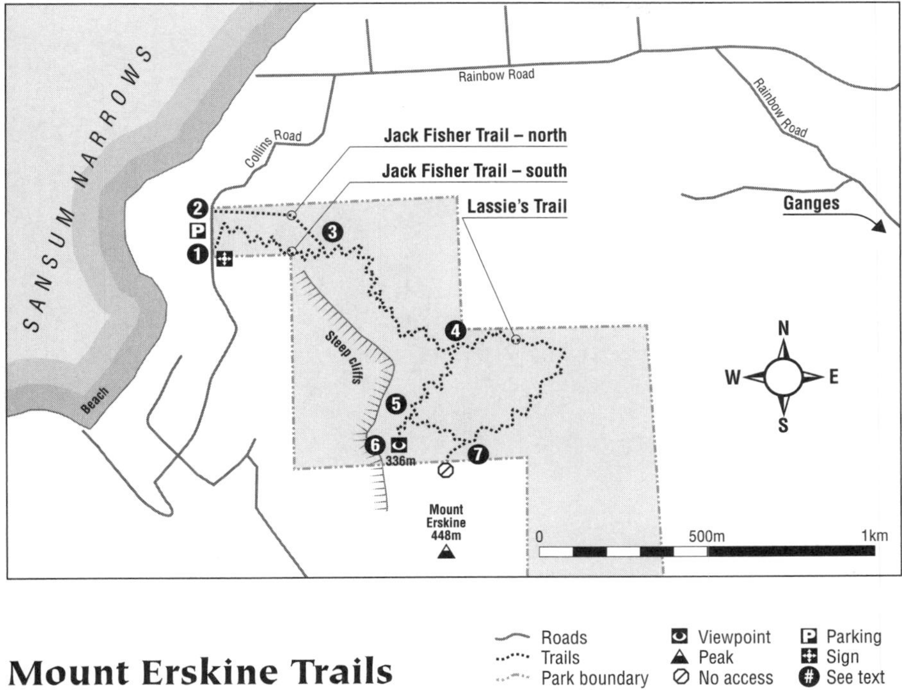

Mount Erskine Trails

on your return. As you continue, look for small elfin doors placed in front of large rocks or tree stumps. In recent years, several of these charming miniatures have been anonymously installed, often accompanied by curtained windows, baskets of firewood and other accoutrements.

After another 20 minutes, you will reach another junction (5). Continue straight ahead to the viewpoint (6). It looks west over Sansum Narrows; north to Tent, Kuper and Galiano Islands; north over Booth Bay and Saint Mary Lake on Salt Spring; and both west and north over Vancouver Island. At time of writing, a public trail was being planned to connect this area with Manzanita Ridge (see hike 14).

If you decide not to continue to Manzanita Ridge, return to the main trail and turn right when you get to the junction (5). Be sure to turn left when you get to the next junction (7), as the trail to the right is on private property. This section of trail is called Lassie's Trail, after Lassie Dodds, who laid out some of the island's hiking trails. From here, make your way to the beginning of the loop (4) and return the way you came. At the next junction (3), you can take the alternate trail down and then walk along the road to your vehicle.

Remnants of Salt Spring's early architecture still exist. Fortunately, they aren't all this dilapidated. K. Hagerty

14. Manzanita Ridge ★★★

Trail length	3 km; more if combined with Mount Erskine Trails
Time required	1–2 hours; more if combined with Mount Erskine Trails
Description	A very steep climb to a 20-ha nature reserve with views toward Galiano Island and the Shepherd Hills
Level	Moderate to strenuous
Access	North side of Toynbee Road (less than 1 km from where Cranberry Road becomes Mount Maxwell Road). Look for the trailhead just past the gate for the tree farm at 101 Toynbee Road.
Caution	Stay on the well-marked trail to the reserve, as the adjoining property and the nearby hydro access road are private. Some of the land adjoining Manzanita Ridge (including the summit of Mount Erskine) is also privately owned.

This 20-ha piece of land was acquired by the Salt Spring Island Conservancy in 2003 from long-time resident Martin Williams. It includes beautiful rocky terrain, a stand of 200-year-old Douglas firs, and has views over Trincomali Channel to Galiano Island and over the Shepherd Hills to Sansum Narrows. The trail in the nature reserve connects with well-established trails that cross Crown land, and in the future, will connect with the Mount Erskine trails that lead down to Collins Road (see hike 13).

15. Channel Ridge Trails ★★★

Trail length	4.5 km each way
Time required	80 minutes each way
Description	A ridge walk through Douglas fir and arbutus forest with occasional views
Level	Easy to moderate with some steep sections
Elevation	265 m
Accesses	A. North end: Across from 1110 Sunset Drive (just south of West Eagle Road). The trailhead (1) is marked with a red metal marker. There's limited parking along the edge of Sunset Drive. B. South end: On the right (east) side of Canvasback Road (off Broadwell Road, 1.7 km from Vesuvius Bay Road). You'll see two grey concrete water tanks on your right as you drive up the road. The trailhead (9) is just to the right of the second water tank, about 400 m from the intersection of Canvasback and Broadwell Roads. You must park on the side of the road, where there is limited parking.
Caution	Although there are many trails through the 600-ha Channel Ridge development, this description concentrates chiefly on the main trail through the publicly owned lands that make up the watershed for Saint Mary Lake. At time of writing, Channel Ridge Properties welcomed hikers to use most of the other trails at their own risk. However, as the development proceeds, some of the trails will be closed or moved. Observe signs posted throughout the trail system, for your own safety and so the developer will continue to allow the public to use these trails.

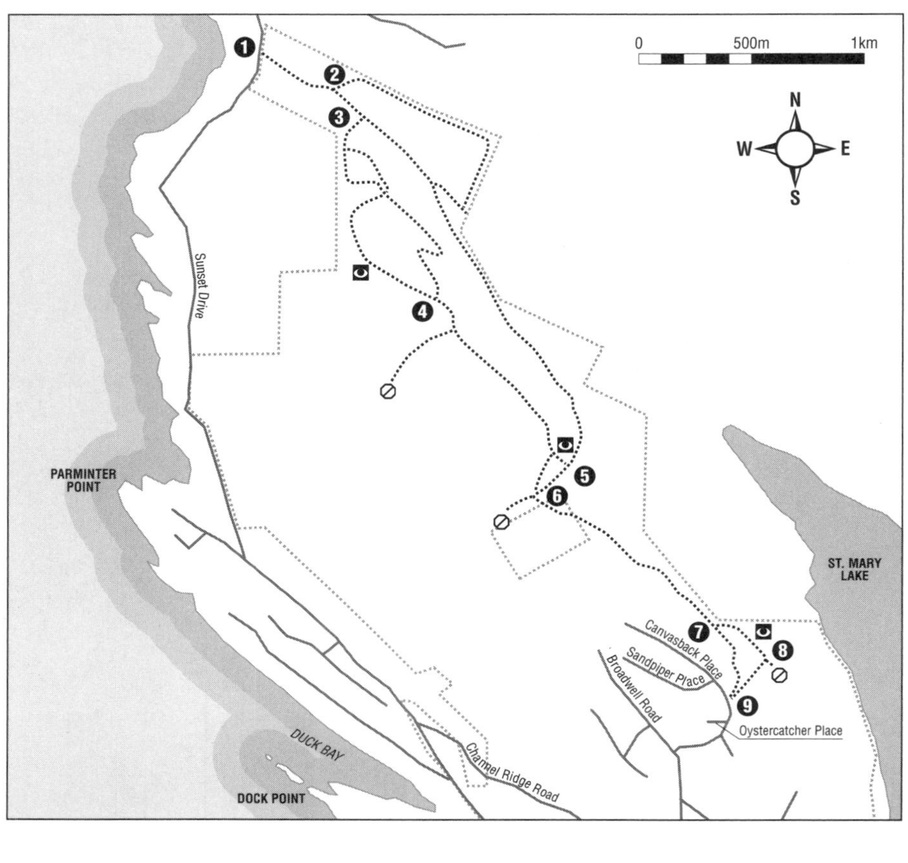

Channel Ridge Trails

Channel Ridge is formed of sandstone and conglomerate rock. Much of the area between the two access points is watershed and is owned by the Salt Spring Water Preservation Society.

From Sunset Drive (access A), the trail rises steeply up an old logging road. Keep to the right (west) at the first intersection (2), to stay on the main trail. About 10 minutes from the trailhead, you'll cross a field. From here, the trail begins to climb quickly and, soon, you'll pass through wooden gateposts.

You'll pass another junction (3) with a trail heading off to the left (east). As you can see on the map, this trail follows a parallel course to the viewpoint (5) that overlooks the north end of Saint Mary Lake and the Coast Mountains and Mount Baker in the distance. However, it is less used and often overgrown, so I recommend continuing on the main trail.

After about 25 minutes of hiking, you will come to a junction with another trail on the right (4). Continue straight ahead, as the other trail returns the way you've already come. (This trail leads through the development's private land and has views west toward Chemainus and Ladysmith, on Vancouver Island. It is also a good alternate trail to take on your return.)

You will reach another major junction about 3 km from the trailhead, near a boggy area (6). Turn left here, walking by the swampy area, and then follow the trail markings for the rest of the way. Toward the end of the trail, there's a junction (7) with a trail heading left. This trail leads to a lookout with a view of Saint Mary Lake and Galiano Island and then continues to the concrete water tank (9); the trail straight ahead is less interesting but ends in approximately the same place. You can return to Sunset Drive the way you came or by using one of the alternate routes mentioned above and indicated on the map.

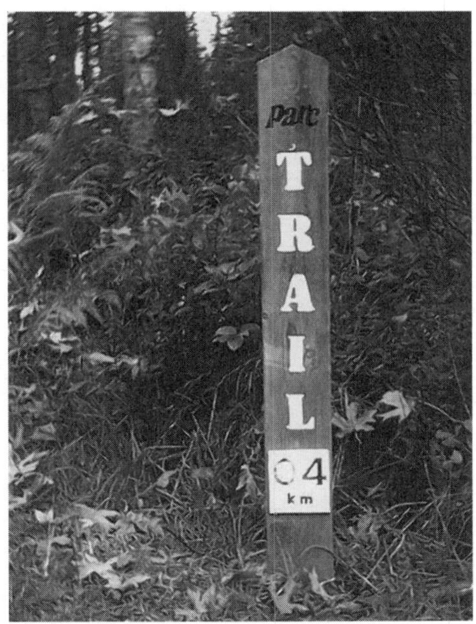

Plans are underway to mark Salt Spring's trails, beach accesses and local parks with these signs. Philip Grange

16. Duck Creek ★★★

Trail length	1.5 km each way
Time required	45 minutes
Description	A pleasant stroll along a creek
Level	Easy
Access	A. On the east side of Sunset Drive less than 500 m from Vesuvius Bay Road (directly across from the mailboxes just south of 208 Sunset Drive) B. On the west side of Broadwell Road just north of Vesuvius Bay Road

The trail stretches from Sunset Drive east to Broadwell Road and includes a series of stairs, bridges, viewpoints and rest spots. As it follows the creek, it passes through some old-growth fir and cedar forest. Salmon-enhancement workers adjusted the flow of water in the creek to create rearing pools and spawning beds for salmon and steelhead trout. The creek is a rushing stream in the rainy months but dwindles to a trickle in the summer.

17. Jack Foster Trail (Southey Point) ★★★

Trail length	4 km round trip (at low tide)
Time required	70–80 minutes total
Description	A circle route that begins in a lovely wooded area, continues on the beach along Trincomali Channel and returns along a road
Level	Moderate
Access	A. On the east side of Southey Point Road at its junction with Sunset Drive and North End Road. The trailhead is marked with a red metal marker. There's limited parking just across the road but be sure not to block any driveways. B. From the right (east) side of the driveway to the farm at 2521 North End Road
Cautions	This hike must be done at very low tide (definitely not more than 0.5 m). Be careful on the steep descent to the beach on the first part of the hike. Be sure to stay on the trail and off the neighbouring private property. The last section of the beach is covered with large boulders, which you will have to scramble across. Be careful, as the rocks can be slippery. If you have a dog, keep it leashed on the last part of the trail, as you will be passing a sheep farm.

From access A, the first section of this hike is through a fine forest of arbutus, cedar and fir. This area can be quite wet at times. It will take you about 20–25 minutes to reach the beach.

When you reach the shore, you can follow it in either direction; however, if you turn left (toward Southey Point), you cannot leave the shore without trespassing on private property. So turn right (south) and walk along the beach for about 1 km (20 minutes), until you reach a small breakwater. Along the way, you will have views of other islands in Trincomali Channel: the Secretaries to the northeast, Wallace directly to the east and Galiano behind it.

You could choose to turn around at this point, as you have just completed the most beautiful part of the hike. However, just before the breakwater, a boulder stairway leads to a public trail that joins North End Road (access B). The trail comes out just before the end of the driveway to 2521 North End Road. Continue along the driveway to the road, turn right (west) and walk about 1 km to the trailhead on Southey Point Road.

18. DUNBABIN TRAIL ★★★

Trail length	1.6 km return
Time required	30 minutes return
Description	A pleasant trail following a small creek through rain forest
Level	Easy
Access	A. On the south side of Stark Road, 500 m west of Robinson Road B. On the west side of Robinson Road, 200 m south of Stark Road

While this trail is much shorter than any of the other hikes, I have included it here because of its beauty. The walk features large cedars, firs and ferny hollows. It is accessible to most walkers and is well worth the visit.

19. QUARRY DRIVE PARK–BAKER RIDGE TRAIL LOOP ★★

Trail length	2 km
Time required	30–40-minute loop trail
Description	A pleasant trail through forest and along the shore
Level	Moderate
Access	A. From Quarry Drive Park just past 221 Quarry Drive on the south side of the street (Quarry Drive runs east off Chu-an Drive.) B. On the north side of Baker Road near its end

From access A, a 400-m trail leads up and over a mossy ridge to the shore, where you can walk in both directions, for some way. The trail will take you about 10 minutes. On the way, you will pass a bench at a point where there is a view of the water. Once on the beach, you can return the way you came or turn left (east) and walk for about another 10 minutes, until you reach a wooden stairway that leads to the public access at the end of Baker Road. From here, walk a short way east along the road, until you see the start of the Baker Ridge trail on your left. This 10–15-minute trail is steep at the beginning but is well flagged and easy to follow. It emerges on the north side of the end of Quarry Drive (about 2 minutes from where you started).

SHORE WALKS

There are a number of fine walks along Salt Spring's mostly rocky shore, though finding the poorly signed (at time of writing) public accesses to the shore can sometimes be a challenge. The following selection of public accesses are listed roughly from north to south and have been grouped by area. Some of the accesses indicated on the Salt Spring map have not been described, as they offer limited walking opportunities. However, they are often excellent places to launch a kayak or canoe.

Southey Point area: One of the prettiest spots on Salt Spring is the pock-marked sandstone shore at the foot of Arbutus Road. At low tide, you can walk south, enjoying the views toward Kuper and Thetis Islands and examining tidal pools and sea stars clinging to the rocks. You can also walk north, for a short distance, along this shore. In the summer, swimming from the sandstone rocks is lovely.

There is a second beach access at the end of Southey Point Road (a narrow path between two private properties). Although you cannot walk very far (little beach is exposed even at low tide), this is a pretty place to swim, to clamber over the rocks or just to enjoy the view.

You can also walk some distance along the east shore of Southey Point (see hike 17, page 178).

Sunset Drive: Between 1076 and 1100 Sunset Drive (south of West Eagle Road), a path descends west to the shore and provides excellent views of Idol Island just offshore and Tent Island in the distance. At low tide, you can walk south along the beach, for a short distance.

A second access just south of 856 Sunset Drive (across and to the south of Sir Echo Way) has a short trail to an appealing little bay that dries at low tide.

Hudson Point: A road descends to the beach, 800 m north of Fernwood. This access doubles as a boat launch. At low tide, you can walk along the shore for some way in both directions. In the distance is Wallace Island and behind it Galiano Island.

Fernwood: A government dock is located at the foot of Fernwood Road (where North Beach Road becomes Walker's Hook Road). It's possible to reach the shore just to the right of the dock and then walk south along the beach.

Maliview Drive: The beach at the foot of Maliview Drive is the same beach accessed at Hudson Point, Fernwood Road and along Walker's Hook Drive. This long beach is a good place to examine intertidal life and to watch great blue herons fishing.

Vesuvius Beach: A short flight of stairs from Langley Street (off Vesuvius Bay Road) leads to the most popular bathing beach on Salt Spring. This lovely bay is known to have the warmest ocean swimming on the island; however, the walking here is limited.

Quarry Drive Park: See hike 19, page 179.

Booth Bay: At the end of Baker Road (off Lower Ganges Road), stairs lead to the beach. At low tide, you can walk for some distance in both directions, although if you walk southeast and turn into Booth Canal, you soon begin to sink into the mud.

Collins Road: The beach at the end of Collins Road (off Rainbow Road), beneath Mount Erskine, is known locally Cranberry Outlet (a.k.a. Bader's Beach, Erskine Beach and Collins Beach). The best walking here is right (north) along the shore at

While blue herons are on the endangered species list, they are frequently seen in the Gulf Islands, where there are many rookeries. Kim Thompson

low tide. You might also like to hike the short trail that parallels the beach at a slightly higher elevation. It begins beside the parking area, at the end of Collins Road, near where Maxwell Creek (a.k.a. Cranberry Creek) flows into the sea.

Long Harbour area: There are two accesses to the shore of Long Harbour: one by a path at the end of Beachside Drive (off Harbourside Place) and the other at the bottom of Ontario Place (off Quebec Road), at the boat launch. At low tide, both accesses offer limited walking.

Churchill Road: Stairs lead down to the pretty beach at the end of Churchill Road (off Upper Ganges Road), where you can walk a short distance along the shore at low tide. From here, there's a good view of the Chain Islands in Ganges Harbour and the shoreline along Long Harbour Road.

Price Road: Take Beddis Road to Price Road (about 1.8 km). Turn left (east) onto Price Road and continue for 900 m. This excellent access (which looks like a driveway to the south of 289 Price Road) allows you to walk the beach either way for some distance at low tide.

Beddis Beach: Toward the end of Beddis Road (about 6 km from the Fulford–Ganges Road), south of the Cusheon Lake Road turnoff and before Beddis turns sharply right (south). Look for the gate across the driveway to the beach.

There's a small parking area on the south side of the road. Many consider this to be the island's loveliest beach. You can walk north for some distance at low tide.

Burgoyne Bay: At the end of Burgoyne Bay Road, you'll find a parking area in the new provincial park. You can combine a beach walk with a walk along the trails higher up above the bank (see hike 8). There are excellent views of Baynes Peak, on Mount Maxwell directly above the bay, and across to Maple Bay on Vancouver Island.

Ruckle Park: This outstanding park, at the end of Beaver Point Road, has a rocky shoreline with beautiful little coves and bays that you can explore at length. (See hike 1).

Eagles Way: See Forest Ridge Park, page 184.

Musgrave Landing: See hike 7, page 165.

Drummond Park: Take the Fulford–Ganges Road to Isabella Point Road. The parking area is on the left of Isabella Point Road, just past the intersection. At low tide, this small local park opens on a wide beach where you can walk in either direction, for some way. This flat beach is likely to be quite muddy just after the tide has gone out. Under some cedar trees next to the north end of the parking lot, you'll find a petroglyph of a seal on a large, smooth boulder.

Hamilton Beach: Park on the left side of Isabella Point Road, in an open area about 1.8 km from the Fulford–Ganges Road, and walk down to the beach. (The road is adjacent to the beach.) This is the same kind of walk as Drummond Park (above). There is a public trail in Fern Creek Park, a 2-ha park across the road (on the west side). You might like to combine this with your shore walk.

The author and friend check on the dinner menu from Hope Hill. Lynn Thompson

ROAD WALKS

There are many beautiful roads to walk on Salt Spring, although few of them are as peaceful as they were once. The following selection is based on tranquillity and beauty. These walks are described in roughly a north-south order. (I have also included a few short and easy off-road walks.)

Southey Point area: Arbutus Road, Southey Point Road and Dogwood Lane are all pleasant. They are well treed and quiet, but provide few glimpses of the water.

Sun Eagle Road to North View Road: This steep, 10-minute connector trail descends west from just left (south) of 268 Sun Eagle Road to the south side of the end of North View Road. The trail offers views west to Kuper and Tent Islands from its top end.

North Beach Road to Walker's Hook Road: This is the longest stretch of low-bank seaside road walking you'll find on Salt Spring. For much of the way, the houses are on the west side, while the east (water) side is clear. The views are of Wallace and Galiano Islands. You might like to combine this with a beach walk.

Saint Mary Lake area: There are good water views from Tripp Road on the quiet, west side of the lake, where you'll also find a few relatively private swimming spots. The walk along North End Road, on the east side of the lake, is also pretty but the traffic is heavy. The area along and off Lang's Road, at the north end of the lake, is lovely but there is no public access to the water here.

Vesuvius: This residential area off Vesuvius Bay Road, southeast of the ferry dock, is a lovely, quiet area for walking. Start with Chu-An Road, which runs south off Vesuvius Bay Road, and then meander through the labyrinth of neighbourhood roads. There's another small pocket of interesting, quiet roads off Langley and Bayview Roads, which also run south off Vesuvius Bay Road just before the ferry dock. You might want to combine this walk with a swim at Vesuvius Beach.

Long Harbour area: Some of Salt Spring's most interesting homes and loveliest shoreline are along Old Scott Road and Scott Point Drive. Start walking on either of these from Long Harbour Road. Both roads are narrow, well treed and quite beautiful.

A 10-minute off-road walk beside the ferry terminal (on the north side of Long Harbour Road) climbs to a beautiful view over Welbury Bay and then descends to rejoin Long Harbour Road opposite Welbury Road. Try this one while you wait for the ferry.

Ganges area: To ensure that the village of Ganges remains a pedestrian-friendly area, the Parks, Arts and Recreation Commission (PARC) is developing pathways to connect the various parts of the village. Inquire at the Tourist Information Centre or the PARC office for a map of the entire pathways system and use some of these paths to explore the village. Some of these paths connect with the trails in Mouat Park (see below).

Mouat Park: At the end of Seaview Avenue (off the Fulford–Ganges Road) in Ganges. The trails follow McPhillips Creek and go through second-growth forest.

Grace Point Park: Walk along the water beside the Grace Point condominium compound at the end of Purvis Road in downtown Ganges. Continue past the condominiums on the left and through the condominium gate out to Grace Point, at the end of the peninsula. Be careful, as the trail climbing the rocky headland is a bit treacherous. From the point, you'll have lovely views of Ganges Harbour and the surrounding shore. Nearby Grace Point Island is privately owned.

Beddis Road: Beddis is a joy to walk. It meanders like a country road should, affording good views of the water, every so often, and lovely vistas of the surrounding land. If you have the stamina, walk the 8.5 km from the Fulford–Ganges Road as far as Beddis Beach.

Sky Valley–Cusheon Lake circuit: This walk goes through arbutus forest and along Cusheon Lake, where you can swim. Park on Sky Valley Road, just off the Fulford–Ganges Road (about 3.5 km south of Ganges). Walk to the end of Sky Valley Road and take the trail heading off on the left (east). When you have choices, keep to the right or go straight (the offshoots to the left lead to private property). This is a very short trail, and in about 5 minutes, you will emerge on the continuation of Sky Valley Road. Follow it 200 m to Lord Mikes Road and turn right. Walk along Lord Mikes for 500 m, then turn right again on Cusheon Lake Road. There are good views of the lake and of Bruce Peak. When you return to the Fulford–Ganges Road, turn right (north) toward Ganges and walk the short distance back to Sky Valley Road, where you started. The whole walk will take you about an hour.

Beaver Point Road area: Beaver Point Road is a great country-road walk along a verdant valley lined with farms encircled by cedar-rail fences. Two of Salt Spring's prettiest lakes—Stowell and Weston—are on this road. Be sure to look at charming Beaver Point Hall (at the corner of Bridgman Road) and the little, red Beaver Point School behind it.

If you walk down Bridgman Road to the end of Menhinick Drive, you might like to combine this with a hike through the Indian Reserve (see hike 2, page 157).

Forest Ridge Park: This beautiful area is often overlooked because it's so close to Ruckle Provincial Park. From Beaver Point Road, walk down Forest Ridge Road to its end, at Stevens Road. Just before the Stevens Road junction, you'll see a soon-to-be-signed trail entering the forest. Follow it for a short distance through some mature trees until you see a giant Douglas fir on your left. Known to locals as the Grandmother Tree, this is the second-largest Douglas fir I've seen on Salt Spring (the largest is in Ruckle Park) and seems to be a popular spot for some islanders to leave tributes either to the tree or to important people in their lives. From here, you can walk east along Stevens Road, continuing along Eagles Way to a grassy unmarked roadway on the right that leads to the shore at Eleanor Point. From this vantage point, you have an excellent view of Russell Island just offshore and the Swartz Bay ferry terminal in the distance.

Fulford Harbour: From the ferry, walk along Morningside Road, exploring the side roads as you go. There are good views of Fulford Harbour along the way. This is a good walk to combine with hike 3.

Fern Creek Park: Walk about 1.8 km along Isabella Point Road until you get to Hamilton Beach. Across the road is 2-ha Fern Creek Park. Look for the trailhead about 25 m south of the road leading into a development. This pretty trail follows a creek bed through a fern-filled ravine. Look for western hemlock, immense red cedars and some large holly trees. The trail meanders through the woods around this development, making it a pleasant place to spend an hour or so.

Isabella Point Road–Roland Road: Walk south along Isabella Point Road from Drummond Park. Turn left at Roland Road to continue along the shore. The road is quiet and pretty, and there are good views of Fulford Harbour. It's about 4 km from Drummond Park to the end of Roland Road. You might like to combine this road walk with a shore walk, at low tide. (See the Drummond Park shore walk, page 182.)

Mountain Road: Mountain Road runs southwest off Isabella Point Road, slightly over 3 km from the Fulford–Ganges Road. You can walk this beautiful, seldom-travelled, forested road for at least 4 km before you reach a private development. From here, a public road allowance continues toward Musgrave Landing. Look for one of Salt Spring's two waterfalls, on the north side of the road, about 3 km from Isabella Point Road. You will also find a number of well-used trails to explore in the Mount Tuam Ecological Reserve, which straddles Mountain Road.

Refrigerator Trail: This trail at the end of Isabella Point Road is so named because of a discarded appliance at one end of it. The trail leads to Mountain Road, close to the Mount Tuam Ecological Reserve, which has very well-developed trails throughout and is regularly used by locals.

AND IF YOU PADDLE . . .

With many good launch spots and mostly protected water, Salt Spring has some of the best paddling in the Gulf Islands. In addition to the cautions detailed below, be very careful to avoid Salt Spring's three ferries and other boat traffic. Here are a few ideas from the easiest of Salt Spring's launch sites:

Arbutus Road: Put in at the end of Arbutus Road and paddle south along the well-developed shore of Stuart Channel to Vesuvius; or east to Wallace Island (see page 233); or even farther east to Dionisio Point Provincial Park (see page 74) or Montague Harbour Provincial Park on Galiano Island (see page 72); or west around the beautiful sandstone formations of the Tent and Kuper Island shoreline, possibly stopping for lunch at the pub in Telegraph Harbour on Thetis Island (see page 221).

Hudson Point: This popular boat launch on North Beach Road gives you access to Salt Spring's fairly developed northeast shore and an easy trip to Wallace Island (see page 233) or farther south to Montague Harbour Provincial Park on Galiano Island (see page 72). *Caution:* The wind can come up suddenly in Houstoun Passage, especially on summer afternoons.

Cranberry Outlet: Put in at the end of Collins Road and paddle south along the mostly undeveloped shoreline to Burgoyne Bay, or paddle north along the island's more heavily developed northwest shore to Southey Point, or paddle west over to Maple Bay on Vancouver Island for lunch at the pub.

Quebec Drive: Launch at the end of Quebec Drive, in the middle of Long Harbour, and paddle along the Athol Peninsula shoreline to Nose Point. From here, you could paddle east over to James Bay on Prevost Island (part of the Gulf Islands National Park Reserve). Local paddlers enjoy the paddle all around Prevost Island, which offers some of the most scenic and varied shoreline in the Gulf Islands. Alternatively, if you prefer something less remote, you can paddle west around heavily developed Scott Point into Welbury Bay and on to busy Ganges Harbour. *Cautions:* If you paddle to Prevost Island, be careful of turbulence around Nose Point when the current is running; strong tidal flows where Captain Passage meets Trincomali Channel, especially on a flood tide (time your paddle for slack current); and rough water around Selby Point on Prevost.

Churchill Road: From the beach access at the end of Churchill Road, you have easy access to the Chain Islands (Goat, Deadman and the Sisters). While all of these islands are privately owned, you are allowed to stop on the beaches below the high tide line. Plan to stop for tea or lunch at the stunning shell beach on privately owned but uninhabited Third Sister Island. The beach access on Price Road is another good

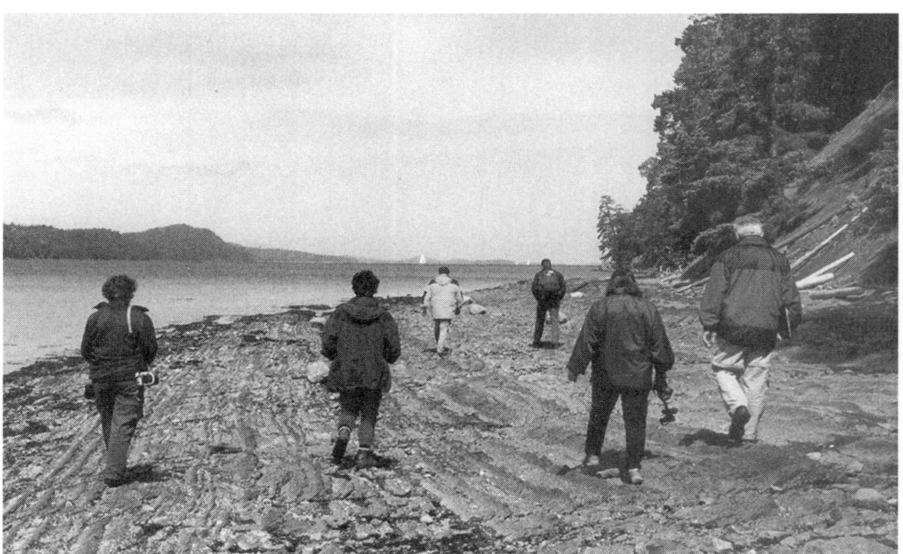

Most of Prevost Island still belongs to the descendants of Digby Hussey de Burgh, the Irish farmer who bought it in 1924. Kayakers can camp and hike on the Gulf Islands National Park Reserve's land around James Bay and Selby Cove and explore the land around Portlock Point and Richardson Bay, where the light beacon established in 1895 still shines its warning. Parks Canada

launch site for visits to these islands. *Cautions:* The beach at the end of Churchill Road is almost non-existent at very high tides. Walter Bay, on the south side of Ganges Harbour, is a protected bird sanctuary.

Beddis Beach: From this launch site, you can paddle to Prevost Island and the islands on its western shore. Of particular interest is little Owl Island (beside Secret Island) in the spring when it is covered with wildflowers. Beddis Beach is also a good place to put in for a paddle along Salt Spring's southeast shore toward the Channel Islands and the beautiful Ruckle Park shoreline.

Burgoyne Bay: From the end of Burgoyne Bay Road, launch from the government dock or the nearby beach and paddle south to Musgrave Landing, north to Cranberry Outlet, or west to Genoa Bay or Cowichan Bay on Vancouver Island. The shoreline to the south of Burgoyne Bay is largely undeveloped. Musgrave Landing is a fascinating little backwater that contains a lot of Salt Spring history. There's a small, upscale strata development here. *Caution:* The water around Bold Bluff Point in Sansum Narrows can be rough, especially when a southerly wind meets an ebbing tide. To avoid paddling against a potentially strong current, paddle north with the flooding tide or south when the tide is on the ebb.

Menhinick Road: Launch from an access across from 130 Menhinick. This access is down a right-of-way beside a house. Walk down the path to the water and carefully take your boat down the rickety stairs to the small beach below. From here, you can cross to Russell and Portland Islands. Either of these makes a good lunch stop and both have trails to walk. (For more information on Portland Island, see page 230.) You can then tour the shoreline or continue to Ruckle Park. You can also launch at Ruckle Park, if you want to dedicate more time to this area. From the Menhinick launch site, you can also paddle to the shoreline of the Indian Reserve and the beautiful shoreline along the east side of Fulford Harbour. There is a second public launch site from the end of Seabright Road, which runs south off Menhinick. The only disadvantage with this water access is that the beach disappears at very high tides.

Drummond Park or **Hamilton Beach:** Either of these launch sites on Isabella Point Road gives you access to the diverse shoreline of Fulford Harbour. From Hamilton Beach, you can easily round Isabella Point to tour the exquisite Isabella Islets and continue along the relatively undeveloped southern shoreline of the island to Cape Keppel.

Saturna ISLAND

Located at the end of a chain of islands that includes Mayne and Galiano, Saturna is the most southern Gulf Island and considered by many the most lovely. Much of Saturna's 31 square km is part of the Gulf Islands National Park Reserve, including Saturna Island Ecological Reserve, Brown Ridge, Taylor Point, Narvaez Bay, land around the summits of Mount Elford and Mount David, and Winter Cove. Its lovely beaches and ridge walks make Saturna one of the best hiking destinations in the Gulf Islands, and because of its small population (only 319), its charming roads are serenely quiet. East Point Road, on the north shore, has sea views and beach access for almost all of its length. Other roads lead to delightful coves and bays, and one leads to a splendid cliff walk overlooking other Gulf Islands, the San Juan Islands and the peaks of Washington state. Two ridges run the length of Saturna, the deep valley between them extends from Narvaez Bay in the east to Lyall Harbour in the west, with Narvaez Bay Road running through it. Most of the island's limited services are located near the ferry terminal, from where there are daily sailings to Swartz Bay (near Victoria).

HISTORY

Saturna Island was named after the *Saturnina*, a Spanish ship that explored the area in 1791. This island grew more slowly than its neighbours—Mayne, the Penders, Salt Spring and Galiano—largely because it had little good farmland and was the farthest away from the main shipping routes. The first settlers had orchards and cows (for milk and butter) but kept mostly sheep, as is still the case with the few farmers on Saturna today. At the end of the 19th century, some sandstone quarries were established on the island. Although these were never profitable ventures, sandstone quarried at Taylor Point was exported to Victoria and as far away as Winnipeg.

The riptides and strong currents in Boundary Pass, east of Saturna's East Point, have always made it a dangerous waterway. The lighthouse was built in 1888, two years after a ship went aground on Boiling Reef.

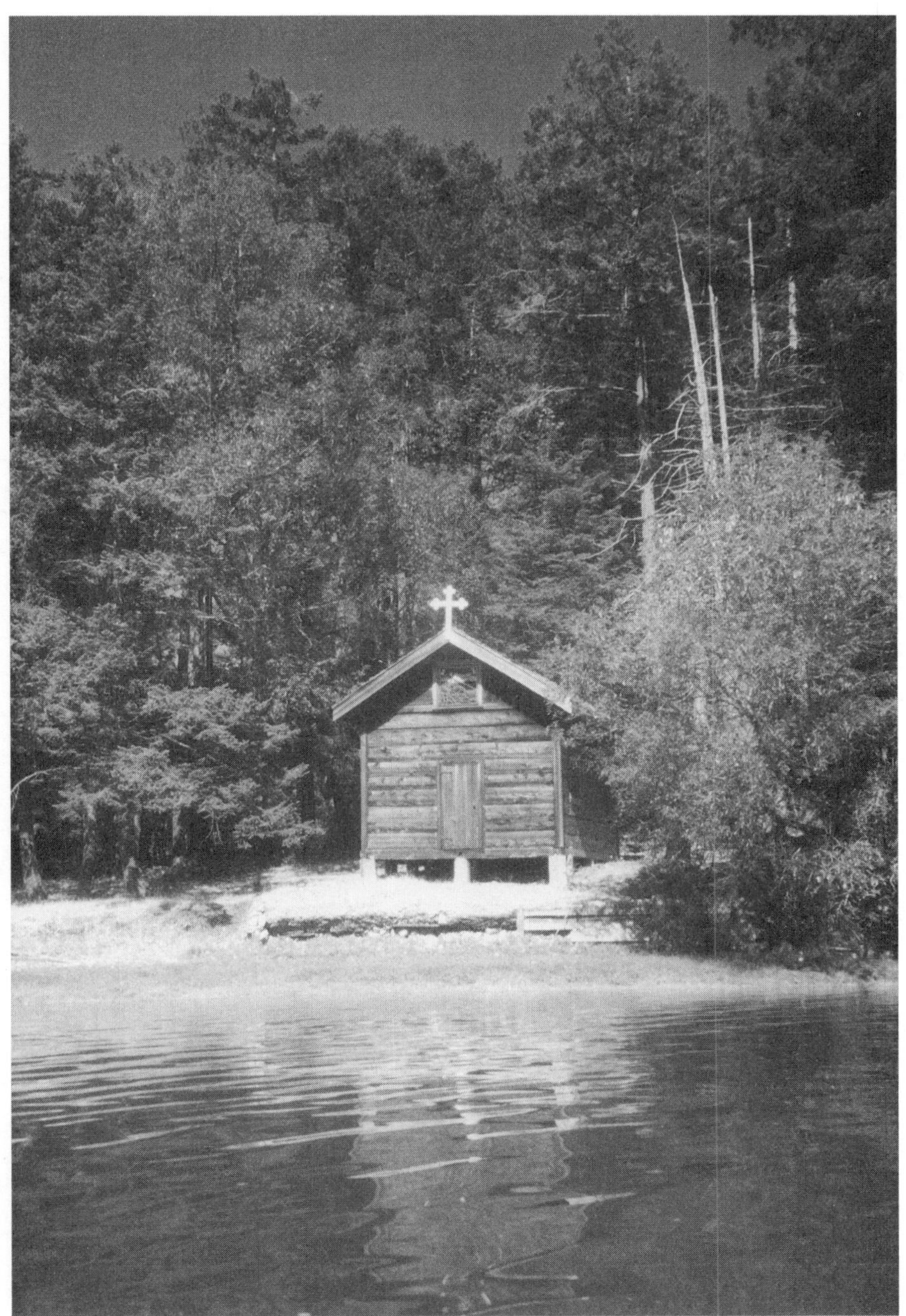

This charming little church was once used by visitors to Saturna but is now on private land and best viewed from the water.

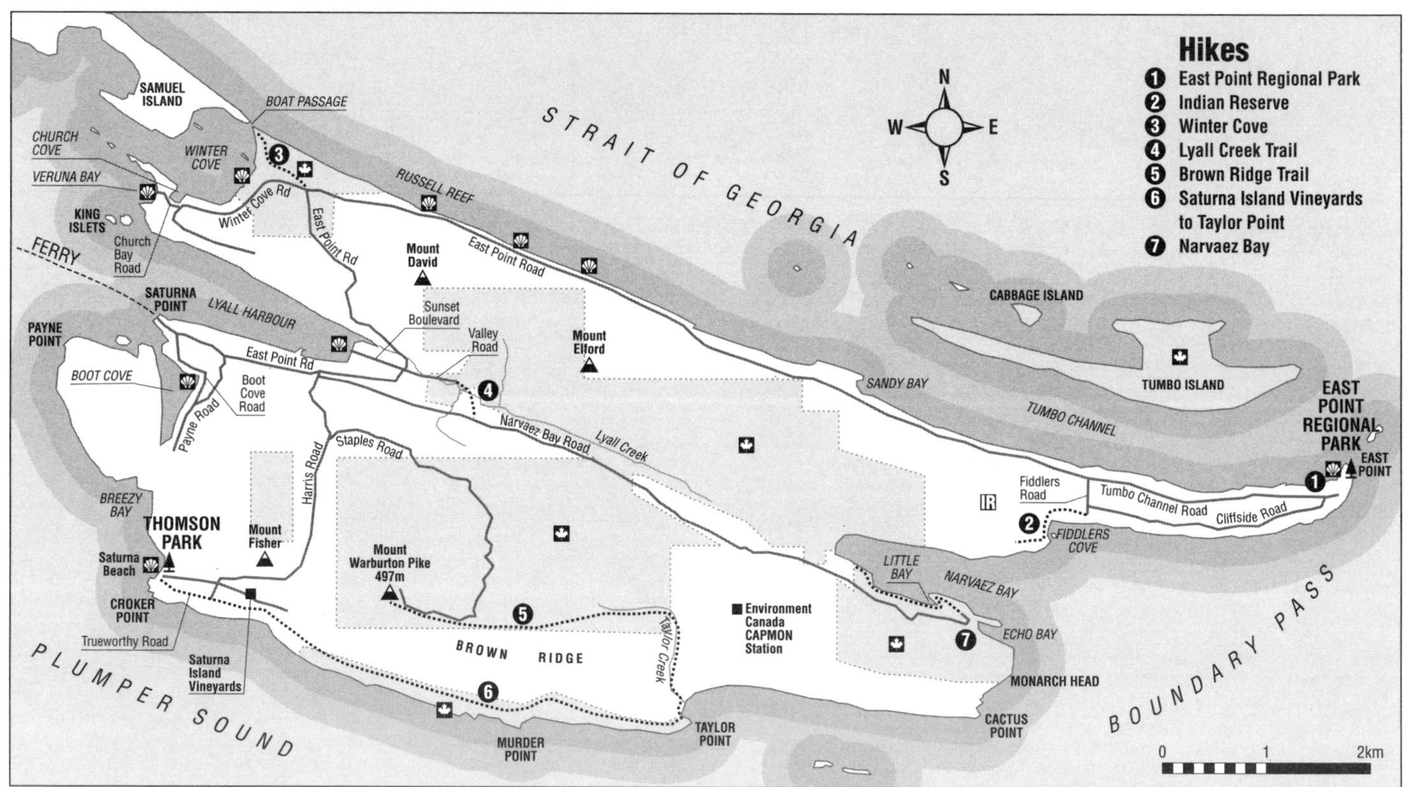
Hikes
1 East Point Regional Park
2 Indian Reserve
3 Winter Cove
4 Lyall Creek Trail
5 Brown Ridge Trail
6 Saturna Island Vineyards to Taylor Point
7 Narvaez Bay
N
W
E
S
STRAIT OF GEORGIA
SAMUEL ISLAND
BOAT PASSAGE
CHURCH COVE
WINTER COVE
VERUNA BAY
KING ISLETS
Church Bay Road
Winter Cove Rd
East Point Rd
RUSSELL REEF
Mount David
East Point Road
FERRY
SATURNA POINT
LYALL HARBOUR
PAYNE POINT
Sunset Boulevard
Valley Road
Mount Elford
East Point Rd
BOOT COVE
Boot Cove Road
Payne Road
CABBAGE ISLAND
TUMBO ISLAND
SANDY BAY
TUMBO CHANNEL
EAST POINT REGIONAL PARK
EAST POINT
Narvaez Bay Road
Lyall Creek
Staples Road
Harris Road
Fiddlers Road
Tumbo Channel Road
Cliffside Road
FIDDLERS COVE
BREEZY BAY
THOMSON PARK
Mount Fisher
Saturna Beach
Mount Warburton Pike 497m
LITTLE BAY
NARVAEZ BAY
CROKER POINT
Environment Canada CAPMON Station
ECHO BAY
Trueworthy Road
Saturna Island Vineyards
BROWN RIDGE
Taylor Creek
MONARCH HEAD
PLUMPER SOUND
MURDER POINT
TAYLOR POINT
CACTUS POINT
BOUNDARY PASS
0
1
2km
Roads
Trails
Gulf Islands National Park Reserve
Park
Beach access
Peak
Indian Reserve
See text
Saturna Island

GETTING THERE

There are direct ferries to Saturna from Swartz Bay (near Victoria) four times a day, from Tsawwassen (near Vancouver) about twice a day, and ferries to Galiano, Mayne and the Pender Islands two or three times per day. Reservations are recommended for travel between Saturna Island and Tsawwassen. For more information, obtain a Southern Gulf Islands schedule or contact BC Ferries. Pacific Spirit Air, Harbour Air and Seair Seaplanes fly to Saturna (see Resources, page 235).

SERVICES AND ACCOMMODATION

The ferry landing is at Lyall Harbour, adjacent to most of Saturna's few services, including one of two general stores on the island (which sells gas and diesel fuel), a pub and the community hall. The second general store (which sells delicacies from the island's excellent bakery) is not far away, on Narvaez Bay Road, where you will also find a café, post office, mechanic and liquor store. At time of writing, there were no doctors, pharmacies, banks or ATMs on Saturna.

Many of the island's bed and breakfasts are within a few kilometres of the ferry dock. At time of writing, there were no public or private campgrounds on Saturna. Be sure to make arrangements for lodging in advance, as accommodation is extremely limited, especially during the summer.

An information pamphlet is published annually and is available on the ferries and in island stores. For more information on Saturna, contact the Saturna Island Tourism Association, Box 45, Saturna Island, BC V0N 2Y0, or www.saturnatourism.com.

ESPECIALLY FOR WALKERS

In addition to the Shore and Road Walks listed at the end of this chapter, there are many easy walks on Saturna. Try the following:

- Brown Ridge Trail (see hike 5, page 195) from Mount Warburton Pike. Here, for once, is a ridge walk that you can drive up to and then enjoy magnificent views as you walk along gentle terrain right on the edge of a cliff.
- the short loop in Winter Cove (see hike 3, page 193)
- the area around East Point Lighthouse (see hike 1, page 192)
- the walk down to the anvil in Narvaez Bay (see hike 7, page 198)
- Lyall Creek Trail (see hike 4, page 194). If you don't like steep terrain, access this trail from the end of Valley Road and don't climb the last bit to its end; the Narvaez Bay Road access is very steep.

Three cultural spots are worth visiting.

- A short walk from the ferry, along East Point Road, is St. Christopher's Anglican Church, which I found appealing.
- The exterior of the original St. Christopher's Church can be seen from Church Bay Road. From its intersection with East Point Road, walk along Winter Cove Road 1 km to Church Bay Road and then down this road to where you can see Church Bay. The charming little church (capacity 20) started out as a Japanese boathouse. It is now on private property and no longer in use.
- If you like exploring old cemeteries, visit the Saturna Cemetery, 1.3 km along Narvaez Bay Road east of the store.

HIKES

At time of writing, the National Park Reserve was new and a network of trails on park lands, as well as linkages to other trails on the island, had not been developed. Park managers recommend you hike only on officially designated trails. These trails will be indicated on park maps, at trailheads and on park information boards. They also will have been assessed for public safety concerns and routed to ensure that sensitive ecosystems are not impacted.

1. East Point Regional Park ★★★

Trail length	1.5 km
Time required	35 minutes or more
Description	This walk along the beach surrounding the East Point Lighthouse offers great views of the churning waters and Washington's majestic Mount Baker, as well as the chance to see killer whales.
Level	Easy
Access	The end of Tumbo Channel Road. Trails go off to both the left and the right of the parking area.
Facilities	Outhouses, benches, telephone, bicycle rack

The views from East Point over the busy, churning waters of Boundary Pass are magnificent. This is perhaps the best place in the Gulf Islands to see killer whales—pods of whales pass by the lighthouse regularly, from May to November.

The trail to the left of the parking area accesses the beach below the lighthouse. Walk along the stunning shoreline, with its intricate sandstone formations, as far as you can. At low tide, you can walk right around the point on the boulders, examining tidal pools and admiring the large rocks. Then walk around the meadow surrounding the lighthouse and other buildings.

From here, return to the parking area and try the trail along the fence to the right (east) of the parking area. This trail will lead you to the rocky ledge above the swirling waters of Boiling Reef.

2. Indian Reserve (Fiddlers Cove) ★★★

Trail length	1.5 km each way
Time required	Up to 40 minutes each way, more if you descend to Fiddlers Cove
Description	A beautiful walk along the grassy and arbutus-strewn cliffs overlooking Fiddlers Cove and Narvaez Bay
Level	Easy for the first bit and then moderate

Access	The end of Fiddlers Road off Tumbo Channel Road. The trail leads right (west) through the Indian Reserve.
Cautions	The Indian Reserve is private land, owned jointly by the Tsawout (250-652-9101) and Tseycum (250-656-0858) bands. Permission to hike this land should be obtained from either of these bands. Be sure not to hike on the reserve when logging is taking place, as happens from time to time. The cliff is steep; be careful to keep well away from the edge.

The first part of this hike follows open woods along the edge of the cliff and has great picnic spots, with spectacular views of Fiddlers Cove, Narvaez Bay and Monarch Head beyond. The unsigned trail is very easy to follow for some distance but it gradually becomes little more than a deer trail that rises and falls along the cliff edge, leading inland to where you will get only occasional glimpses of the sea. I followed the trail for about 40 minutes, before turning back. Finding the trail on my return was tricky in places and I recommend you turn back before the trail becomes difficult to follow.

Less than 1 km from the trailhead, you will see another trail leading down to Fiddlers Cove. You can descend this trail about 90 m to the beach below but be aware that the trail is very steep and difficult.

3. Winter Cove (National Park Reserve) ★★★

Trail length	1.5 km loop
Time required	35 minutes
Description	A walk through forest and along the shore of Winter Cove to the open water of the Strait of Georgia
Level	Easy
Access	To the west of the intersection of East Point Road and Winter Cove Road. The trail enters the woods on the right (east) side of the picnic area, just up from the water.
Facilities	Picnic tables, outhouses, boat launch, sports fields. The park has no campsites.

Winter Cove Park occupies 75 ha of land and an additional 16 ha of intertidal foreshore. The park contains a fine salt marsh and the typical dry coastal Douglas fir vegetation. The shoreline is made up of sandstone, shale and midden left over from aboriginal use in the past.

This short hike is well worth doing for the fine views of Winter Cove and the Strait of Georgia, as well as the restful ambience of the park. After about 10 minutes, you reach a point at the edge of Boat Passage, the narrow stretch of water that rushes between Saturna and neighbouring Samuel Island. Park benches on the edge of these rocks and elsewhere make pleasant places to stop and contemplate the power of the water. Continue along the edge or, if the tide is out, you can return by the beach. Winter Cove appears remarkably different at high and low tide.

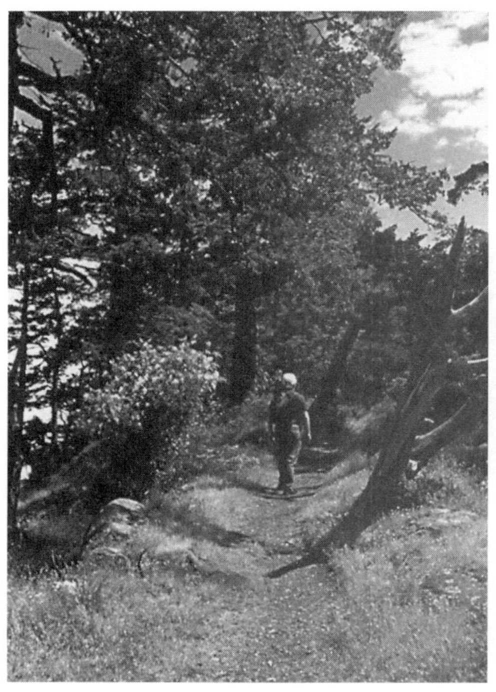

This trail in Winter Cove Park passes through lush forest and along the ocean's edge.
Richard Blier

4. Lyall Creek Trail (National Park Reserve) ★★

Trail length	1.5 km one way
Time required	20 minutes each way
Description	A descent to a ferny forest and along a creek. This trail was developed by the local parks and recreation department and is now part of the National Park Reserve.
Level	Easy
Access	A. At the end of Valley Road (east off East Point Road) B. On the north side of Narvaez Bay Road 1.4 km east of the store

From the Narvaez Bay Road access, the trail drops steeply about 50 m to the ferny canyon floor below. On the way, about 5 minutes from the trailhead, you will find a bench where you can sit and watch an exquisite seasonal waterfall as it flows gently over a mossy rockface. The well-developed trail, with boardwalks and steps, joins the two accesses and passes through a great number of large cedar, mature alder and fir.

5. BROWN RIDGE TRAIL FROM MOUNT WARBURTON PIKE ★★★★★

Trail length	Up to 8 km round trip if you stay on the ridge; another kilometre if you descend to Taylor Point; about 21 km round trip if you drop down to Taylor Point and then combine this hike with hike 6
Time required	Allow 2 hours for the ridge walk. Don't rush; this is one of the finest hikes in the Gulf Islands.
Description	Glorious cliff walk looking southwest over Plumper Sound and the Pender Islands and south to the San Juan Islands and the mainland peaks in the US beyond.
Level	Easy if you stay at the top; strenuous if you descend to Taylor Point
Elevation	497 m
Access	The trail begins at the end of Staples Road (4 km southeast off Harris Road) at the top of Mount Warburton Pike and continues east along Brown Ridge.
Cautions	The TV tower is on land leased from the federal government. It is private property and should not be disturbed in any way. This trail follows the edge of a steep cliff. Proceed carefully.

As you descend from Mount Warburton Pike you'll see the tip of Taylor Point curling out into the sea. Parks Canada

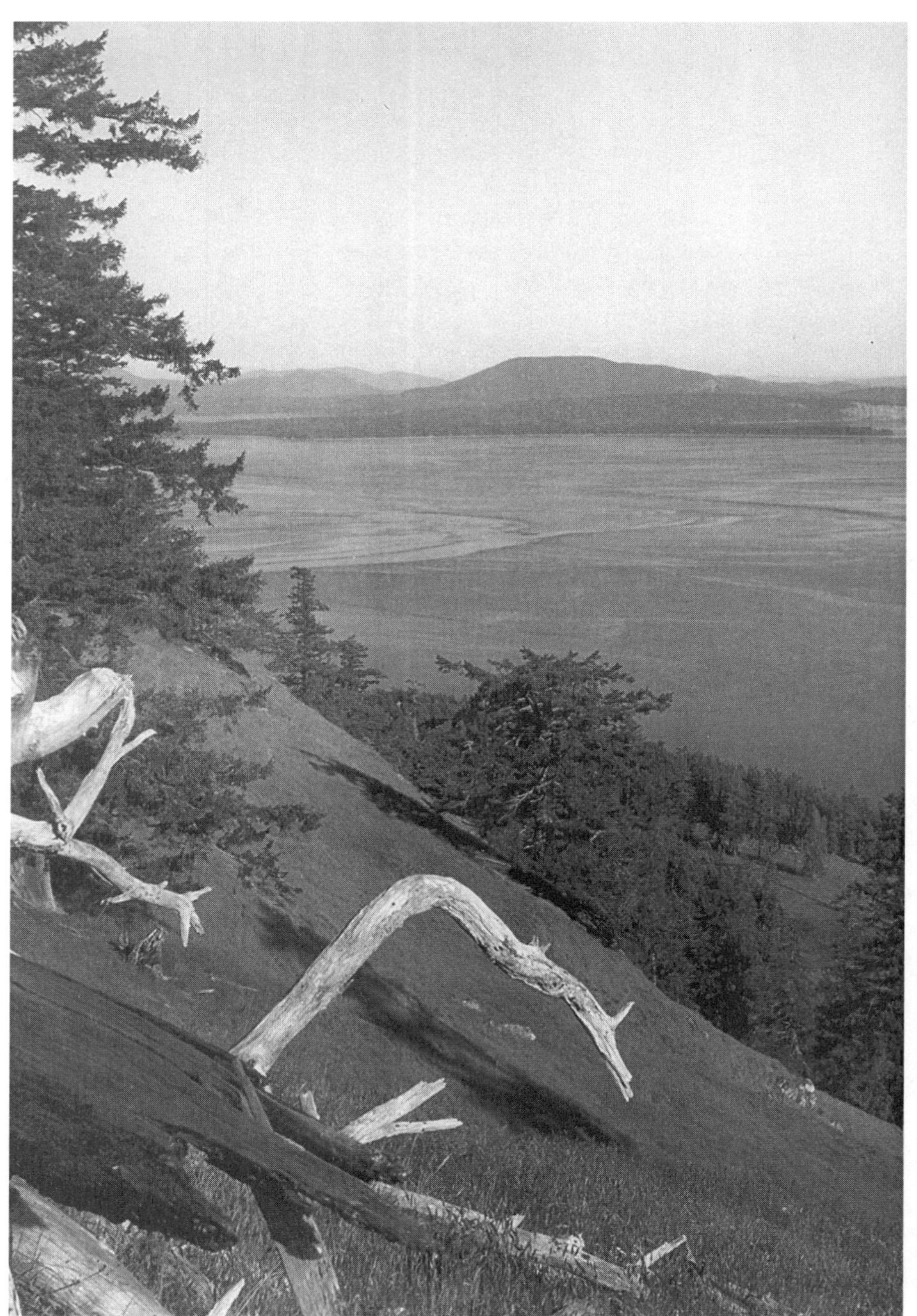

From Mount Warburton Pike, you look over South Pender Island to Stuart Island in Boundary Pass and to the many islands that border Haro Strait.
Parks Canada

Mount Warburton Pike is on land once owned by its namesake, the youngest son of an upper-class English family. At one time Pike owned 1,400 acres of land on Saturna. Lynn Thompson

Mount Warburton Pike is the highest point on Saturna. The trail that follows the edge of Brown Ridge is to the left (east) of the TV towers, at the end of Staples Road. From here, drop down until you find a trail; otherwise you will be in the woods. You will probably find several trails, as you make your way east along the ridge. Many of these are goat trails, and if you're lucky, you'll see the large feral goats that inhabit the ridge area.

On a clear day—and there is really no point in doing a hike like this if it isn't clear—the views are fantastic. At the beginning of the hike, you look down over the Pender Islands and beyond to Moresby, Portland and Salt Spring Islands. As you proceed farther, you can see the San Juan Islands and the Washington coast. Below, grassy meadow drops away, at first gradually and then very steeply, to the farm below. Behind you is a magnificent stand of, perhaps, the largest firs on the island.

At the east end of the ridge, you can return the way you came or follow a creek bed south down toward Taylor Point. At time of writing, there was no developed trail to Taylor Point but islanders have been taking this route for years. Parks Canada has obtained a trail easement through the Campbell farm property, and this roughly follows Taylor Creek. Undoubtedly, Parks Canada will develop this route as a proper trail in the future. Until this happens, the going is rough, so caution is advised. In some places, locals have placed ropes to help the descent. It will take you about 40 minutes to reach the shore.

Taylor Point is an exquisite headland where you will want to have your lunch or stop for tea. Nearby is the ruin of a stone house built by George Taylor, a stonemason who settled here around 1900. The house burned down some years later.

6. Saturna Island Vineyards to Taylor Point ★★★★

Trail length	4 km each way
Time required	1–2 hours each way
Description	A precipitous walk along the top of a bluff with occasional magnificent views out across Plumper Sound to the Pender Islands
Level	Moderate to strenuous
Access	A. The eastern end of Trueworthy Road (off Harris Road), where you will find a gate and a National Park Reserve signboard B. From Taylor Point if you combine this with the previous hike. Be aware that, unless you are prepared for a long hike, the distance from the vineyards to the top of Mount Warburton Pike may present some problems if you left your car or bike at the access to hike 5. However, it could work well if you have a friend with a second vehicle so that you can leave one at each end.
Cautions	At time of writing, Parks Canada is discouraging people from hiking this route until public safety concerns have been addressed and routing determined that minimizes impacts on sensitive ecosystems. The animal trails that now exist cross steep terrain. The Campbell farmland is to the north of the parkland; respect the private property and stay within the parkland.

It is possible to follow a route along animal trails below the Campbell farm between the Saturna Island Vineyards and Taylor Point. This 54-ha strip of parkland falls sharply toward the sea, rising to over 100 m in places. There is no developed trail, although when I did it, I found flagging that followed an animal trail. You will often find yourself on rocky ledges, and in a couple of places, you will have to descend down one side of a shallow gorge and then climb up the other side.

7. Narvaez Bay (National Park Reserve) ★★★★

Trail length	Variable
Time required	1–4 hours
Description	A walk to stunning shoreline with possible additional hikes to a bluff and connections to longer hikes on Brown Ridge and along the shoreline

Level	Moderate to strenuous, depending on what you choose to do
Access	The end of Narvaez Bay Road (6.4 km from the general store on Narvaez Bay Road). Other accesses to this section of the National Park Reserve are on the south side of Narvaez Bay Road (2.8 km from the store) and on the north side of the road (4.1 km from the store).
Facilities	Outhouses, picnic tables, signboards
Cautions	Monarch Head is not part of the National Park Reserve. While private landowners have been accepting of hikers in the past, you should obtain their permission to use their land. Having done so, you can stay on the high ground and walk west, for some way, along the top of the bluff.

At the end of Narvaez Bay Road, you'll find Parks Canada's signboard marking what I consider the most beautiful part of the 252 ha of the Narvaez Bay section of the National Park Reserve. The 2-km walk, which is indicated on the park map, takes you down to the water. You'll need only a half hour or so, but you'll want even more time to enjoy the ambience of this lovely spot.

If you follow the main roadway to its end, ignoring the grassy logging roads that branch from it, you'll find yourself on the left point of an anvil-like protrusion in the shoreline that creates Little Bay on the west and Echo Bay on the east. You'll find another park sign, picnic tables, an outhouse and the beautiful shoreline along Narvaez Bay. From here, you can see Fiddlers Cove and the houses along Cliffside Road to the northeast and, to the east, Washington State.

When you're ready to return, start back up the road. Where the road turns sharply to the right, around the fenced field you've been walking around, proceed straight ahead (along the grassy roadway you passed on your way down to Little Bay) to explore Echo Bay on the eastern side of the anvil. Here the trail crosses a small peninsula of classic Gulf Islands rocky, forested terrain, complete with wildflowers.

On your way back to Narvaez Bay Road, you'll pass a couple of old, now grassy logging roads. If you take the first one and head mainly east and a bit south, for about 10–15 minutes, you'll find yourself above Monarch Head, about 115 m above sea level, with a good view of exquisite Cactus Point below and to the south. Locals say that you can eventually reach Brown Ridge (see hike 5) by continuing along the top of the bluffs, although you would then be on private property outside of the National Park Reserve. Be careful on the trails in this area, as many visitors have gotten lost. You'll need a good compass and orienteering skills to find your way back.

SHORE AND ROAD WALKS

The roads on Saturna are almost always quiet and pleasant for walking. East Point Road from just east of Winter Cove to the Indian Reserve is a particularly pleasant walk because it follows beautiful shoreline and provides easy access to the rocky beach. At low tide, this makes a good beach walk.

Both Cabbage Island (4.5 ha) and Tumbo Island (121 ha), just north of Saturna and now part of the National Park Reserve, are accessible only by watercraft. While there are no hiking trails on Cabbage Island, you can walk around the island and the views are excellent. The park allows camping and provides picnic tables and outhouses but no drinking water. In addition to beachcombing, you can swim and fish from the island's beautiful beaches. Tumbo Island has no camping, but it is interesting to walk around. It too has beautiful views and beaches.

The beach at Winter Cove (National Park Reserve) is another good place to spend time. There is some beach access at both East Point Lighthouse and Saturna Beach. Here are some other beach accesses, none of which are currently well marked:

Tumbo Channel Road: Access is on the north side of the road, west of 701 Tumbo Channel Road (at the end of East Point Road). There's a large, grassy parking area but the access to the beach is difficult. To get to the lovely sandstone beach, you have to clamber down over boulders and logs. Once there, the walking is relatively easy.

Russell Reef (National Park Reserve): The access to this little park is on the north side of East Point Road, 1.1 km east of Winter Cove Road. At low tide, you can walk on this beach for some distance.

Veruna Bay: The access is at the end of Church Bay Road, down an unmarked roadway to the left. Walk along the shore of this pretty bay.

Sunset Boulevard: At the end of Sunset Boulevard (off East Point Road), this sand beach is in the middle of Lyall Harbour. I'm told that the beach can be very muddy, although it was fine when I walked it.

Thomson Park (Saturna Beach): The access is from the western end of Trueworthy Road (behind Saturna Vineyards) off Harris Road or through the right of way at the end of the vineyards parking lot. Named after the Thomson family, one of Saturna's oldest families, this beach was the original home of the Saturna Canada Day lamb barbecue, an island tradition now held in Winter Cove. The park has picnic tables and an outhouse. The dock is privately owned.

AND IF YOU PADDLE . . .

Saturna's deep bays and coves, as well as the many neighbouring islands, make paddling here a delight. However, the currents in Boat Passage and around East Point Regional Park can be dangerous, and only experienced paddlers should even consider paddling here without a guide. If you do go, study your tide and current tables carefully and only paddle these areas at slack tide. Here are some good places to launch:

Winter Cove: The boat launch at Winter Cove (National Park Reserve) is an easy place to launch. From here, you can paddle southwest around the cove and along

At high tide, the water furiously funnels through Boat Passage between Saturna and Samuel Islands. Some small boats use this shortcut to reach the open water of the Strait of Georgia. Rick Tipple

the shore to Veruna Bay and on to Lyall Harbour. If you are an experienced paddler, you can also paddle around neighbouring Samuel Island, but do this in a counter-clockwise direction, returning the way you came and avoiding Boat Passage except at slack tide. The stories of dumpings in Boat Passage are legendary. The flood tide also flows swiftly northwest in Georgeson Passage between Samuel and Lizard Islands. Be very cautious in these narrow channels.

Veruna Bay: The access is at the end of Church Bay Road, down an unmarked driveway and to the left. Paddle south to the King Islets and around the shoreline of Lyall Harbour.

Sunset Boulevard: At the end of Sunset Boulevard, this boat launch puts you in the middle of Lyall Harbour which, though large, is not very interesting.

Boot Cove: The access is across from 121 Boot Cove Road, to the right of 120 Boot Cove Road. This is a good place to launch at high tide. However, at low tide you will find yourself in oozy mud. Boot Cove is a pleasant and interesting place to paddle. From here, you can paddle north across Lyall Harbour to the King Islets, Veruna Bay, Winter Cove and Samuel Island, or south to Breezy Bay and Saturna's Plumper Sound shoreline.

Thomson Park (Saturna Beach): The access is from the western end of Trueworthy Road (behind Saturna Vineyards) off Harris Road or through the right-of-way at the end of the vineyards parking lot. This gives you easy access to the Plumper Sound shoreline east as far as Narvaez Bay, or north to Breezy Bay and Payne Point.

Texada ISLAND

Not only is Texada the largest of the Gulf islands, at 50 km long and up to 10 km wide, it is also the tallest—its highest peak, Mount Shepherd, is an impressive 891 m. Like the other islands in this book, it has a mild climate and lush forests. However, it is often overlooked as a tourist destination, as it has long been considered an industrial island. Its three massive limestone quarries produce about six million tonnes of limestone a year for the chemical, cement and pulp industries. Its 988 residents are largely employed by the quarries, don't depend on tourism and are happy to keep their abundant wildlife and trail systems a secret. Its links are to the mainland, with ferries connecting it to Powell River rather than to Vancouver Island or to another island. Good farmland is scarce, there are few safe anchorages and the island's main towns of Van Anda and Gillies Bay reflect its working-class roots, with little in the way of typical island craft boutiques or tourist-savvy shops. Despite this harder, less tourist-friendly exterior, Texada's hikes, Mount Grant and Mount Davies in particular, offer some of the more stunning views in the Gulf Islands and make it well worth a visit.

HISTORY

Discovered by Spanish explorers in 1791, Texada was named after Felix de Tejada, a rear admiral in the Spanish navy. Following the discovery of iron ore in 1871 and copper and gold in about 1880, Texada's Van Anda became a boom town. By 1910, the island had a population of about 3,000 and Van Anda had three hotels with saloons, a hospital, several stores, a bimonthly newspaper (the *Coast Miner*) and even an opera house. During these heady days of the early 20th century, Texadans were known for their moonshine, setting up stills that were almost impossible to find. The island's colourful history is well exhibited in the Texada Island Heritage Museum, on your left as you come off the ferry from Powell River.

Many of the hikes on Texada Island are in "big tree country" and have views like this peekaboo one of Powell River on the mainland. Craig Carpenter

GETTING THERE

The ferry from Powell River to Blubber Bay makes ten 35-minute round trips each day. For more information, obtain a Mainland–Vancouver Island–Sunshine Coast schedule or contact BC Ferries. KD Air has daily flights to Texada from Vancouver to Gillies Bay (see Resources, page 235).

SERVICES AND ACCOMMODATION

Most of the services on Texada are in Van Anda, toward the north end of the island (8 km from the ferry). These include an inn with a restaurant and bar, a grocery store, a service station and laundromat, and the Texada Branch of the Powell River Credit Union, which offers full-service banking on weekdays. Gillies Bay (20 km south of the ferry) has an ATM and a grocery store that sells takeout food. Shelter Point Regional Park (604-486-7228) has excellent camping, telephones and a concession stand that cooks some of the best food on the island. From June to October, there is a farmer's market in the Gillies Bay ball park, from 12:30 p.m. to 2:30 p.m., every Sunday.

There are primitive campsites off forestry roads at Bob's Lake and Shingle Beach, and some private campsites and RV sites. There is also limited accommodation in bed and breakfasts, cottages, a motel at Shelter Point and a hotel in Van Anda.

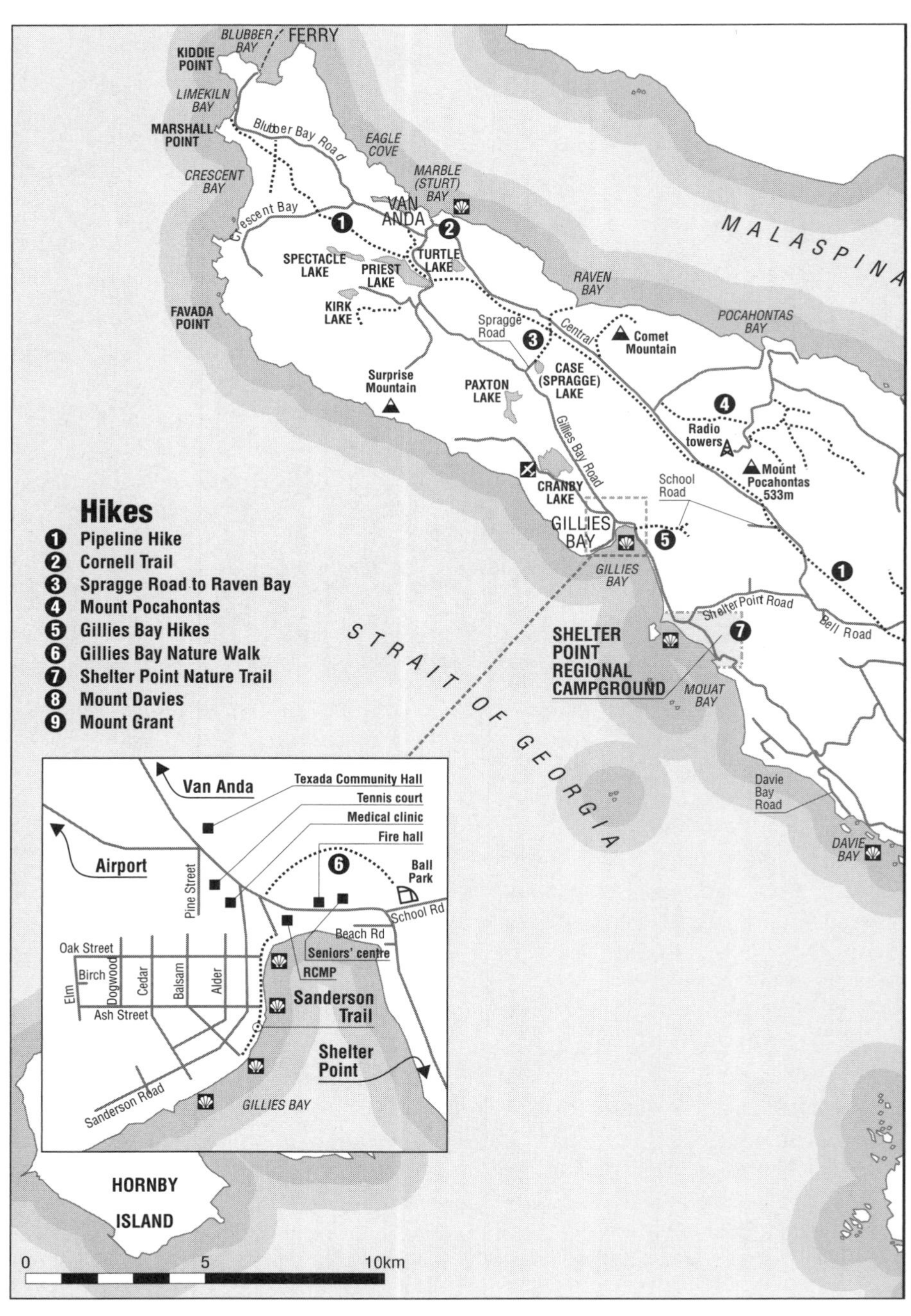

Texada Island

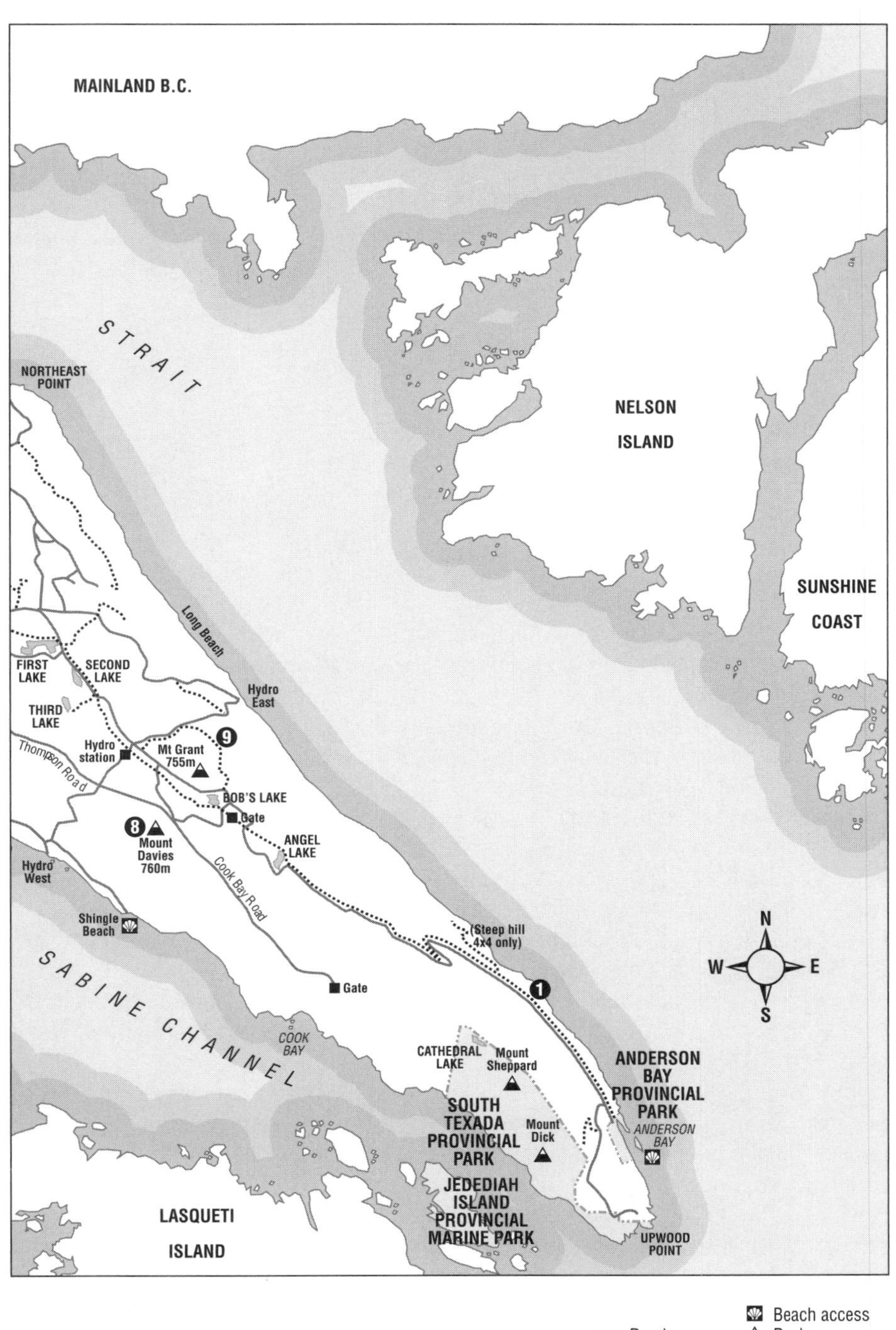
MAINLAND B.C.
STRAIT
NORTHEAST POINT
NELSON ISLAND
SUNSHINE COAST
Long Beach
Hydro East
FIRST LAKE
SECOND LAKE
THIRD LAKE
Hydro station
Thompson Road
9
Mt Grant 755m
BOB'S LAKE
Gate
8
Mount Davies 760m
ANGEL LAKE
Hydro West
Cook Bay Road
Shingle Beach
(Steep hill 4x4 only)
N
W
E
S
1
SABINE CHANNEL
Gate
COOK BAY
CATHEDRAL LAKE
Mount Sheppard
ANDERSON BAY PROVINCIAL PARK
ANDERSON BAY
SOUTH TEXADA PROVINCIAL PARK
Mount Dick
JEDEDIAH ISLAND PROVINCIAL MARINE PARK
LASQUETI ISLAND
UPWOOD POINT
Roads
Trails
Park boundary
Beach access
Peak
See text
Airport

Information on Texada is available from the Powell River Visitors Bureau Society (4690 Marine Avenue, Powell River, BC V8A 2L1; tel: 604-485-4701 or 1-877-817-8669; fax: 604-485-2822; e-mail: info@discoverpowellriver.com. You can also get information on Texada from www.thesunshinecoast.com/texadaisland and www.discoverpowellriver.com.

ESPECIALLY FOR WALKERS

There are many easy walks, for those not wishing to ascend one of Texada's peaks. In addition to the Shore and Road Walks outlined at the end of this chapter, try one of the following:

- the Cornell Trail (see hike 2, page 207)
- Spragge Road to Raven Bay (see hike 3, page 208)
- Gillies Bay hikes (see hike 5, page 209)
- Gillies Bay Nature Walk (see hike 6, page 210)
- Shelter Point Nature Trail (see hike 7, page 211)

HIKES

Much of the hiking on Texada is on old logging roads, many of them now moss-covered and ingrown. Most hikes are on uninhabited Crown land on the southern half of the island.

Some trails are on private land managed by a company called Texada Island Forest Reserve. You will see many of the company's red-and-white signs with its telephone number and, often, a No Trespassing sign. A spokesperson for the company said that hiking was permitted on the land but bicycles and motorized vehicles are strictly prohibited. Before using the land, call the company representative on Texada at 604-486-7362 to obtain permission.

There is one paved main road (with changing names) that extends from the ferry dock, through Van Anda and Gillies Bay, ending 4 km past Shelter Point. From there, Central Road (known locally as High Road) is a good gravel road back to Van Anda. Bell Road runs southeast from Central Road at its intersection with Shelter Point Road. Bell connects with many of the forestry roads in Texada's south end and this is where you'll find the best hiking on the island.

The hikes described here are listed roughly from north to south. Distances on Texada can be fairly long, so some kind of transportation is almost essential. None of the hikes described are within walking distance of the ferry.

In addition to the trails listed here, you might like to inquire about the trails to Surprise Mountain, Black Mountain northeast of Mount Pocahontas, Mount Flicker (local name) and Mount Shepherd in 900-ha South Texada Provincial Park. At 891 m, Mount Shepherd is the highest peak in the Gulf Islands. Texada's 35-ha Anderson Bay Provincial Park includes a small island and a peninsula and is on Texada's southeastern shore. You need a four-by-four or a boat to get to these parks, which, I am told, offer extensive hiking opportunities. Unfortunately, I was not able to explore them myself.

Much of the information for this chapter was made possible by Texada's master trekker, John Dove. John came to Texada more than 30 years ago, to work as a geologist. He has hiked the island from end to end and knows the trails intimately, especially since he is responsible for creating many of them. John welcomes visitors to the island's hiking club, the Texada Trekkers, which has an outing every Saturday. All you have to do is show up at 10 a.m., usually at the parking area in the Gillies Bay ball park but sometimes at the service station in Van Anda. For more information, call John at 604-486-7100 or email jdove@prcn.org.

1. PIPELINE HIKE ★

Trail length	Up to 40 km one way
Time required	Variable
Description	Fairly level hike along pipeline right-of-way
Level	Easy
Access	The natural gas pipeline runs the length of the island and the right-of-way can be accessed in many places, including along Central Road, about 4 km south of Van Anda. Yellow signs identify the pipeline path and red-ribboned sticks mark its route.
Cautions	No vehicles, including mountain bikes, are allowed on this grassy corridor. Walk with care, as there are open ditches and gravel barriers, in places.

Walking along this pipeline is not unlike walking along a hydro right-of-way cut through the forest. Nevertheless, the countryside is pretty. Don't walk farther than you wish to return, since this is not a circular route.

2. CORNELL TRAIL ★★

Trail length	1.5 km each way
Time required	About 30 minutes each way
Description	Pretty hike through forest and along a lake
Level	Easy
Access	Drive or walk south on Prospect Street (this road starts to the left of 2516 Van Anda Street in Van Anda) for about 500 m, until you reach an old logging road going off on your left. The hike starts here.
Cautions	There are houses along Central Road north of the hike but out of view. Respect private property.

This hike is in the area of the old Cornell gold mine. You walk along the logging road at the beginning of the hike for about 10 minutes, until you reach a foot trail going down to the left. Take this trail. Soon you will cross a little bridge. The trail then follows an old railway bed.

This fine path leads south along the east side of Turtle Lake (a.k.a. Emily Lake). There are many offshoots along the way, some leading to houses along Central Road. Follow the railway bed beyond the south end of the lake to reach the site of the Cornell Mine. Where the mine tunnel used to be visible near the bottom of a steep hillside, there is now just an area of broken rocks below a small quarry. A short distance beyond the mine, the trail ends on Central Road, next to a small log cabin. You can then, if you wish, return along the trail or use the road to circle back to the trailhead in Van Anda. The distance is about the same either way.

3. Spragge Road to Raven Bay ★★

Trail length	About 3 km each way
Time required	35–40 minutes each way
Description	Pleasant hike through mixed forest
Level	Easy
Access	Spragge Road is a short road to the east of Gillies Bay Road, about halfway between Van Anda and Gillies Bay. Park at the end of Spragge Road. You will see a private property on the right. Turn left onto a dirt road. You will almost immediately see a gate to another private property on the left. Take the old logging road just to the right of this gate.
Caution	Be very careful to respect the private property in this area. I had a close encounter with one rather large dog protecting his turf.

The logging road descends to pond-like Case (or Spragge) Lake, which it follows for a short distance. It then climbs a small hill to the left. There are several offshoots along the way but the main trail is wide and unmistakable. After about 20 minutes of pleasant downhill walking, you will come out on Central Road. This is as far as I walked. However, I understand that if you walk left (north) along Central Road for a few hundred metres, you will find another old logging road heading right (east). (If you are driving from Van Anda, this point is about 5 km from the town or 1.6 km past the Imperial Limestone Company quarry.) About 20 minutes walking along this road will take you to Raven Bay on Texada's east side.

4. MOUNT POCAHONTAS ★★★

Trail length	2.5 km each way
Time required	About 1 hour up, 45 minutes down
Description	A climb to a fine lookout that provides outstanding 360-degree views
Level	Moderate; some steep sections
Elevation	533 m, although your climb is only about half this
Access	The logging road to Pocahontas Bay runs off Central Road about 8.5 km from Van Anda (on the left) or 6.2 km from the intersection of Shelter Point Road if you're coming from the southeast. Park about 800 m along this logging road, where a rough road goes off to the right. The hike starts here.

The trail follows an old logging road for most of the way. While the surrounding forest is fairly young, there are many rocky outcrops along the left side as you climb and some mossy areas on the right. You'll pass large patches of evergreen huckleberry, many different varieties of fern, and both white and jack pine.

Continue straight on the road for about 40 minutes until it begins to descend. At this point, look for a trail to the left. At time of writing, the turnoff was well flagged with surveyor's tape and the trail itself marked by red metal squares. The trail leads to the remains of the first forestry lookout in BC. The views from here are spectacular. On a clear day, you will see as far as Savary Island to the north, Jervis Inlet to the east, and Hornby and Denman Islands to the west. While this lookout is not the summit of Mount Pocahontas, which has a number of radio towers and which you can see to the west, it has better views.

5. GILLIES BAY HIKES ★★

Trail length	5–10 km, depending on route taken
Time required	1–2 hours, depending on route taken
Description	Trails on old forestry roads through mixed forest
Level	Easy
Access	Take the section of School Road opposite the Gillies Bay grocery store and park at the field. Follow the logging road until you see a sign for Texada Island Forest Reserve.
Cautions	As this hike is on private land, first obtain permission to hike by calling Texada Island Forest Reserve (604-486-7362). The company accepts no liability should any mishap occur.

This network of logging roads criss-crosses an area of second-growth alder and fir. There are some low, wet areas. Most of the roads go nowhere in particular but one leads to a bluff with a good picnic spot and view over Gillies Bay. Another road leads to a beaver-dammed lake that contains painted turtles, while School Road (really just an old logging road, most of the way) is a 5-km walk to Central Road, due east of Gillies Bay.

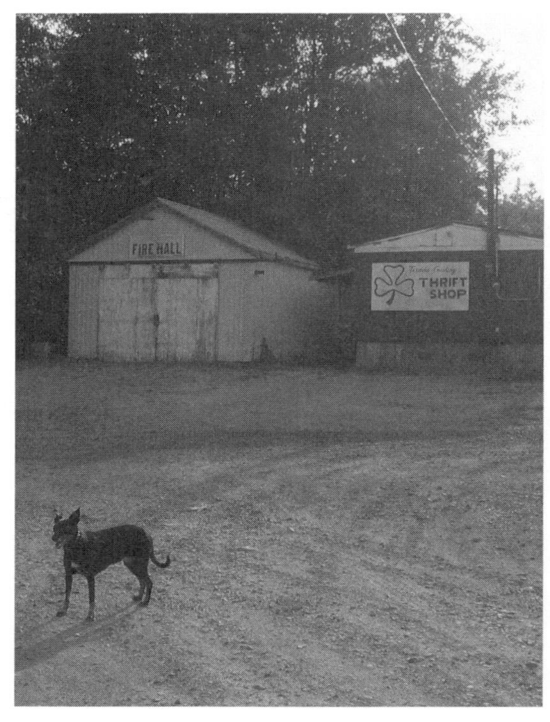

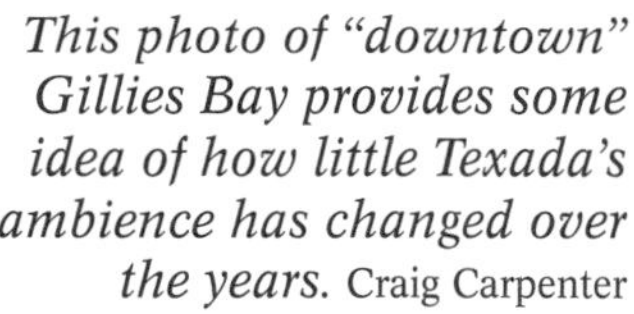

This photo of "downtown" Gillies Bay provides some idea of how little Texada's ambience has changed over the years. Craig Carpenter

6. Gillies Bay Nature Walk ★★★

Trail length	2 km each way
Time required	1 hour
Description	A captivating walk through old-growth forest and wetland
Level	Easy
Access	From behind a dilapidated house across from the RCMP station
Cautions	Parts of the trail cross wet areas on log rounds placed as stepping stones or on long, overgrown nurse logs, so be very careful of your footing.

This beautiful forest walk, constructed for community use by the Texada Island Forest Reserve on its own property, has a bit of almost everything. You will pass perhaps the largest old-growth Douglas fir trees on Texada, immense cedars and Sitka spruce, large patches of giant devil's club, wet areas filled with skunk cabbage and a heronry in the tree tops at the reserve's west end.

7. SHELTER POINT NATURE TRAIL ★★★

Trail length	1 km each way, plus additional forest trails
Time required	30 minutes each way, plus 45 minutes if you try all the forest trails
Description	A very pretty hike through old-growth forest and along the ocean
Level	Easy
Access	The south side of Shelter Point Road at the entrance to the park

This delightful hike on a well-manicured trail follows a bank along the water. The forest is fairly open with some lovely old-growth trees and glimpses of the ocean and the beach below, all along the trail. There are several accesses to the beach, although some are rather steep. There are also some fine benches to sit on and enjoy the view.

The trail loops to the left at the Ponderosa (a spot on the beach where a road access comes in on the left). At this point, you can choose to continue by the trail (which is still flat, although slightly rougher than the first section), return by the beach (if it's low tide), or take the road until it crosses Davie Bay Road, where you turn left to return to your starting point. If you follow the beach and the tide is out, look for the low stone walls of the old Native fish traps, which can be clearly seen at the south end of the hike.

There are several forest trails that join the nature trail here and there. If you decide to hike these too, you will add about another 1.5 km to your outing.

The Texada Trekkers taking a break on one of their weekly outings, this time on a coastal hike near Davie Bay. David Martin

8. Mount Davies ★★★★	
Trail length	4 km
Time required	2 hours
Description	A very enjoyable hike along a diverse trail through old-growth forest to two sensational viewpoints
Level	Moderate; some steep sections
Elevation	760 m; elevation gain: 150 m
Access	From the junction of Shelter Point, Central and Bell Roads, take Bell Road south for 9.3 km to a fork and then take the left road toward Bob's Lake. (Do not turn right to the BC Hydro Reactor.) From here, drive 1.3 km to a second junction, where you turn right into Texada Forest Service Road 5829 Branch 09, known locally as Cook Bay Road because it leads to Cook Bay. (A sign here directs you to the Anderson Bay Pipeline Route.) Continue for 2 km to the intersection of Texada Forest Service Road 5829 Branch 02 (Thompson Road) and turn right. Drive for another 100 m and park on the left side of the road. The flagged trailhead (several round boulders and a small cairn) is just a little farther down the same side of the road as the parking area.

Note: The forest service roads mentioned were signed at time of writing.

This 35-minute trail to the summit of Mount Davies passes through mixed forest with a pine-needle and moss ground cover. The well-flagged trail (red surveyor's tape) circles the mountain and provides views at the top. Along the way, you will pass massive moss-covered boulders from which ferns and other plants manage to grow.

About 15–20 minutes along the trail, you will pass a trail on the left (east). This trail passes through old growth, a wet area and a viewpoint on Bloody Mountain (a local name). Try this on your way back. For now, continue to the summit.

From the top of Mount Davies, you have magnificent 360-degree views. To the south is Lasqueti Island and to the west are Hornby and Denman Islands. You can even see Chrome Island Light Station to the south of Denman. To the north are the mainland mountains. In both directions, you have good views of the huge expanse of Texada Island.

It will take you about 15 minutes to descend to the flagged trail to Bloody Mountain, so named because a Texada Trekker once cut a finger here and bled profusely for a few minutes. This trail meanders through lovely old-growth forest and soon

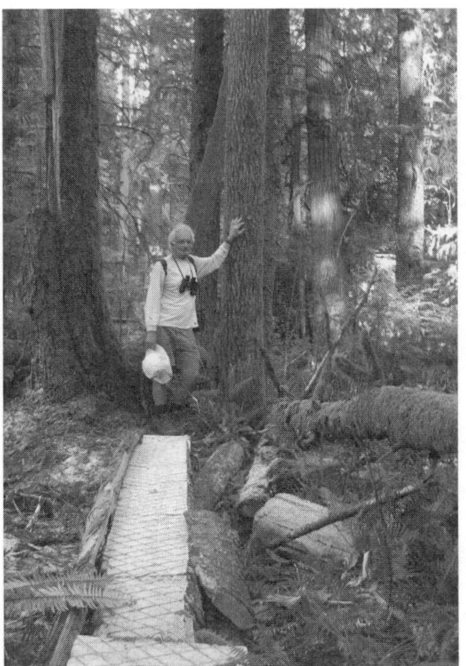

John Dove—trail maker, trailblazer, guide and naturalist—enjoying the peace of the Gillies Bay Nature Walk.
Craig Carpenter

reaches a large lily pond where beaver live. After hiking for about 25 minutes, you will reach another trail, marked with a cairn, that leads to a viewpoint.

The 20-minute (there and back) detour to the viewpoint is well worth the time and effort. It crosses a logged and replanted area before reaching the viewpoint. Here you are looking across Sabine Channel over Jedediah, Paul and Jervis Islands to the eastern end of Lasqueti Island. To the southeast, you can see Mount Shepherd.

Once you return from the viewpoint to the main Bloody Mountain trail, it's only another 5–10 minutes down to the Texada Forest Service Road 5829 Branch 09 (the Cook Bay Road). Turn left (north) on the road and continue to an intersection where you will again turn left (northwest). At a third junction, take the left fork once again, which will put you back on Texada Forest Service Road 5829 Branch 02 (Thompson Road), about 100 m from where you parked.

9. Mount Grant ★★★★

Trail length	4 km
Time required	1.5–2 hours
Description	A superb trail with many fine views north and south of Texada Island
Level	Moderate; some very steep sections
Elevation	755 m; elevation gain: 135 m
Access	From the junction of Shelter Point, Central and Bell Roads, take Bell Road south for 9.3 km to a junction, then take the left fork toward Bob's Lake. (Do not turn right to the BC Hydro Reactor.) Continue 1.6 km (past another turnoff) and park on the grass off the right side of the road (Texada Forest Service Road 5829 Branch 03). Walk back about 60 m to the flagged trailhead on the right (north side of the road).

John Dove, Texada Island's master hiker and creator of many of the island's trails, pauses for a "nature moment" to enlighten a group of hikers. Craig Carpenter

About 5 minutes from the trailhead, you'll come to a junction. You can choose to go either way, as this is a loop trail. I recommend turning right and have described this route below. The climb is more gradual this way, although the descent from the summit is steeper.

The trail up follows a logging road east-southeast around the mountain. Along the way, you'll pass white, jack and ponderosa pine. The white pine here, as elsewhere on Texada, is being killed by a disease called "blister rust." Other plants to look for along this trail include juniper, Labrador tea, adder's tongue, grape fern and ground cedar.

After you have walked for about 20 minutes, take a flagged trail heading off to the left (northeast). (At time of writing, the logging road was blocked here with tree limbs to indicate that you are not to continue along it.) The new trail, which heads steeply uphill, is well marked with red flagging. You'll soon reach a viewpoint from which you can see Denman and Hornby Islands to the west. After another 10 minutes, you will reach another viewpoint providing views of Nelson and Hardy Islands and Jervis Inlet to the northeast. This view is even more spectacular from the summit. It took us an hour to reach the top, but we spent time examining some rare plants that are distantly related to ferns.

The trail down from the top is steep. Its descent begins in a southwesterly direction. Soon you will reach a cairn, indicating a change of direction to the north. This trail is well flagged. Shortly after this, you will see a side trail to the right. It is a short detour to a spectacular viewpoint atop a rocky outcrop. The rest of the return trail descends steeply, and you can easily return to the starting point in about 40 minutes.

SHORE AND ROAD WALKS

Erickson Beach: There is a very short beach walk along Erickson Beach to the east of the government dock in Van Anda.

Sanderson Trail: This trail along the Gillies Bay shore parallels Sanderson Road and runs from the RCMP station on Gillies Bay Road to Balsam Avenue (off Sanderson Road). You can access the trail from several of the beach accesses off Sanderson Road (opposite Balsam Avenue, Ash Street or Oak Street) or from the access beside the RCMP station. The trail weaves in and out along the shoreline in front of houses and passes through blackberry bushes that drip with the luscious fruit in August. You might consider walking one way along the trail and then returning along the road. The trail provides sweeping views of the large bay.

Shelter Point Regional Park beach access: This beach is a lovely place to walk at low tide.

Davie Bay beach access: South of Davie Bay, you can park at the hydro station and walk on the beach, for some distance. If you walk south for about 3 km on the forest road, just above the hydro station, you'll reach Shingle Beach.

AND IF YOU PADDLE . . .

Texada's position in the middle of the Strait of Georgia means that it is more exposed than most of the islands described in this book. Waves and wind can build up in the strait and create dangerous conditions on both sides of Texada. Sabine Channel has quite strong currents that create steep seas. This, combined with Texada's few bays and inhospitable shores, makes paddling here more difficult—and dangerous—than on many other Gulf Islands. I recommend that only experienced paddlers, or paddlers in the company of a guide, use the launches described below. I have not launched from any of these accesses, although I have kayaked to the southwestern shore of Texada from Jedediah Island (about a 20–30 minute paddle).

Van Anda marina: You can launch from here to explore Texada's northeastern shore.

Raven Bay: This is another launch site for visiting Texada's northeastern shore.

Pocahontas Bay: From here you can explore Texada's eastern shore.

Sanderson Road: There are beach accesses opposite most of the side roads that intersect Sanderson Road. While they give you access to Gillies Bay, the bay dries out at low tide, thus limiting the time when you can use these accesses.

Shelter Point Regional Park: This is a good place to launch and will allow you to explore the Texada shore both to the north and south. If you paddle south, be careful of the currents around Mouat Bay, which I've been told can be particularly swift.

Hydro West: This is a good place to launch but there is limited parking. If you paddle northwest to Davie Bay, there are several islets to visit along the way.

Shingle Bay: You can launch from the beach, at this forestry site. It will give you access to the south Texada shoreline, as well as the opportunity to paddle north.

Anderson Bay: This is an excellent place to launch and to camp, but you need a four-wheel drive vehicle to reach this part of the island. Much of Anderson Bay is provincial park.

Thetis ISLAND

Thetis is the smallest island discussed in this book and, except for about 14 km of public road and 19 km of shoreline, everything on Thetis is private. Most of its 10.4 square km is forested, with some farmland, meadows and wetlands. While the owners of Thetis's three Christian study centres have kept much of the island from being developed, many new lots have been created by a recent strata development near the centre of the island.

Although serviced by a ferry, many visitors to Thetis are boaters who spend much of their time in and around the two marinas in Telegraph Harbour, where most of the island's services are found. Those who venture inland find a small, tranquil island that has changed little over the decades. Like other Gulf Islands, Thetis has attracted a wide variety of strong-minded, independent individuals, including one who makes his living catching slugs to supply to science labs. The permanent population of 349 swells in summer with the seasonal residents who own cottages here. While the hiking is curtailed by private property, the island's serene roads are delightful to explore on foot or by bicycle.

HISTORY

Thetis Island was named after the British frigate H.M. *Thetis*, which operated in the Gulf Islands under Captain Augustus I. Kuper between 1851 and 1853. Originally, Thetis and Kuper Islands were one, but in 1905, a channel was dredged between them to allow boats passage. This channel, now known as Canoe Pass, was originally about 2 m at low tide but has since silted in and become much shallower.

Almost all of Thetis's early European settlers were from Great Britain, including its first resident, William Henry Curran, an Irishman who felled trees and sold them to the Chemainus sawmill in the 1870s. Two pioneering families—the Hunters and the Burchells—arrived in the early 1890s and soon owned almost all the island between them. The Hunters eventually donated land to the Intervarsity Christian Fellowship, which now operates the Pioneer Pacific summer camp here. The Burchells ran a successful store and farm where the Capernwray Harbour Bible School now stands. In 1904, Alfred Heneage and his sister Eveline Mary bought land on Thetis. Eveline grew lavender, which she distilled into perfume, and Alfred grew a fine vegetable garden. In keeping with island tradition, Alfred left the land to the

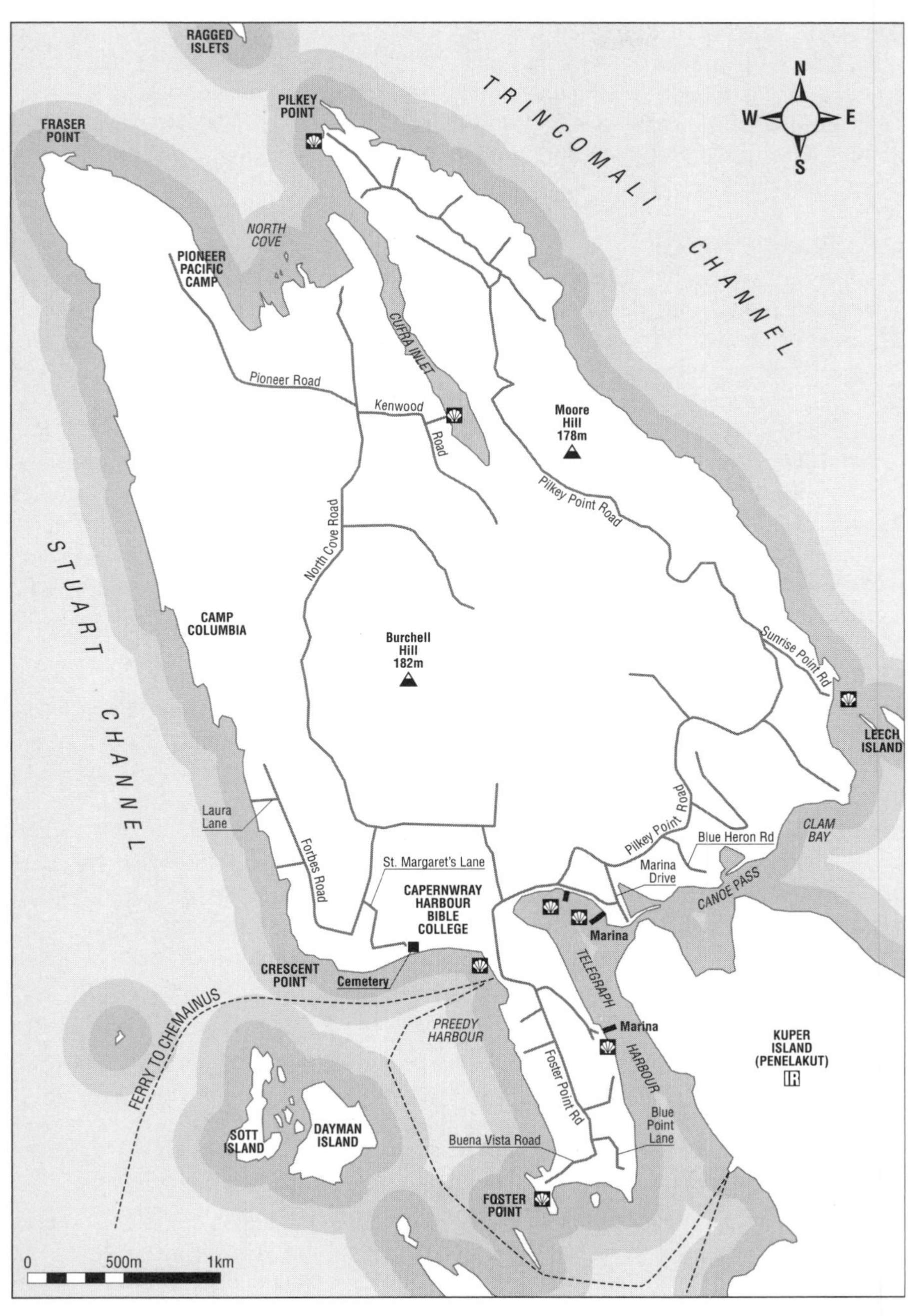
RAGGED ISLETS
TRINCOMALI CHANNEL
N
W
E
S
PILKEY POINT
FRASER POINT
NORTH COVE
PIONEER PACIFIC CAMP
CUFRA INLET
Pioneer Road
Kenwood
Road
Moore Hill 178m
Pilkey Point Road
North Cove Road
STUART CHANNEL
CAMP COLUMBIA
Burchell Hill 182m
Sunrise Point Rd
LEECH ISLAND
Laura Lane
Forbes Road
Pilkey Point Road
Blue Heron Rd
CLAM BAY
St. Margaret's Lane
Marina Drive
CANOE PASS
CAPERNWRAY HARBOUR BIBLE COLLEGE
Marina
TELEGRAPH HARBOUR
CRESCENT POINT
Cemetery
Marina
FERRY TO CHEMAINUS
PREEDY HARBOUR
KUPER ISLAND (PENELAKUT)
IR
Foster Point Rd
SOTT ISLAND
DAYMAN ISLAND
Blue Point Lane
Buena Vista Road
FOSTER POINT
0
500m
1km

Roads
Beach access
Peak
Indian Reserve

Thetis Island

Anglican Church and it became Camp Columbia, another summer camp for children. Rupert Forbes arrived with his family in 1905. He built small boats, which were admired for their workmanship and lovely lines. Today, the Forbes home—Overbury Farm Resort—is still in the family. Thetis grew slowly and by 1914 had a population of only 70, most of whom supported themselves by growing vegetables for the Chemainus market.

GETTING THERE

The ferry makes twelve 30-minute trips between Thetis Island and Chemainus on Vancouver Island every day. For more information, obtain a Southern Gulf Islands schedule or contact BC Ferries. Harbour Air, Seair Seaplanes, Amigo Airways and Tofino Air fly to Thetis (see Resources, page 235).

SERVICES AND ACCOMMODATION

Limited groceries can be purchased at the two marinas in Telegraph Harbour, the Howling Wolf Farm or Dragon Rock Farm. The Telegraph Harbour Marina also has a café and gift shop, while the Thetis Island Marina has a restaurant, pub, post office and laundromat. There are several bed and breakfasts, cabins for rent and a small resort but no public campground. Accommodation is listed on the community web site at www.thetisisland.net. In the summer, there is often a water shortage on Thetis.

SHORE AND ROAD WALKS

Thetis has no Crown land or public parks and, therefore, no public hiking trails. However, the roads are pretty and have little vehicle traffic, making Thetis a pleasant place to spend a day walking or cycling. Perhaps the best shore walk is just north of the ferry dock. Here, at low tide, you can walk along Thetis's western shore for some distance.

Residents walk, with permission, on their neighbours' land, but these trails are not available to the general public. If you want to follow a trail to the island's interior or to access the shore, you must ask the property owner's permission first.

Most of the walking is along either Pilkey Point Road or North Cove Road. If you walk up the hill from the ferry, you will have the choice of turning right (east) along Pilkey Point Road or left (north) up North Cove Road.

Pilkey Point Road (7 km one way): Before turning onto Pilkey Point Road, stop and enjoy the view down over Capernwray Harbour Bible Centre and the ferry dock. Take Pilkey Point Road east, skirting the head of Telegraph Harbour. Take a small detour by turning right down Marina Drive to the nicely landscaped grounds of the Telegraph Harbour Marina (about a 10-minute walk from the ferry).

Continuing along Pilkey Point Road, you'll pass a few farms, some boggy areas and stands of trees. Be prepared for a stiff climb as the road goes up Moore Hill, which provides some glimpses of the sea. It will take you about 90 minutes to reach the end of Pilkey Point Road. Here you'll find a public beach access. Pilkey Point is a popular place for residents to come on summer nights to picnic, swim and watch the sun set.

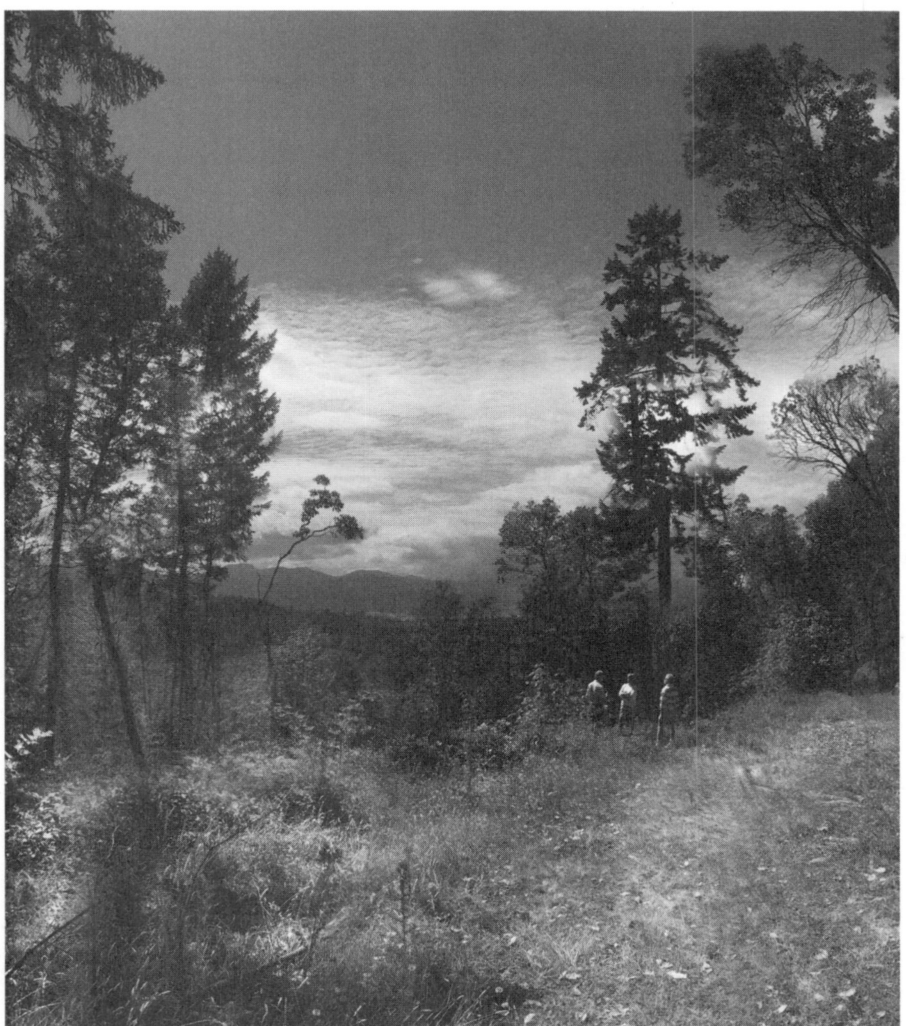

Along Pilkey Point Road you'll pass farms and boggy areas but be prepared for a steep climb as the road goes up Moore Hill, which provides glimpses of the sea. Veronica Shelford

North Cove Road (3.5 km one way): A few minutes walk from the ferry terminal, North Cove Road passes the Community Hall and the Thetis Island Elementary School (to the right). A little farther on, you can make a worthwhile detour to the left, onto Forbes Road, and continue to St. Margaret's Lane (left again) and Thetis Island's historic St. Margaret's Cemetery. This pretty little graveyard, about 2.5 km from the ferry terminal, contains the graves of many of the island's pioneers.

Moore Hill, toward the northeastern end of Thetis Island, is the second highest point on Thetis. Unfortunately for hikers, it is private land and you have to obtain permission from the landowner to use the trails here. Veronica Shelford

North Cove Road continues past Forbes Road about 3 km to North Cove (where there is no public beach access). If you turn off North Cove Road onto Kenwood, you'll reach narrow Cufra Inlet, which stretches over 1 km toward the centre of the island. Commercial clam beds and soft ground make it hard to walk along the inlet's banks and the unwelcoming shoreline, with little human habitation, does not invite exploration.

Foster Point (2 km one way): From the ferry, it is possible to walk south along Foster Point Road for about 2 km. At the end of the road (where it turns off into Buena Vista), you'll find a somewhat overgrown path that provides public access to Foster Point. From here, you have good views south to tiny Hudson Island, east to Kuper Island and west to Vancouver Island.

AND IF YOU PADDLE . . .

If you wanted to circumnavigate Thetis Island, you'd be looking at about 11 nautical miles (20 km), a good day's outing including a stop or two for lunch and tea. Nearby Kuper, Tent and some of the Shoal Islands belong to the Penelakut Band.

There are only a few places to put in on Thetis since so much of the island is private. Here are a few suggestions:

Preedy Harbour: Try the beach or the public dock, where the ferry lands. This gives you access to Thetis's western shore and the cluster of small but pretty islands just offshore. You can also paddle south and view the stunning sandstone sculpture on nearby Kuper and Tent Islands.

Telegraph Harbour: You can launch from the public boat ramp (on the right, just as you turn down Marina Drive) or, with permission, from one of the marinas in Telegraph Harbour. There's a small beach to the north of the Thetis Island Marina's store, which is very convenient. From here you can explore Telegraph Harbour and exit either by narrow Canoe Pass at its northern end or from the open end to the south. The former gives you access to Thetis's northern end, as well as Penelakut Spit on Kuper Island and the cluster of privately owned islands north and east of Kuper. The latter gives you access to the Kuper Island shoreline and Thetis's western shore. While Canoe Pass can be very shallow at low tides, it only dries completely at the lowest tides.

Sunrise Point Road and Pilkey Point: I don't recommend these beach accesses, mainly because the previous accesses are so handy. Sunrise Point gets you on Thetis's eastern shore and Pilkey Point puts you on the north shore with possibilities of exploring, at high tide, some of shallow Cufra Inlet that cuts into the island for some distance.

Marine Parks

Marine parks provide recreational opportunities for boaters, throughout the year. Most of them also provide safe overnight anchorages, camping, picnic tables, fresh water and outhouses. They don't usually have extensive trail networks, although most of them have some trails, often along beautiful shoreline.

The marine parks described in this chapter are administered by either BC Parks or Parks Canada. Most Marine Parks are accessible only by boat; however, a few of them, mostly those on larger islands, with regular ferry service, are accessible by land. Marine parks on islands discussed elsewhere in this book are described in the chapters devoted to those islands and include Beaumont on South Pender, Mansons Landing on Cortes, Montague Harbour on Galiano, Rebecca Spit on Quadra and Winter Cove on Saturna Island.

The marine parks included here are all on small islands that are not discussed elsewhere in this book, have at least 3–4 km of trails and can be reached by either a private passenger ferry or a relatively short paddle. Parks that are more interesting as destinations for experienced paddlers than they are for hikers are not described here. BC Parks includes more detailed information about its marine parks on its web site: wlapwww.gov.bc.ca/bcparks/explore/explore.htm. Information on parks in the Gulf Islands National Park Reserve can be found on the Parks Canada web site: www.parkscanada.gc.ca.

Marine Parks are popular with paddlers and boaters. Parks Canada

The following rules should be observed in all marine parks:

- All wildlife is protected and should be left undisturbed.
- There are no disposal facilities; take out all your garbage.
- Where mooring buoys are provided, no more than one boat should be moored to a buoy; rafting of boats is not allowed.
- Fresh water is not always available, so bring your own.
- Cutting trees is not allowed.
- In provincial marine parks, where no camping facilities are provided, onshore camping is permitted; however, in the Gulf Islands National Park Reserve, camping is only allowed in designated camping areas.
- Where campfires are allowed, follow the usual precautions. Make fires only in firepits, as these islands receive little rain and are very dry. At times, open fires may not be allowed on any of the islands.
- Quiet hours are from 11 p.m. to 7 a.m.
- Excessive noise is not permitted at any time.

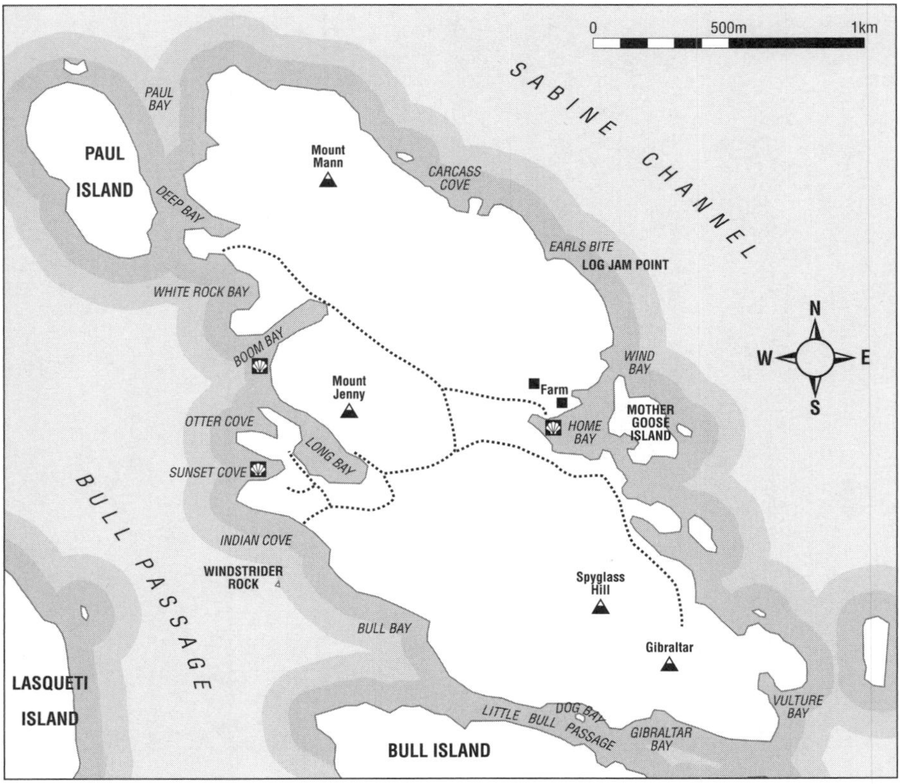

Jedediah Island Provincial Marine Park

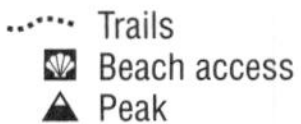

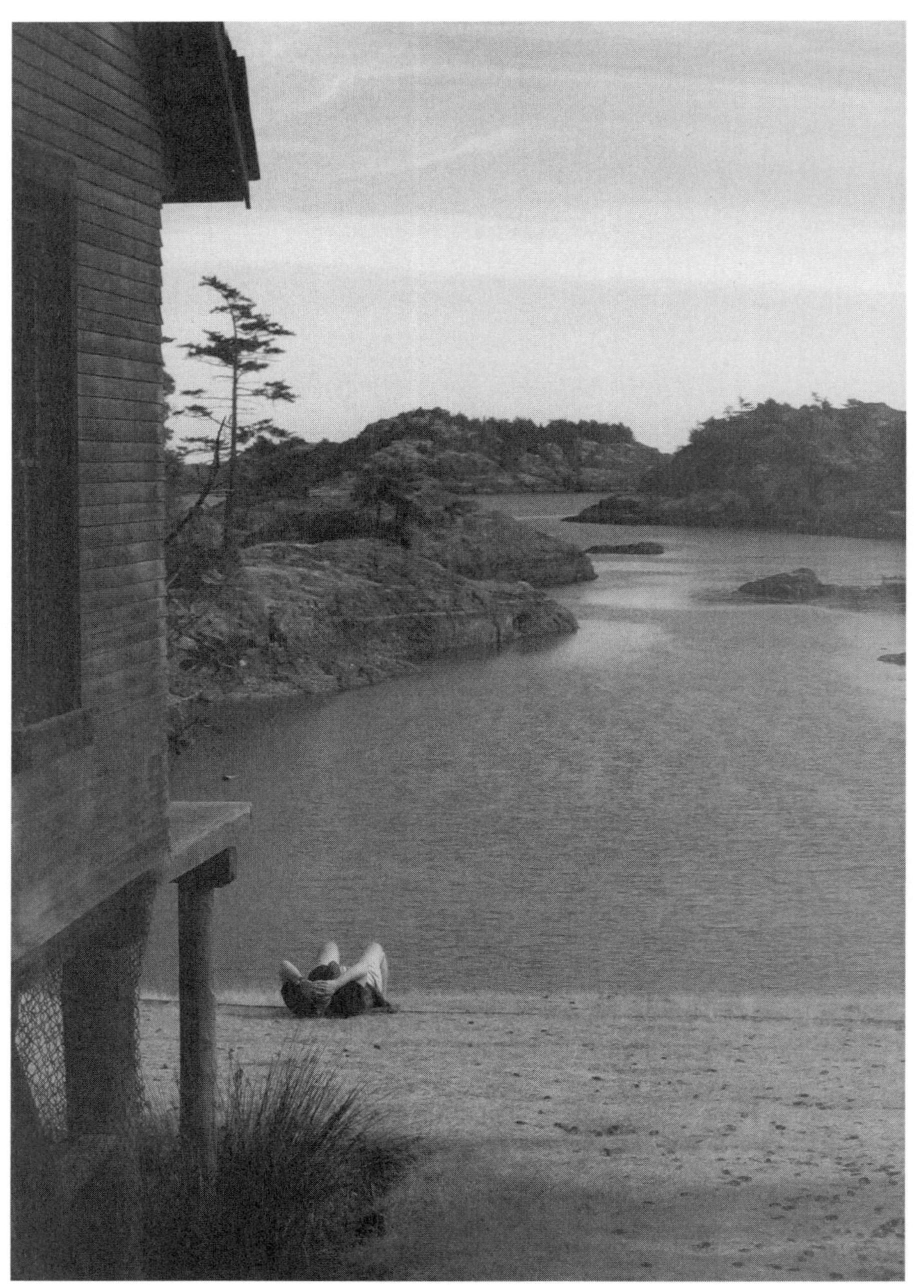

Home Bay, Jedediah Island. This house was built by a Mr. Foote of Vancouver, who purchased the island soon after it was Crown-granted in 1885. The house was occupied until 1990, most recently by the last owner, Mary Palmer, who bought the island with her first husband in 1949. Craig Carpenter

- Boats are prohibited from discharging sewage or grey water while moored or anchored in marine parks.
- Dogs may not be permitted in some parks. When they are, they should be leashed and you must clean up after them.
- Consumption of alcohol is permitted only in your campsite.
- Firearms are prohibited.
- Barbecues can be used only on the ground, unless a barbecue attachment is provided on the picnic table.

1. JEDEDIAH ISLAND ★★★★

Jedediah Island lies in Sabine Channel, between Lasqueti and Texada Islands, and is accessible only by private boat. It is a popular destination for kayakers, who often reach it from either Lasqueti Island or Schooner Cove on Vancouver Island, where private boat operators offer kayak ferry service to the island.

One of the largest island parks in the province (243 ha), Jedediah is named after the son of Lord Tucker of England, who sponsored a survey expedition of the Gulf Islands in the late 19th century. The island had only a handful of owners before Evan and Mary Mattice of Seattle, Washington, purchased it in 1949. In 1972, Mary and her second husband, Albert Palmer, retired to the island, where they lived until 1990, when they put it up for sale. The BC government bought it in 1995 with the help of many private donors, several environmental organizations and $1.1 million from the estate of the late Daniel Culver, a mountaineer from North Vancouver who died on his descent from the summit of K2.

The interior of Jedediah contains mature Douglas fir and arbutus and rocky outcrops. The island's homesites, farm fields and orchards are still evident. Sheep, feral goats and a horse were left on the island. The horse has since died but the other animals still roam free.

There are several good camping areas near the shoreline around Long Bay and in the small bays on the east side of the island.

Hiking/Walking Trails

The 3.5 km of walking trails cross the island and connect Jedediah's many bays. The main trail passes through old-growth forest to an open field, linking up with several other trails. Animal trails meander through open forest and reach the island's peaks.

2. NEWCASTLE ISLAND ★★★★

Newcastle Island is a 306-ha park in Nanaimo Harbour. From May to September, you can reach it by a 10-minute foot-passenger ferry from Maffeo-Sutton Park, just north of downtown Nanaimo (behind the Civic Arena) on Highway 1. The ferry departs hourly between about 10 a.m. and 7 p.m. with additional later sailings in the high season. It is run by the Snuneymuxw First Nation. Outside of summer months, you can take a water taxi to the island. Private boats can anchor in Mark Bay or tie up at the wharf, where there are berthing facilities for more than 50 boats.

Middens remain from the residents of two Salish villages, which were deserted by the time coal was discovered here in 1849. The island was given the same name as

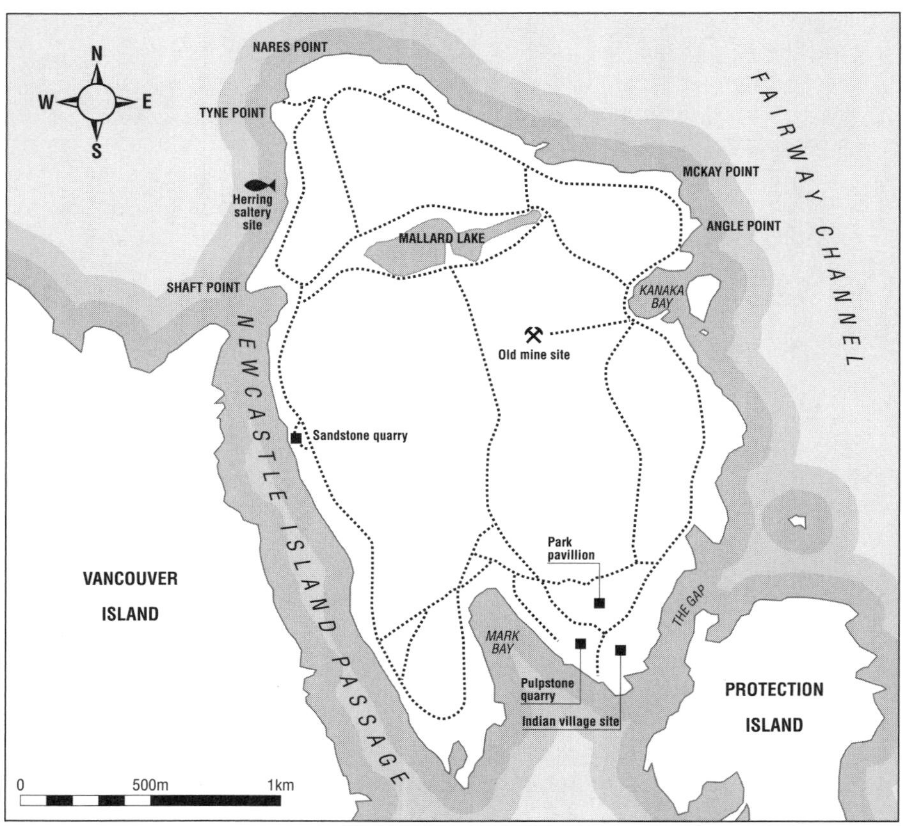

Newcastle Island Provincial Marine Park

the famous northern English coal town, and for 30 years coal was mined here. Sandstone quarried on the island from 1869 to 1932 was used in buildings such as the San Francisco mint and for pulpstones used in paper mills. From about 1910 to 1941, Newcastle was home to a small settlement of Japanese who operated a herring saltery, cannery and shipyard.

In 1931, the Canadian Pacific Steamship Company acquired the island and built a dance pavilion, a tea house, picnic areas, a soccer field and a wading pool. The company successfully competed with the Union Steamship Company's similar operation on Bowen Island by bringing pleasure-seekers on one-day outings from Vancouver. Until World War II, Vancouverites regularly flocked to the island on Sunday outings and company picnics. In 1955, the island became the property of the City of Nanaimo, and in 1961, it was established as a provincial marine park.

Newcastle Island is one of BC's most developed marine parks. The dance pavilion has been restored and is now a visitor centre, complete with displays and a restaurant. There are individual and group campsites, picnic facilities, washrooms, pit toilets, picnic and barbecue shelters, an adventure playground, a soccer field, swimming areas and about 20 km of well-developed trails.

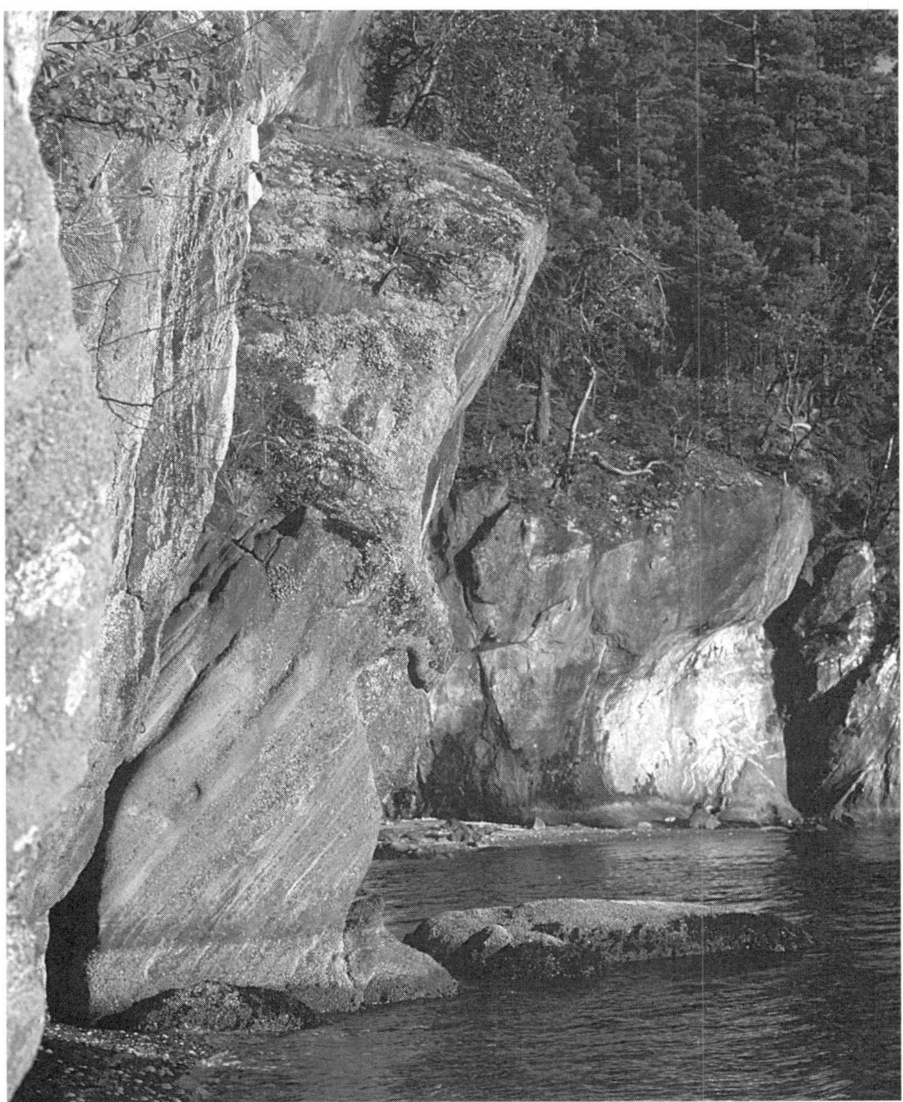

Newcastle Island is a microcosm of Gulf Islands history, having been the site of a centuries-old Salish village, a coal mine and a sandstone quarry from 1869 to 1932, and a pleasure resort from 1931 to 1955, when as many as 1,500 people at a time came from Vancouver to picnic and party. Mark Kaaremaa

Hiking/Walking Trails

You can walk all around and through the centre of the island. Along the way, you will pass sandstone cliffs, sandy gravel beaches, middens and even a small lake. The caves and caverns along the shoreline were reputedly used for burials by the Coast Salish. There are also many fine views of the mainland mountains and of Vancouver Island. The trails pass the remains of Newcastle's industrial past and middens. Among the animal life are blacktail deer, otters, rabbits, raccoons and squirrels, as well as muskrats and beaver on Mallard Lake. The forest contains Garry oak, dogwood, arbutus and Douglas fir.

3. PIRATES COVE (DE COURCY ISLAND) ★★★★

Pirates Cove, on De Courcy Island, is about 16 km southeast of Nanaimo. The marine park is on 38 ha of land on the southeast tip of the island; the rest of the island is privately owned.

De Courcy Island has a mystique because of its association with Edward Arthur Wilson, a cult leader known as Brother XII. Despite being the subject of several books, the details of Wilson's life are sketchy and will probably never be completely known. It's generally agreed that, after travelling extensively, he came to British Columbia from England in 1927 as the leader of a theosophist cult called the Aquarian Foundation. Fuelled by the donations of his followers, Brother XII built a commune first in Cedar, south of Nanaimo, and then on De Courcy and Valdes Islands. In time, he began to psychologically and physically abuse his followers. They, in turn, took him to court to recover their financial contributions. The resulting lawsuits and counter lawsuits made headlines in the Nanaimo newspapers. In the end, Brother XII disappeared mysteriously with Madame Zee, his female partner. His legendary hoard of gold also disappeared.

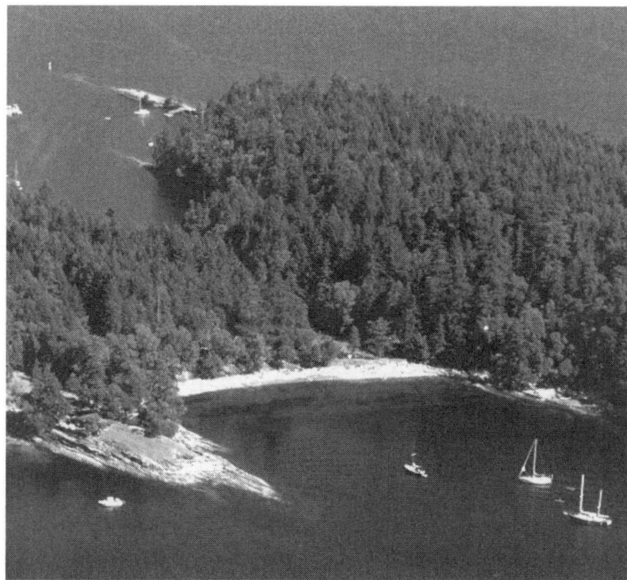

Pirates Cove, De Courcy Island. The natural shelter of this well-protected little harbour probably led to its name and definitely accounts for its popularity with boaters. The hiking trails follow the shoreline of the cove and continue along Pylades Channel, circumnavigating the park. Mark Kaaremaa

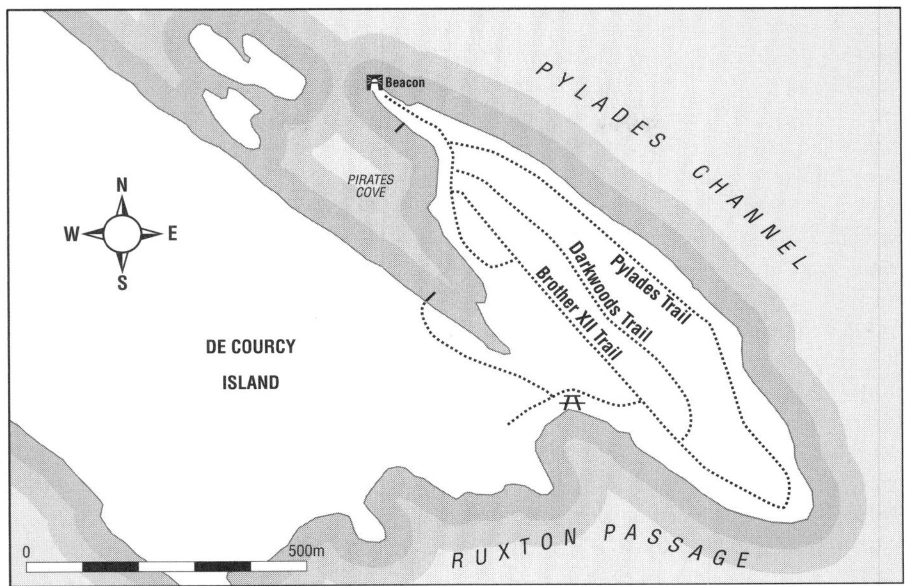

Pirates Cove Provincial Marine Park

In addition to the usual coastal plants, Pirates Cove contains Rocky Mountain juniper, satinflower and poison oak (you'll want to avoid this one, so stay on the trails). Pipsissewa, a low-growing evergreen plant with pink flowers and leathery, shiny leaves is abundant on the park's east side in June and early July. Among the park's animal inhabitants are blacktail deer, river otters, mink and raccoons. Offshore, look for harbour seals, Steller's and California sea lions, porpoises and killer whales. Wilson's warblers, Pacific-slope flycatchers, black oystercatchers, white-crowned sparrows, bald eagles and great blue herons are among the birds most frequently sighted on the island.

Hiking/Walking Trails

There are about 4 km of trails in Pirates Cove. The Pylades Trail, along the cliff above the eastern shore of the island, provides good views of the sandstone rocks on Valdes Island to the east. It ends at the tip of the rocky peninsula at the entrance to the cove. From here, you can return by either the Darkwoods Trail through the centre of the park or the Brother XII Trail that follows the eastern shore of the cove. At the beginning of these return trails, you will find excellent views of both the cove and the boats that frequent this popular anchorage. All the trails are well established and easy to follow.

A short, unnamed trail leads from the beach on the south side of the park to camping spots and picnic tables along the western edge of the park. You will find a fresh water pump and outhouses in the camping area.

4. PRINCESS MARGARET (PORTLAND ISLAND), GULF ISLANDS NATIONAL PARK RESERVE ★★★★

Princess Margaret Marine Park is south of Salt Spring Island, west of Moresby Island and about 3 km north of the Saanich Peninsula. It can be reached by private boat or water taxi. It's about a 45-minute paddle from one of the launch sites near Sidney or from the launch sites on Menhinick Road on Salt Spring (see page 187).

As evidenced by the many middens, the 575-ha island was once used by First Nations people. In the mid-1800s, the Hudson's Bay Company contracted up to 400 Hawaiian workers (known as Kanakas) to work in the company's fur and timber businesses and some of these people settled on the island. They stayed until 1907 and are remembered by such place names as Kanaka Bluff and Pellow Islets. The island had several owners over the years, the most memorable one being Frank A. Sutton, a one-armed ex-soldier, who bought the island in 1928 to raise horses. Sutton constructed a large stable, planted an orchard and planned to build a hotel, a golf course and 30 summer cottages. However, he had to give up the island the following year when the stock market crashed, taking his money with it. In 1957, Portland Island became the property of the province, which gave it to Princess Margaret when she visited BC the next year. She was good enough to return it to the province in 1967, when it became a park named in her honour. Today, it is part of the Gulf Islands National Park Reserve.

There are many small islands around Portland. To the south, Brackman Island, also part of the Gulf Islands National Park Reserve, is an ecological reserve and is off-bounds unless you receive permission from BC Parks (see Resources, page 235).

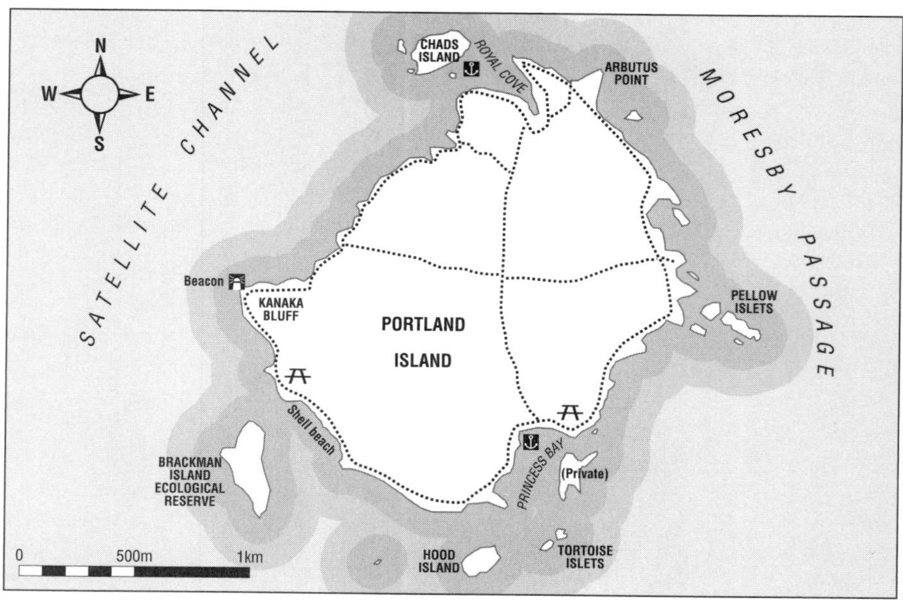

Princess Margaret Provincial Marine Park

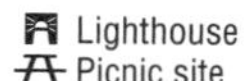

There are two anchorages off Portland, one in Royal Cove and the other in Princess Bay. (A trail connects them.) Camping is allowed in the open field at Princess Bay, on Shell Beach and at Arbutus Point. There is a hand pump for water, outhouses and picnic tables. Campfires are allowed in the firepits, except during summer months, when the island is extremely dry.

Hiking/Walking Trails

About 10 km of hiking trails run all along the circumference of the island and criss-cross the centre, as well. You will see the fruit trees, roses and garden plants that have survived from when people lived here. You will also find Rocky Mountain juniper and yellow-flowering cactus on rocky outcrops, as well as arbutus and Garry oak trees south of Princess Bay. The island's growth is still sparse in places as a result of feral sheep (removed in the 1980s) and the large population of indigenous blacktail deer (which remain).

You will also pass a beautiful shoreline, including Royal Cove, where you may see mink, river otters and such shore birds as oystercatchers, great blue herons and glaucous-winged gulls. Bald eagles and turkey vultures are commonly spotted in the sky, along with the occasional red-tailed hawk.

5. SIDNEY SPIT (SIDNEY ISLAND), GULF ISLANDS NATIONAL PARK RESERVE ★★★★

Sidney Spit is at the northern end of Sidney Island, 5 km from the town of Sidney on Vancouver Island. A foot-passenger ferry leaves the Sidney dock at the bottom of Beacon Street hourly during the summer from 10 a.m. to 5 p.m. on weekdays and until 6 p.m. on weekends. There is more limited service available in May and June and in September and October. You can also reach the park by private boat (the park has many mooring buoys) or by water taxi.

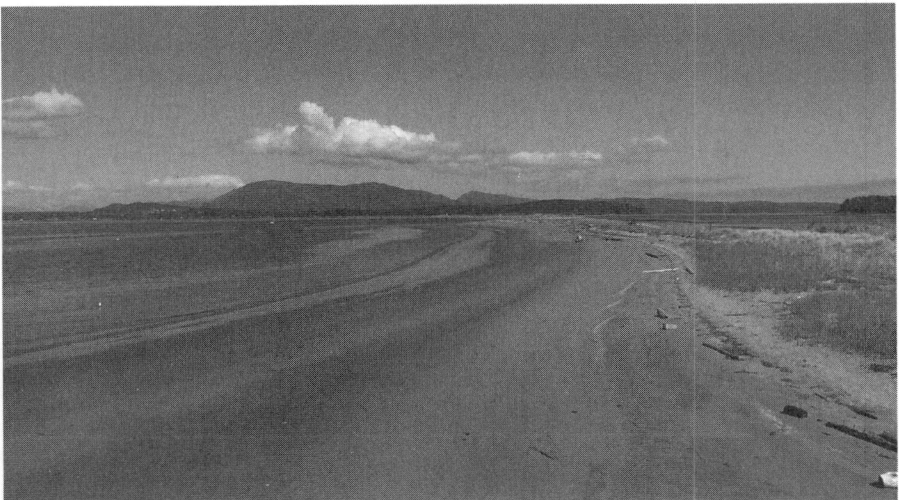

Sidney Spit is a long sandy finger of land extending far into the sea.
Parks Canada

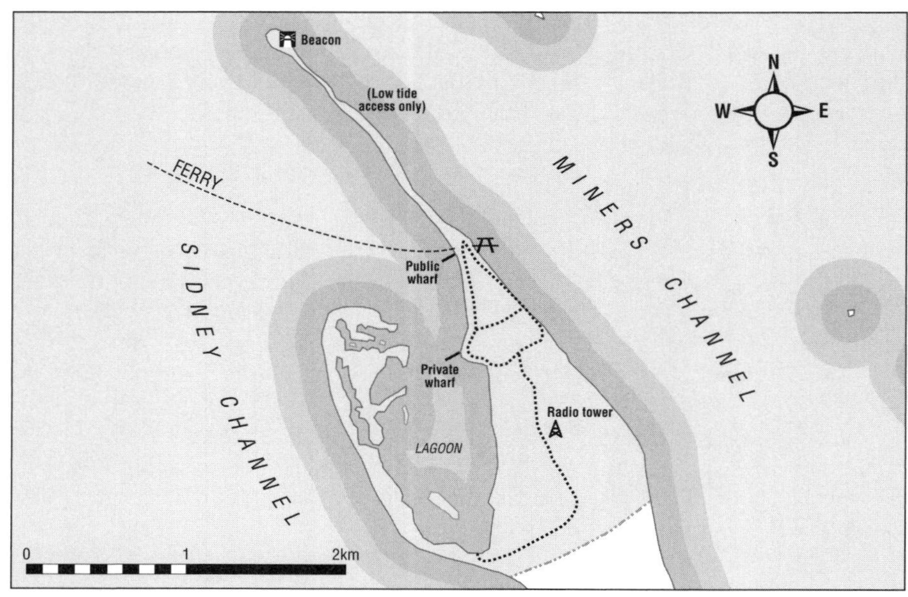

Sidney Spit Provincial Marine Park

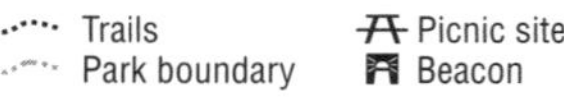

Called Sallas Island by officers of the Hudson's Bay Company in about 1850, Sidney Island was renamed by Captain George Henry Richards, who surveyed the area in 1859. A year later, when the island was offered for sale at six shillings an acre (0.4 ha), few people wanted to buy. Today, most of Sidney Island is private property but the spit is part of the Gulf Islands National Park Reserve. The park occupies the northern third of the island, about 400 ha that includes 223 ha of foreshore.

In addition to hiking, there is excellent swimming, birdwatching and camping on Sidney Spit. Bring your own drinking water as the water provided, while drinkable, can be very salty.

Hiking/Walking Trails

Several hiking trails cross the park. One leads to the site of the Sidney Island Brick and Tile Company, which functioned in the early 1900s and employed, on average, 70 men. Other trails lead to Sidney Lagoon, a popular birdwatching area, especially in the spring, and the lookout for the seabird colony on nearby Mandarte Island (an Indian Reserve). You can also explore the more than 20 km of Sidney Spit's sandy beaches. It will take you about two hours to walk to the spit's lighthouse from the ferry dock. Be sure to stay on the trails, as the clay-and-sand banks erode easily.

6. WALLACE ISLAND ★★★

Wallace Island is located in Trincomali Channel, midway between Galiano and Salt Spring Islands (about a 20-minute paddle from either). You can get here by private boat or water taxi from Salt Spring. The park covers 72 ha.

Jeremiah Chivers, a Scot, lived on Wallace by himself from 1889 to 1927, when he died at the age of 92. He planted a garden and orchard, bits of which are still visible. In 1946, Americans Jeanne and David Conover bought the island, built a home and, ultimately, a small resort. Some of the resort's cottages and the Conover home can still be seen on the island. Conover sold the island in 1966 but it did not became a park until 1990. There are still a couple of private cottages and a small piece of private property northwest of Princess Cove; the land and privacy of these property owners should be respected.

Wallace Island is a great place to visit in the off-season, and especially in the spring when the island is covered with wildflowers, the bald eagles are nesting and there are plenty of harbour seals on the rocky islets to the west. You may also see blacktail deer, river otters and mink. Steller's and California sea lions are often sighted in the winter.

The park is a very popular destination for boaters, especially in the summer months. There are protected anchorages in both Conover Cove and Princess Cove. (Conover Cove also has a small dock.) There is camping on the island, picnic tables, outhouses, a picnic shelter and fresh water, which must be boiled before drinking. Fires are not permitted on the island.

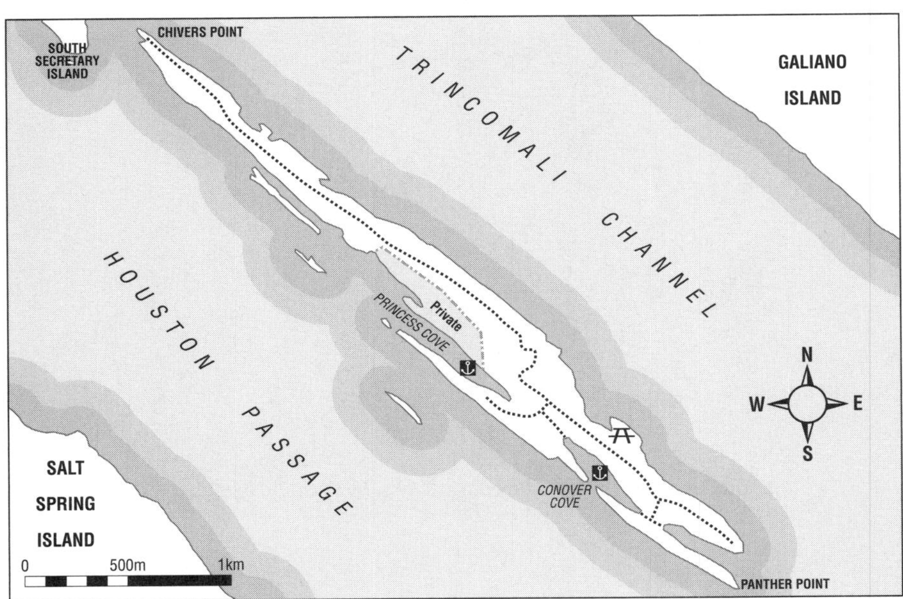

Wallace Island Provincial Marine Park

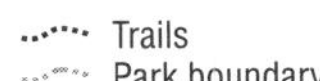

Hiking/Walking Trails

There are several trails here. The 4-km main trail runs down the centre of the island, from Panther Point in the southeast to Chivers Point in the northwest. It passes through lovely woods and provides access to Conover Cove and the public side of Princess Cove on the way. Side trails lead to some of the many beautiful, sheltered coves around the island. Among the many excellent spots for picnics, Chivers Point is perhaps the loveliest. The main trail passes by the remnants of David Conover's resort, which make interesting exploring and are being renovated for some future park use. The trail also passes an old garden area, complete with the remains of old farm equipment.

Judy Norget

Resources

BOOKS

Andersen, Doris. *Evergreen Islands: A History of the Islands of the Inside Passage*. Vancouver: Gray's Publishing/Whitecap Books, 1979.

Assu, Henry, with Joy Inglis. *Assu of Cape Mudge: Recollections of a Coastal Indian Chief*. Vancouver: University of British Columbia Press, 1989.

Baron, Nancy, and John Acorn. *Birds of Coastal British Columbia*. Vancouver: Lone Pine Publishing, 1997.

BC Historical Association, Gulf Islands Branch. *A Gulf Islands Patchwork: Some Early Events on the Islands of Galiano, Mayne, Saturna, North and South Pender*. Sidney, BC: Peninsula Printing Co., 1961.

Bentley, Mary and Ted. *Gabriola: Petroglyph Island*. Victoria: Sono Nis Press, 1981.

Blier, Richard K., ed. *Hiking Trails III: Northern Vancouver Island*. 9th ed. Victoria, BC: Vancouver Island Trails Information Society, 2002. Distributed by Orca Book Publishers.

Bovey, Robin, Wayne Campbell, and Bryan Gates. *Birds of Victoria and Vicinity*. Edmonton: Lone Pine Publishing, 1989.

Cannings, Richard and Sydney. *British Columbia: A Natural History*. Vancouver: Greystone Books/Douglas & McIntyre, 1996.

Darwin, Betty J., and Patricia J.M. Forbes. *So You Want to Know About Lasqueti Island: A Visitor's Guide to Its Past And Present*. Parksville, BC: Parks West Printing and Stationery, n.d.

Elliott, Marie. *Mayne Island and the Outer Gulf Islands: A History*. Mayne Island, BC: Gulf Islands Press, 1984.

Fladmark, Knut R. *British Columbia Prehistory*. Ottawa: National Museum of Man, National Museums of Canada, 1986.

Fletcher, Olivia. *Hammerstone: A Biography of Hornby Island*. Edmonton: NeWest Press, 2001.

Gulf Islands' Branch, British Columbia Historical Federation. *More Tales from the Outer Gulf Islands: An Anthology of Memories and Anecdotes*. Pender Island, BC: Gulf Islands' Branch, BC Historical Federation, 1993.

Hamilton, Bea. *Salt Spring Island*. Vancouver: Mitchell Press, 1969.

Hill, Beth and Ray. *Indian Petroglyphs of the Pacific Northwest.* Saanichton, BC: Hancock House Publishers, 1974.

Howard, Irene. *Bowen Island, 1872–1972.* Bowen Island, BC: Bowen Island Historians, 1973.

Isbister, Winnifred A. *My Ain Folk: Denman Island, 1875–1975.* Courteney, BC: E.W. Bickle, 1976.

Isenor, D.E., E.G. Stephens, and D.E. Watson. *Edge of Discovery: A History of the Campbell River District.* Campbell River, BC: Ptarmigan Press, 1989.

Jones, Elaine. *The Northern Gulf Islands Explorer: The Outdoor Guide.* Vancouver: Whitecap Books, 1991.

Kahn, Charles. *Salt Spring: The Story of an Island.* Madeira Park: Harbour Publishing, 1998.

Kelsey, Sheila, ed. *The Lives Behind the Headstones.* Duncan, BC: Green Gecko Electronic Publishing, 1993.

Kirk, Ruth. *Wisdom of the Elders: Native Traditions on the Northwest Coast.* Vancouver: Douglas and McIntyre/British Columbia Provincial Museum, 1986.

Lewis-Harrison, June. *The People of Gabriola: A History of Our Pioneers.* Gabriola Island, BC: June Lewis-Harrison, 1982.

Ludvigsen, Rolf, and Graham Beard. *West Coast Fossils: A Guide to the Ancient Life of Vancouver Island.* Rev. ed. Madeira Park: Harbour Publishing, 1997.

Lyons, C.P. *Trees, Shrubs, and Flowers to Know in British Columbia.* Toronto: J.M. Dent, 1974.

Macnair, Peter L., Alan C. Hoover, and Kevin Neary. *The Legacy: Tradition And Innovation in Northwest Coast Indian Art.* Vancouver: Douglas and McIntyre/Seattle: University of Washington Press, 1984.

Murray, Peter. *Homesteads and Snug Harbours: The Gulf Islands.* Ganges, BC: Horsdal and Schubart, 1991.

Palmer, Mary. *Jedediah Days: One Woman's Island Paradise.* Madeira Park, BC: Harbour Publishing, 1998.

Pender Islands Parks Commission. *Community Parks Guide.* Pender Island: Pender Islands Parks Commission, 2002.

Pojar, Jim, and Andy MacKinnon, eds. *Plants of Coastal British Columbia.* Edmonton: Lone Pine Publishing, 1994.

Reimer, Derek, ed. *The Gulf Islanders.* Victoria: Aural History, Provincial Archives of British Columbia, 1976.

Roberts, Eric A. *Salt Spring Saga: An Exciting Story of Pioneer Days.* Ganges: Driftwood, 1962.

Sept, J. Duane. *Common Wildflowers of British Columbia*. Sechelt, BC: Calypso Publishing, 2002.

Sept, J. Duane. *Common Birds of British Columbia*. Sechelt, BC: Calypso Publishing, 2003.

Smith, Elizabeth, and David Gerow. *Hornby Island: The Ebb and Flow*. Campbell River, BC: Ptarmigan Press, 1988.

Snowden, Mary Ann. *Sea Kayak the Gulf Islands*. Rev. Ed. Heritage House, 2004

Steward, Elizabeth. *Galiano: Houses and People—Looking Back to 1930*. Galiano Island, BC: Elizabeth Steward, 1994.

Sweet, Arthur Fielding. *Islands in Trust*. Lantzville, BC: Oolichan Books, 1988.

Taylor, Jeanette, and Ian Douglas. *Exploring Quadra Island: Heritage Sites and Hiking Trails*. Quathiaski Cove, BC: Fernbank Publishing, 2001.

Thompson, Bill. *Texada Island*. Powell River, BC: Powell River Heritage Research Association, 1997.

Toynbee, Richard Mouat. *Snapshots of Early Salt Spring and Other Favoured Islands*. Ganges, BC: Mouat's Trading Co. Ltd., 1978.

Walbran, John T. *British Columbia Coast Names: Their Origin and History*. Vancouver: Douglas & McIntyre, 1971.

Walter, Margaret (Shaw). *Early Days Among the Gulf Islands of British Columbia*. 2nd ed. Hebden Printing Co. Ltd., n.d.

MAPS

Road maps for individual islands can usually be obtained from local real estate offices, tourist offices and chambers of commerce.

Gulf Islands Recreation Map (1:50 000). 1st ed., 1992. ISBN 0-9214-6333-3. Published by ITMB (International Travel Maps and Books) Publishing Ltd. for World Wide Books and Maps, 530 West Broadway, Vancouver, BC V5Z 1E9 (tel.: 604-879-3621, fax: 604-879-4521; web site: www.itmb.com; email: itmb@itmb.com).

Terrain Resource Information Management (TRIM) maps (1:20 000) are available from Base Mapping and Geomatic Services Branch, PO Box 9355, Station Provincial Government, Victoria, BC V8W 9M2; 250-952-4050; web site: http://srmwww.gov.bc.ca/bmgs/ or www.landdata.gov.bc.ca.

These maps are also available from Nanaimo Maps and Charts and ITMB (see previous two listings).

The National Topographical Series (NTS) (1:50,000) contains individual topographic maps of the Gulf Islands prepared by Natural Resources Canada. For information, visit http://maps.nrcan.gc.ca/topographic.html. The maps are available from authorized local map dealers such as Crown Publications, 521 Fort St., Victoria, BC V8W 1E7, 250-386-4636; fax: 250-386-0221; Nanaimo Maps and Charts, 8 Church St., Nanaimo, BC V9R 5H4; 1-800-665-2513; fax: 1-800-553-2313 and ITMB (see previous listing).

Map 92 G/6 of this series covers Bowen; 92 K/2 covers Cortes; 92 F/10 covers Denman and Hornby; 92 G/4 covers Gabriola; 92 B/14 covers Galiano; 92 F/8 and 92 F/9 cover Lasqueti; 92 B/14 covers Mayne; 92 B/11 covers the Penders; 92 K/3 (1:50,000) covers Quadra Island; 92 B/11 and 92B/00 cover Salt Spring; 92 B/14 Canada covers Saturna; 92 F/9 and 92 F/00 cover Texada; and 92 B/13 covers Thetis.

ACCOMMODATION

You can obtain some information on accommodation from *British Columbia Approved Accommodation*, Tourism BC's free, annual booklet, which you can obtain from Travel Infocentres or by calling 1-800-435-5622 (toll free) or 604-435-5622 in the Vancouver area. However, this booklet does not include any information on the vast majority of the islands' bed and breakfasts. You can also visit Tourism BC's web site: www.HelloBC.com.

SOURCES OF INFORMATION

Amigo Airways, 1-866-692-6440; www.amigoairways.ca.

BC Ferries. 1112 Fort Street, Victoria, BC V8V 4V2. Tel.: 1-888-223-3779 (anywhere in BC except Victoria), 250-386-3431 (Victoria or from outside of BC), 250-335-0323 (Buckley Bay), 250-286-1412 (Campbell River), 250-753-9344 (Gabriola), 604-921-7414 (Horseshoe Bay), 250-539-2321 (Mayne Island), 250-753-1261 (Nanaimo), 250-629-3344 (Pender Islands), 604-485-2943 (Powell River), 250-653-4245 (Fulford Harbour) or 250-537-5313 (Long Harbour, Salt Spring); 1-888-724-5223 (for reservations when calling from within BC), 604-444-2890 (reservations Vancouver); fax: 250-381-5452 (Victoria); web site: www.bcferries.com.

BC Ministry of Forests. Communications Branch, PO Box 9529, Station Provincial Government, 3rd Floor, 1520 Blanshard St., Victoria, BC V8W 3K2; 250-387-5255; web site: www.gov.bc.ca/for/. Campbell River Forest District, 370 South Dogwood St., Campbell River, BC V9W 6Y7; 250-286-9300.

BC Parks. 2nd Floor, 800 Johnson Street, Victoria, BC V8V 1X4, www.gov.bc.ca/wlap; or *Ministry of Water, Lands and Air Protection*, PO Box 9398 Stn. Prov. Govt. Victoria, BC V8W 9M9, or http://wlapwww.gov.bc.ca/bcparks/.

BC Tourist Information. 1-800-435-5622; www.HelloBC.com.

Capital Regional District Parks, 490 Atkins Avenue, Victoria, BC V9B 2Z8; 250-478-3344; fax: 250-478-5416; web site: www.crd.bc.ca/parks.

The Federation of BC Naturalists, 307-1367 West Broadway, Vancouver, BC V6H 4A9; tel.: 604-737-3057; fax: 604-738-7175; web site: www.naturalists.bc.ca.

Greater Vancouver Regional District Parks, 4330 Kingsway, Burnaby; tel.: 604-432-6350; fax: 604-432-6251.

Gulf Islands Water Taxi, 250-537-2510.

Harbour Air, 1-800-665-0212 or 604-274-1277; www.harbour-air.com.

HarbourLynx, 250-753-4443; www.harbourlynx.com.

KD Air, 1-800-665-4244 or 604-752-5884.

Lasqueti passenger ferry, Western Pacific Marine, 604-681-5199 or 250-333-8787.

Newcastle Island passenger ferry, 250-754-7893.

Regional District of Comox-Strathcona, Parks and Recreation Department, 600 Comox Rd., Courtenay, BC V9N 3P6; 1-800-331-6007 (if calling from within the 250 area code) or 250-334-6000.

Regional District of Nanaimo, Recreation and Parks Department, 830 Island Highway, Parksville, BC, V9P 2X4; 1-888-828-2069, 250-248-3252; fax: 250-248-3159; email: recparks@rdn.bc.ca; web site: www.rdn.bc.ca.

Salt Spring Air, 250-537-9880 or 1-877-537-9880; www.saltspringair.com.

Seair Seaplanes, 604-273-8900 or 1-800-447-3247; www.seairseaplanes.com.

Tofino Air, 1-800-665-2359; or 250-247-9992; www.tofinoair.ca.

Tourism Association of Vancouver Island, #203–335 Wesley St., Nanaimo, V9R 2T5; tel: 250-754-3500; fax: 250-754-3599; web site: www.islands.bc.ca.

Index

Additional Reading
FROM HARBOUR PUBLISHING

The Beachcomber's Guide to Seashore Life in the Pacific Northwest
by J. Duane Sept
5.5" x 8.5" • 240 pages, 500 colour photos • 1-55017-204-2 • $24.95

274 of the most common animals and plants found along the saltwater shores of the Pacific Northwest are described in this book. Illustrating each entry is a colour photo of the species in its natural habitat.

Coastal Villages by Liv Kennedy
9" x 12" • 176 pages, photos throughout • 1-55017-057-0 • $42.95

Fascinating local history and more than 300 photographs, from archival photos to lush contemporary images of BC's picturesque coastal villages.

Exploring the BC Coast by Car by Diane Eaton and Alison Eaton
5.5" x 8.5" • 400 pages, 150 photos, 50 maps • 1-55017-178-X • $24.95

This indispensable book shows how you can use BC's world-class ferry and coastal road system to reach the coast's most spectacular places in the comfort of your family car.

Paddling The Sunshine Coast by Dorothy and Bodhi Drope
5.5" x 8.5" • 192 pages, 40 photos, illustrations and maps
1-55017-164-X • $19.95

This book will introduce both new and experienced sea kayakers to the matchless paddling opportunities of the Sunshine Coast, from Howe Sound in the south to Desolation Sound in the north, including Sechelt Inlet, the islands of Georgia Strait and Jervis Inlet.

Jedediah Days: One Woman's Island Paradise by Mary Palmer
6" x 9" • 224 pages, 100 photos • 1-55017-184-4 • $26.95

For 45 years, Mary Palmer was owner of Jedediah Island, a picturesque 640-acre jewel in British Columbia's Strait of Georgia. This book is her story, a wonderful tapestry of life on the island between 1949 and 1994.

Kayaking Vancouver Island: Great Trips from Port Hardy to Victoria
by Gary Backlund and Paul Grey
6" x 9" • 295 pages • 1-55017-318-9 • $24.95

Veteran paddlers Gary Backlund and Paul Grey describe more than 20 kayaking trips ranging from a lazy day excursion in Victoria's historic Gorge waterway to an exciting multi-day voyage around Meares Island in Clayoquot Sound. Includes maps, photographs, information on launch sites, camping places, currents and tides.

Pacific Reef and Shore: A Photo Guide to Northwest Marine Life
by Rick M. Harbo
5.5" x 8.5" • 80 pages, 300 colour photos • 1-55017-304-9 • $9.95

A brilliant full-colour field guide to the marine life of coastal British Columbia, Alaska, Washington, Oregon and northern California is perfect for divers, boaters, beachwalkers and snorkellers.

Pacific Seaweeds: A Guide to Common Seaweeds of the West Coast
by Louis Druehl
5.5" x 8.5" • 192 pages, 80 colour photos, illustrations
1-55017-240-9 • $24.95

The authoritative guide to over 100 common species of seaweed. Includes interesting facts, scientific information and tasty recipes.

Salt Spring: The Story of an Island by Charles Kahn
6" x 9" • 344 pages, 150 photos • 1-155017-262-X • $24.95

Chronicles the island's rich history through some 150 years of settlement by many diverse groups. This is the engaging and thoroughly researched story of all these special people, and the very special place they called home.

Shells and Shellfish of the Pacific Northwest by Rick M. Harbo
5.5" x 8.5" • 272 pages, 350 colour photos • 1-55017-146-1 • $25.95

This easy-to-follow, full-colour guide introduces more than 250 species of mollusks found along the beaches and shallow waters of the Pacific Northwest.

continued...

Visions of the Wild: A Voyage by Kayak Around Vancouver Island
by Maria Coffey and Dag Goering
8" x 9.5" • 182 pages, colour photos • 1-155017-264-6 • $36.95

Brimming with breathtaking colour photographs and compelling journal entries from all stages of their three-month kayaking journey, this book is at once an inspiring chronicle of an adventure of a lifetime, and a beautiful book of photographs that rejoices in the untamed spirit of Canada's West Coast.

Where to See Wildlife on Vancouver Island by Kim Goldberg
5.5" x 8.5" • 174 pages, 100 colour photos • 1-55017-160-7 • $20.95

Info-packed and user-friendly, this guide introducess the 50 best wildlife viewing hot spots on Vancouver Island, from the busy Victoria waterfront to Nanaimo's Buttertubs Marsh to "Gator Gardens" in Alert Bay.

Whales of the West Coast by David A.E. Spalding
6" x 9" • 256 pages, 100 photos • 1-55017-199-2 • $21.95

Huge, powerful, intelligent and beautiful, whales have fascinated human beings for millennia. From the better-known orcas, greys and humpbacks to porpoises, blue whales and sperm whales.

Whelks to Whales: Coastal Marine Life of the Pacific Northwest
by Rick M. Harbo
5.5" x 8.5" • 248 pages, 500 colour photos • 1-55017-183-6 • $25.95

This full-colour field guide to the marine life of coastal British Columbia, Alaska, Washington, Oregon and northern California is perfect for divers, boaters, beachwalkers and snorkellers.